THE
STRANGEST
TRIBE

THE STRANGEST TRIBE

How a Group of Seattle Rock Bands Invented Grunge

STEPHEN TOW

SASQUATCH BOOKS
SEATTLE

Printed in the United States of America
Published by Sasquatch Books
17 16 15 14 13 12 11   9 8 7 6 5 4 3 2 1

Cover photograph: Charles Peterson
Interior photographs: Charles Peterson, Neil Hubbard, Marty Perez, and Stephen Tow
Cover design: Henry Quiroga
Interior design and composition: Emily Ford

Library of Congress Cataloging-in-Publication Data
Tow, Stephen.
 The strangest tribe : how a group of Seattle rock bands invented grunge / Stephen Tow.
   p. cm.
 Discography: p.
 Includes bibliographical references and index.
 ISBN 978-1-57061-743-0
 1. Grunge music—Washington (State)—Seattle—History and criticism.
 2. Alternative rock music—Washington (State)—Seattle—History and criticism. I. Title.
 ML3534.3.T69 2011
 781.6609797'772--dc23
                              2011020055

Sasquatch Books
119 South Main Street, Suite 400
Seattle, WA 98104
(206) 467-4300
www.sasquatchbooks.com
custserv@sasquatchbooks.com

In memory of my father,
Seymour Tow,
1918–1978.

. . .

CONTENTS

ACKNOWLEDGMENTS

First, I would like to thank my interviewees who graciously shared their life experiences: Grant Alden, Dawn Anderson, Mark Arm, Jon Auer, Peter Barnes, Jim Basnight, Leighton Beezer, Matt Bischoff, Al Bloch, Kurt Bloch, Jane Brownson, James Burdyshaw, Shirley Carlson, Tina Casale, Chad Channing, Art Chantry, John Conte, Blaine Cook, Kurt Danielson, Mike Davidson, Amy Denio, Tad Doyle, Duff Drew, Jon Driver, Tom Dyer, Chris Eckman, Jack Endino, Craig Ferguson, Todd Fleischman, Steve Fisk, John Foster, Mike Fuller, Gillian Gaar, Milton Garrison, Jeff Gilbert, Greg Gilmore, Max Godsil, Stone Gossard, Terry Lee Hale, Chris Hanzsek, Faith Henschel-Ventrello, Paul Hood, Neil Hubbard, Ben Ireland, Calvin Johnson, Nate Johnson, Jeff Kelly, Joey Kline, David Kulczyk, Jamie Lane, Michael Laton, Jim Lightfoot, Pete Litwin, Kurtiss Lofstrom, Bret Lunsford, Scott McCaughey, Ben McMillan (R.I.P.), Lance Mercer, Dave Middleton, Courtney Miller, Gary Minkler, Rod Moody, Rob Morgan, Terry Morgan, Mike Musburger, Chris Newman, Kyle Nixon, Steve Pearson, Charles Peterson, Mark Pickerel, Poki (Hugo) Piottin, Tom Price, Chris Pugh, Stephen Rabow, Ned Raggett, Larry Reid, Rich Riggins, George Romansic, Joe Ross, Robert Roth, Ron Rudzitis, Scott Schickler, Nick Scott, Alex Shumway, Rob Skinner, Jeff Smith, Ken Stringfellow, Ben Thompson, Jim Tillman, Damon Titus, Dan Trager, Everett True, Conrad Uno, Steve van Liew, Scott Vanderpool, Bon Von Wheelie, Kim Warnick, Laura Weller-Vanderpool,

Dennis White, Kevin Whitworth, Rusty Willoughby, Kevin Wood, and Blake Wright.

Second, I would like to offer an extra special thanks to the following people who went above and beyond the call of duty: Leighton Beezer for helping me connect the dots between 1983 and 1985; James Burdyshaw for setting up an interview with the U-Men's Tom Price; Kurt Danielson for his brilliant insight and supportive ear; Jack Endino for providing music, fanzines, and general encouragement; Chris Hanzsek for introducing me to Seattle's neighborhoods and surrounding mountains; Jim Basnight and Paul Hood for providing a starting point; and Rob Morgan for being Rob Morgan.

Third, I would like to thank my agents Janet Rosen and Sheree Bykofsky; my editors Whitney Ricketts and Michelle Hope Anderson and everyone at Sasquatch Books who helped turn my vision into a reality; my sister Susan Louis for her unwavering support; Professor Charles Hardy for inspiring me; the helpful librarians at the University of Washington and Evergreen State College; and the photographers who contributed to this book: Charles Peterson, Marty Perez, and Neil Hubbard.

Finally, I want to thank my wife Irisa, my daughter Sami, and my labs Bear (R.I.P.) and Coco for their invaluable support and for putting up with me during this project. This book is dedicated to them.

INTRODUCTION

*When you look at really where the Seattle thing started,
and how it got off the ground . . . I mean once there was
[Nirvana's] Nevermind, it's not hard to figure out why
there was a Pearl Jam and a Soundgarden and everything
else—because the phenomenon fed on itself quite easily.
But how do you get to a Nevermind?*

—Leighton Beezer, the Thrown Ups

Seattle was rock and roll's last best hope. Not since Liverpool
and Memphis has one city so dramatically altered the course of
music history.

For many Americans, Seattle music equates only to
grunge—a style of music exemplified by Nirvana, Pearl Jam,
Soundgarden, and Alice in Chains. Grunge, in the eyes of
the general population, was an early '90s fad remembered
as fondly as that once hip but no longer fashionable pair of
sneakers. Unfortunately, America has been culturally ripped
off by the mainstream media and major labels, who painted a
completely inaccurate picture of the music and portrayed the
grunge band as a dark, angst-ridden group of depressed heroin addicts. Kurt Cobain's 1994 suicide reinforced that notion.
Grunge was serious.

If only they knew.

Seattle's underground music has always displayed a tongue-
in-cheek sense of humor. Rarely did anyone take themselves

seriously, even people that became rock stars. The national media characterized the grunge musician as a dirty, long-haired, angry young man, shouting enraged commentary about his miserable life. "Wait a minute," says Beezer, who played bass for the Thrown Ups, arguably the quintessential grunge band. "These are like the funniest guys I know! Where's the rage come from? [Laughs.] [It was about] getting drunk and having a good time. End of story!"

The outside world just didn't get it, and Seattle wanted it that way. In 1992 a *New York Times* reporter phoned Megan Jasper, then a sales rep at Sub Pop Records. The caller inquired about the hip grunge slang. One problem remained, however: there *was* no hip grunge slang. Jasper, by then completely tired of the incessant media attention, decided to have some fun. She told the reporter to name some common terms, and she would happily provide the corresponding grunge expressions. As the reporter rattled off phrases like "uncool person" and "hanging out," Jasper responded with "lamestain" and "swingin' on the flippity-flop." The exchange was published in the November 15, 1992, issue of the *New York Times* under the title "Lexicon of Grunge: Breaking the Code."* Jasper and Seattle enjoyed a good laugh.

Mudhoney, a Seattle grunge band then receiving international attention, decided to take the joke a step further. After the "Lexicon of Grunge" showed up in the *Times*, the band gave interviews with the made-up terms sprinkled throughout. "When we heard about that," says Mudhoney's front man

---

*From the *New York Times*, © November 15, 1992 *The New York Times* all rights reserved. Used by permission and protected by the Copyright Laws of the United States. The printing, copying, redistribution, or retransmission of the Material without express written permission is prohibited. The material is available online at http://www.nytimes.com/1992/11/15/style/grunge-a-success-story.html?pagewanted=5.

Mark Arm, "[for] our next round of interviews we threw out as many of those terms as often as possible."

While Seattle's humor often bordered on the macabre, it was typically not executed in a mean-spirited way. For instance, local record label owner Tom Dyer had a band called the Icons and desired publicity. He would send press releases to the *Rocket*, then Seattle's monthly music magazine, only to be ignored. Then he came up with an idea: why not kill a fictional band member—Walter E. Gogh—and put that in the next press release? "So we send this press release to the *Rocket*," says Dyer, "how . . . Walter has died in a car wreck in southern Florida while visiting his mother. And the *Rocket*, they run it."

The Icons have announced the death of founding member Walter E. Gogh. Walter died from injuries sustained in an auto accident while visiting his mother in southern Florida.

—Johnny Renton, *The Rocket*, April 1984

"And I'm going, 'Yes! Hook, line, and sinker!' 'Cause of course," says Dyer, "the next month was the follow-up, a letter to the editor from Walter."

I picked up a copy of your fine magazine, The Rocket April issue, and to my surprise found the Icons had announced my death in Southern Florida. . . . I don't know anyone living in Florida, including my mother!

—Walter E. Gogh, letter to the editor, *The Rocket*, May 1984

Even the term "grunge" was a joke. Bruce Pavitt, founder of Sub Pop Records, began using the word in the April 1988 issue of the *Rocket*. Within a few months, local media picked it up. Pavitt could fold his arms and laugh as the international media latched onto grunge to describe *all* music coming out of Seattle.

Not only did the nation fail to notice that wonderful Seattle sense of humor, it also got the style of music completely wrong. Grunge had little to do with the metal grind of Alice in Chains, the mainstream metal Soundgarden, or the hard-rocking Pearl Jam. Rather, the genre featured a more complex and subtle ethos. "[Grunge was] '70s hard rock with '80s punk and postpunk sensibility grafted onto it," says producer Jack Endino, who recorded the early Nirvana and Soundgarden records, "and [had] a specific lack of concern for playing ability or raw musical technique. Instead, it focused on energy and emotion and immediacy, as opposed to finesse or explicit social commentary.

"Whatever," Endino pauses. "Ask me tomorrow. I might give you a different answer."

Time for some myth debunking. Nirvana, although not part of Seattle's original grunge scene, did present an accessible version of the genre with the seminal album *Nevermind*. Yet if grunge did in fact exist as a legitimate style of music, it is arguably best represented by Mudhoney's 1988 debut single, "Touch Me I'm Sick." "Mark [Arm] and Steve [Turner, also in Mudhoney,] made up grunge in my mind," concludes Pearl Jam's Stone Gossard. "That first Mudhoney record . . . the sound of that record. That was it. That describes perfectly grunge. I think in the long run Pearl Jam was lumped into grunge, but it was never really a grunge band."

Within Seattle, bands playing a grungelike style had evolved beyond that by the time the national media ran with it in the early '90s. Seattle's real grunge heyday occurred during the latter half of the '80s, and even then the musical style did not predominate locally. Music within underground Seattle crossed all lines and genres. In addition to grunge, musicians experimented with psychedelia, folk rock, acoustic harmonics, pop hooks, and garage rock. It was Seattle's Sub Pop Records that amplified the grunge scene and made those outside the Northwest believe that Seattle began and ended with grunge.

Sub Pop, an entity that became a full-time endeavor in 1988, created a cachet for itself and its bands. The label's bold marketing approach brought an international spotlight to Seattle, a city long ignored by the world's tastemakers. Clearly, Nirvana's success would not have happened without Sub Pop, but like everything in life, Sub Pop's methods came at a price. Part of that price is a reframing of Seattle music history. Such misconceptions are illustrated in the 1996 documentary, *hype!*

While *hype!* does a fine job documenting the rise of Sub Pop in the latter '80s, the film dismisses pre-Sub Pop Seattle as lame and imitative, as if the label had created all that made Seattle special. Fortunately, that is not the case. Seattle's identity drew from its early punk rock scene, a scene that created an environment for unabashed creativity. *hype!* briefly mentions the U-Men, a band that preceded grunge Seattle and made it out of the Northwest's confines with its own style of avant-garde postpunk. While the U-Men had little national impact, the band's influence upon the local scene was incalculable. The U-Men's musical approach within the punk rock community gave others hope that anything was possible, despite commercial limitations. Prior to the U-Men, bands like the Meyce, the Telepaths, the Blackouts, and Chinas Comidas captured the local imagination and inspired others to add to Seattle's musical diversity.

Therefore, Seattle deserves further historical exploration, which is the purpose of this book: to document the germination and growth of the Seattle punk rock scene that later blossomed into an exciting—and diverse—musical community.

. . .

When I began this book, I approached it from a historian's perspective. I have taught American history for over a decade as an adjunct professor at a small college near Philadelphia, emphasizing popular music's contribution to the American experience. My passion for music led me to create courses on rock and roll and alternative rock history. An interest in Seattle music, as a historian, arose as I developed those classes.

As a fan—and I've told my interviewees this—I wish I could say I was totally plugged into pre-Nirvana Seattle after I picked up that first U-Men EP in 1984. Unfortunately, that would be a lie. Like most of America, I became aware of Seattle music when *Nevermind* hit #1 in 1992. After that initial rush of grungemania, Seattle began tugging at me in other ways that made the city's music scene seem much richer than just Nirvana and Pearl Jam.

So, after nearly five years of research, I discovered, among other things, one consistent fact: Seattle music people are fucking funny, quirky, and brilliant. Through persistence and dumb luck I was fortunate to interview prominent people like Jack Endino, Stone Gossard of Pearl Jam, Mark Arm of Mudhoney, Scott McCaughey of the Young Fresh Fellows and R.E.M., and Chad Channing of Nirvana. Perhaps even more significantly, I also spoke with some non-famous locals who contributed as much if not more to the music scene than their more well-known brethren. In all, I conducted nearly 120 interviews of musicians, writers, promoters, producers, photographers, and fans who created a music scene out of thin air. Unless otherwise noted, all quotes cited throughout this book come from these interviews.

CHAPTER 1

End of the Road

I remember the MacNeil/Lehrer NewsHour *used to always start with a map, with all these little pinpoint stars on it denoting where all the major-network PBS stations were all over the country. It always kind of shocked me to see the entire northwest quadrant . . . was BLACK except for one little star up there all by itself—and that was Seattle.*

—Art Chantry, punk rock graphic artist

The Meyce performing in Jim Basnight's basement, 1976. (Photo by Neil Hubbard)

Seattle's eclectic and perhaps peculiar personality is reflected in its music. This diverse urban personality, born in the city's neighborhoods, has contributed to Seattle's varied musical expression.

Like many larger cities, Seattle identifies itself through its distinctive neighborhoods. Walk north from its gleaming, upscale downtown business district and you'll arrive in Belltown, a hip neighborhood complete with condos, eateries, and clubs. Just south of downtown is Pioneer Square: Seattle's birthplace. Head back north for a mile, take a right on Olive Way, and you'll climb a steep incline and arrive on Capitol Hill. Capitol Hill is an artsy, almost-anything-goes enclave replete with more bars, condos, and clubs. It is also the symbolic center of Seattle's gay community. Then continue north about a mile or so, cross over the University Bridge spanning the Portage Bay leg of Lake Union, and you'll arrive in the University District, otherwise known as the U-District, home to the University of Washington ("U-Dub" per the locals). The neighborhood's heart is University Way NE, or "the Ave." While the U-District has the typical trappings of a college area—bars, record stores, pizza joints, and the like—it is also a home for wanderers and street musicians.

All of the above describes Seattle today, an upmarket multicultural metropolis that bears little resemblance to Seattle thirty-plus years ago, when the punk scene began. In the '70s, Seattle was a large "small town" suffering through a post-Boeing manufacturing recession. Pioneer Square and the downtown business district were virtually abandoned after dark, Belltown was derelict and dangerous, and Capitol Hill and the U-District were similarly run-down. The city had yet to experience the Microsoft-led tech boom.

Belltown

In the early 1980s, Belltown emerged as an important center of pre-grunge Seattle music, featuring two clubs friendly to a gay clientele: WREX and Tug's. Later on, WREX became the Vogue, which hosted midweek shows for the up-and-coming grunge bands.

Belltown also houses the renowned Moore Theater. The Moore became significant in grunge circles for hosting a key 1989 show featuring Mudhoney, TAD, and Nirvana. In some ways, that show symbolized the beginning of Seattle music's emergence into the mainstream.

Pioneer Square

Seattle began in Pioneer Square, which had its boom years in the late nineteenth-century due to its connection to the transatlantic railroad. By the twentieth century, however, businesses and cultural centers increasingly moved north and east to today's downtown business district and Capitol Hill, respectively. The area became known as the original Skid Road as it declined in stature throughout the century.

The neighborhood's declining stature did provide a silver lining: it made for an inexpensive place to live and make music. Pioneer Square became a home for the music community throughout the '80s, hosting a vibrant all-ages scene in 1983 and 1984. In 1986, the Central Tavern (today known as the Central Saloon) began hosting rock shows by Seattle's original bands. Soundgarden, Mudhoney, Nirvana, the Thrown Ups, and Alice in Chains have all played there.

Capitol Hill

Capitol Hill's origins are shrouded in mystery. What we do know is that early Seattle town planners had a vision of moving the state capital from Olympia to Seattle. That never happened, but the name stuck. Like Pioneer Square, Capitol Hill's low cost of living allowed it to become home to many of Seattle's underground musicians. The neighborhood is also home to Oddfellows Hall, a venue essential to the early Seattle music scene. When established bars and clubs refused to host shows by local original music acts, kids found they could rent out the building and hold their shows there. The Hall, a beautiful brick structure built in 1909, is named for the International Order of Odd Fellows, a British organization dating back to the seventeenth century. The social and charitable organization's activities were frowned upon by proper British society, and its members became known as "odd fellows." The Odd Fellows and Seattle's punk community share an outsiders' spirit.

U-District

The U-District is the neighborhood anchored by the University of Washington (U-Dub). During the '60s the U-District—like many college areas of the era—became the center of anti-Vietnam protests. By the '70s and '80s, like Capitol Hill, the neighborhood's inexpensive cost of living allowed it to become musician friendly. The U-District also became home to the Rainbow Tavern (which called itself the "Fabulous Rainbow"), a venue critical to Seattle music. In conjunction with U-Dub's KCMU, midweek shows at the Rainbow became the lifeblood for the growth of Seattle original music until its 1986 closing.

Rock-and-Roll High School

Of all the city's neighborhoods, the U-District became the key breeding ground for the early underground music scene. Perhaps surprisingly, U-Dub did not directly contribute to that early community. Instead, the roots for the punk and later grunge scenes lie about a mile north of the university, in the North End. There sits the true beginning of Seattle underground music: Roosevelt High School.

Many Roosevelt parents are U-Dub faculty and have imbued their children with an appreciation of the arts. Roosevelt kids often ventured down to the U-District in the '70s, frequenting Campus Music, Cellophane Square, and the other record stores on the Ave. Thus it should come as no particular surprise that Roosevelt contributed a number of musicians to the local music scene. In fact, you could argue that Roosevelt—and nearby Nathan Hale—effectively created it.

The list of musicians hailing from the above two schools reads like a primer of early Seattle punk rock and includes Jim Basnight of the Meyce/Moberlys, Paul Hood of the Meyce/Enemy, Bill Rieflin of the Telepaths/Blackouts (and later Ministry and R.E.M.), Gary Minkler of Red Dress, Rich Riggins of Red Dress/Chinas Comidas, three members of the Fastbacks, Duff McKagan of the Vains (and at least three other bands, eventually leading to Guns N' Roses), Tom Price of the U-Men, Steve van Liew of Overlord/My Eye, and many others. Unlike the later grunge era, when out-of-towners made significant contributions, the early Seattle punk scene was a homegrown enterprise. Without this group of young people and their DIY spirit, Seattle's early-'90s international popularity—including Nirvana and their peers—would never have happened.

You could split hairs arguing when the punk scene actually began, but clearly it was sometime in the mid-'70s, although they didn't call it punk back then. As in a number of small scenes in those days, young men so inclined were experimenting with wearing makeup and women's clothing—the gender-bending "glam" movement. Artists like David Bowie, Mott the Hoople, T. Rex, Slade, Iggy & the Stooges, and the New York Dolls appealed to a group of kids growing tired of mainstream rock's blandness. Glam artists blurred the gender lines, often leaving their audiences wondering about their ultimate sexual preference.

While most kids were listening to Chicago and Led Zeppelin, a small group of Roosevelt kids gravitated to glam. Glam represented freedom: the freedom to dress as you wanted, the freedom to not have to act like a full-on dude, the freedom to challenge not only accepted musical expression, but your place in society. Whether you were straight or gay was almost irrelevant. The point was that all were accepted within this little glam subculture.

Roosevelt student Jim Basnight thrived in that atmosphere. Armed with a love of glam and a vast knowledge of music, he became the front man for a band called the Luvaboys.

In 1975 the Luvaboys decided to perform at a Roosevelt High talent show, held after lunch. The band's clear intention was to incite a reaction, and to paraphrase George W. Bush, they accomplished their mission. They played extremely loud, so much so that the vice principal attempted to turn the volume down several times without success. "We came out there wearing makeup," Basnight recalls. "I painted my whole body in silver spray paint, like Iggy. And I put a big, black X on my chest."

The reception was predictable. Some of the jocks became irritated and began heaving vegetables left over from lunch at the band. The scene quickly degenerated into mayhem. Basnight was physically assaulted by angry jocks after the show. But the Luvaboys inspired some students to form bands of their own in a "they did it, why can't we?" fashion. In many ways, this obscure event became the opening salvo for what later would become a pretty big scene.

The Telepathic Foundation

Out of that small Roosevelt scene grew a fanzine called *Chatterbox*. Founded by Roosevelt's own Lee Lumsden, *Chatterbox* focused on glam acts as well as the burgeoning Seattle original music scene. Lumsden, an extremely bright but somewhat reclusive character, is arguably Seattle music's most underrated participant. His fanzine became a communication device and then a support system for young kids starting their own bands.

Bands began to spring up around the *Chatterbox* community, including Basnight's Meyce, the Telepaths, and the Tupperwares. The three bands had disparate sounds, and nobody knew what to call the new music. That changed when the Tupperwares' Tomata du Plenty returned from New York with a cassette recording of a Ramones CBGB's show. Inspired by New York punk, the Seattle glam community quickly identified with it and henceforth viewed themselves as punk rockers.

The Meyce played what we would today call pop-punk, while the Tupperwares had a glam/pre-goth mystique (the Meyce's Paul Hood describes the Tupperwares' sound as a cross between Devo and Marilyn Manson). The Telepaths, however, had a whole other thing going; featuring brothers Curt and Erich Werner, the band ventured in more of a King Crimson prog-rock direction, anchored by Bill Rieflin's stellar drumming.

Despite the stylistic differences, the three bands developed a tight bond. All three were shut out of the small Seattle cover band–oriented club scene. Other than playing basements, the only way to put a show on was to do it yourself: rent the hall, promote the show, sell tickets, and clean up afterward. The *Chatterbox* crew knew they needed to pool their resources to put on a show. At this point, during the infancy of Seattle's punk rock community, one big show could make an enormous difference. One show could demonstrate to the musicians and fans that punk rock was indeed a viable entity. One show could, in fact, define a scene.

That show would come to fruition on May 1, 1976, and would include all three bands. Held at the Oddfellows Hall on Capitol Hill, the event was promoted as the TMT Show—an abbreviation of the bands' names. A friend named Neil Hubbard helped organize and promote the event. Hubbard and his cohorts found creative ways to obtain free radio advertising. They created a fictional nonprofit organization as a way to raise money for the show, which was supposedly a benefit concert. "This one radio station, KILO, gave us free public service announcements," Hubbard remembers, "'cause we had this nonprofit group that we just made up out of thin air called the Telepathic Foundation. We were just pretty resourceful about things."

The show was an enormous success—not financially, but in terms of demonstrating that a viable scene did in fact exist. About a hundred people showed up.

---

*A heavily made-up young girl in a strapless evening gown was selling tickets for $1 and stamping everyone's hand. "How many people inside?" [*Seattle Times *reporter Patrick MacDonald inquired]. "I dunno. A lot. More than we expected, [she responded.]"*

—Staff reporter Patrick MacDonald,
The Seattle Times, May 3, 1976*

No one knows how many audience members went on to form their own bands, but that number is likely significant. One fan in attendance, Damon Titus, was a guitar player for a

---

*From "Telepathic Rock at Odd Fellows Hall," *Arts and Entertainment* section, p A20, May 3, 1976, by Patrick MacDonald, *Seattle Times* staff reporter, © 1976, Seattle Times Company. Used with permission.

cover-oriented country rock act known as the Fruitland Famine Band. As a result of the TMT Show, the band would abandon its format and become known as the Enemy: an original punk band. "It just blew our minds," says Titus. "We just couldn't go back to being a Top 40 band after that."

The TMT Show sent a clear message to the kids: You can form your own band. An original music scene exists in Seattle, and it loosely converges under the umbrella of punk rock.

The show also symbolically defined the first wave of Seattle punk rock bands. In addition to the TMT acts, artists such as the Feelings, Uncle Cookie, Chinas Comidas, and the Lewd added to the mix. Once again, the sounds of the bands were quite diverse—everything from a Sex Pistols–like assault (the Lewd) to the Stooges-influenced Feelings, to the artsy Patti Smith–sounding Chinas Comidas. In the early Seattle punk scene, bands did not pigeonhole themselves stylistically; people were open to trying pretty much anything. The reasons are fairly apparent. First, punk rock was still new, and people were not sure exactly what it was yet. Second, these underground bands were not going anywhere commercially, so why define themselves as commodities?

The Seattle punk scene was still a long way from gaining legs, however. It was almost as if the kids subconsciously thought of the TMT Show as an anomaly, a one-time event never to be repeated. Could the emerging punk community do it again? Hubbard believed it could.

On March 1, 1977, a Tuesday, Hubbard discovered that the Ramones were going to be playing at a bar in town the following Sunday. He was incensed, however, since he and his friends were underage and would not be able to see them. Out of desperation, he began making phone calls to their record company, hoping to persuade the band to play an all-ages show.

Finally, he got hold of the Ramones' tour agent and begged him to change the venue. "And I [told him] . . . 'Nobody is gonna get into this show who gives a damn about the Ramones,'" Hubbard recalls. "'They're not gonna be able to play for their fans.' And the guy said, 'OK, if you can find a place to do the show, it's yours.'"

With only five days to go, Hubbard frantically began calling around town in search of a venue. After nearly exhausting every possibility, he discovered that downtown Seattle's posh Olympic Hotel (now the Fairmont Olympic) had a ballroom available Sunday evening. He told the staff that he was putting on a dance with live music. Little did the hotel's management realize, however, that the lobby would soon be besieged by hundreds of leather-clad punk rockers.

The Ramones agreed to do the show, with the Meyce securing the opening slot.

Clinching an opening billing with the RAMONES for a one-night free-for-all (or was it?) at the prestige [sic] Olympic Hotel (March 6th, '77), it appeared the MEYCE would be going places soon. 400–500 people covered the plushly carpeted room like a snug sheath. This was EXCITEMENT. Seattle was lucky.

—Robert Larsen, *Chatterbox* no. 6

The Olympic Hotel show reinforced the notion that a significant audience existed for the new music, even though punk rock was considered subversive by '70s mainstream culture. The police despised the punks, just as they had their hippie forbearers. Furthermore, the existing club scene had no interest in these new bands, and it didn't matter anyway since much of the audience was underage. So punks resigned themselves to holding these one-off shows at various rental halls around town.

All of that changed with the opening of the Bird—Seattle's first club specifically dedicated to punk rock music.

Flipping the Bird

The Bird opened on March 4, 1978, in an empty storefront at the corner of 1st Avenue and Spring Street in downtown Seattle, a few blocks south of Belltown. The all-ages club took over the second floor of the six-story building. Access was on Spring, the side street. Since Spring is on an incline, the club entrance was at ground level. "The Bird was literally nothing more than our rehearsal space and a Coke machine," says Peter Barnes, drummer for the Enemy.

Initially, Hubbard and members of the Enemy struggled to come up with a name for the club. Hubbard then ventured outside and noticed an old sign on the building. "I went out and I looked at it," he recalls, "and went, 'Well, it says "John L. Bird Office Supplies." Let's just call it "the Bird."' You know, [as in] 'Fuck you!' Perfect!"

The Bird was a clandestine venue within Seattle. Other than the old John L. Bird moniker, the club never displayed a sign outside. Businesspeople entering the Federal Reserve building across the alley had no indication that they were doing business so close to a punk rock club.

Seattle's first punk rock venue was the brainchild of Roger Husbands, the Enemy's manager. Despite providing a venue critical to the scene's development, the Enemy had an uncomfortable position within that scene. Previously known as the country rock Fruitland Famine Band, the members had made a conscious—and commercial—decision to become punk rockers.

Recording engineer Conrad Uno, who at the time played bass in Uncle Cookie, recalls the band's sudden transformation at an Oddfellows Hall show. "So in the middle of their set," Uno remembers, "strobe lights came on. And the Fruitland Famine Band now was dressed in leather and [became] the Enemy. And henceforth they were the Enemy. And then they dumped ketchup on themselves and stuff. And I gotta tell ya, I thought that was such bullshit."

The Enemy were viewed by those outside their inner circle as the unmentionable *p* word: posers. They were a polished band with their own PA system, manager, sound man, and a roadie, and they wanted commercial success. In punk rock's early days, bands were supposed to disdain all those things, despite the fact that punk icons like the Ramones, Clash, and Sex Pistols had all signed major-label deals and desired stardom.

The Bird symbolizes, albeit on a small scale, the beginnings of a true original music scene. It lasted a grand total of just under three months, although Husbands and the Enemy later did shows under the Bird name at the Oddfellows Hall. "If [the Enemy] hadn't talked their manager into steppin' up and trying to milk this new scene," observes Rob Morgan, who worked the door at the Bird, "God knows if anything would've happened on the level that it did."

In some respects, Seattle in 1978 wasn't a whole lot different from other towns. The idea of punk rock seemed foreign, threatening, and obnoxious to the World War II generation. Today, young people cover themselves in tattoos and piercings and rarely draw a second look. Back then, however, when kids dressed in strange clothes, spiked their hair, and especially when men wore women's clothes—their elders took offense. To the older generation, *punk* meant miscreant, a loser with no aspirations, contributing nothing to proper society.

The 1978 Seattle urban punk community contained—and this is no exaggeration—a total of maybe a hundred people, including the bands. This small group coalesced around the Bird. By this time Seattle had arrived at its second punk wave, including the Enemy, the Mentors, the Cheaters, and leftover first-wavers the Telepaths and Chinas Comidas.

The Bird also helped create an underground connection between Seattle, California, and Vancouver, BC. The Enemy would play at San Francisco's Mabuhay Gardens. In return, San Francisco's Negative Trend would come up and play the Bird. So it went with Los Angeles and Vancouver. At this point, a national underground touring network did not yet exist, but suddenly Seattle seemed a lot closer to the rest of the world.

The Bird's closing featured a not-atypical confrontation with the Seattle police. The landlord ordered Husbands to vacate effective June 1, 1978. The closing-night party exemplified the strained and confrontational relationship between the police and the punk rock community.

A small group, including members of the Enemy, exited the Bird and migrated to the roof after midnight. Drummer Barnes describes the aftershow party as "lame" until some people started throwing things off the roof. "Somehow it ended up that the cops were called," Barnes recalls. "And they showed up, and they sent the vice squad after us . . . I mean, the really heavy-duty cops. . . . They slammed badges in peoples' faces and they called us faggots and they threw people on the ground. We had a rather diminutive woman lead singer, Suzanne [Grant], and they twisted her arm around behind her back and broke it." Titus loudly complained about Grant's treatment to the police and was rewarded by having his face smashed into the pavement.

This confrontational climate that existed between the police department and young music fans would continue throughout the next decade. As a result, punk rock clubs—especially all-ages venues—did not stay open for long, and musicians were constantly on the lookout for places to play.

Unfortunately for the police department, a partygoer happened to record the entire roof melee on tape. The band sued the police and won a court-ordered monetary settlement. An excerpt of the confrontation later found its way onto an Enemy single called "Trendy Violence."

Following the original Bird's demise, Husbands continued to run the club at various halls—calling it "the Bird in Exile"—until finding a semipermanent home at the Oddfellows Hall that August. The Bird had essentially and symbolically broken the ice. It hadn't been an overwhelming success financially and it didn't last long. Nonetheless, Husbands and the Enemy had proved it could be done. Open an all-ages club in Seattle and bands will come, and kids will come to see them.

Rosco Louie

In April 1978 local artists Larry Reid and Tracy Rowland opened a gallery in Pioneer Square. The Rosco Louie Gallery would display visual art, as well as provide a forum for performance art, including punk rock bands. The name Rosco Louie is West Coast hot rod slang for right- and left-hand turns. "Nobody really got that, and that's good," Reid proudly states.

The all-ages venue created an atmosphere where punk rock could comfortably exist. Reid even borrowed the Clash's "Only Band That Matters'" tagline for his gallery. "I would frequently market [Rosco Louie] as 'The Only Gallery That Matters,' and everyone in Seattle knew exactly what I was talking about," says Reid.

Rosco Louie in some ways synthesized and defined the attitude of the Seattle urban punk community. Reid and his peers created an aesthetic that manifested itself in a sense of humor that was equal parts self-effacing, macabre, pompous, sarcastic, and playfully irreverent. For example, the gallery would host shows by a local improvisational punk rock band. The band and Reid had an arrangement such that the members agreed to play until he had had enough. At that point, Reid would end the show by unplugging the PA. Usually, he would endure about twenty minutes before turning off the equipment. Sometimes, though, he couldn't wait that long. "I think [the lead singer] one time got mad at me," Reid recalls, "because about ten minutes into [a show], I couldn't take it anymore. I was like, 'Well, you know, ya said . . . '"*

Rosco Louie blurred the lines between visual and performance art, and became a preferred destination for the developing bohemian urban punk community. Unlike the Bird, Rosco Louie had some staying power and remained open until December 1982. Its small space provided exposure not only to local music and artwork, but also national independent acts and performance artists. Rosco Louie's space limitations limited its impact as well, although symbolically, the gallery represented another milepost for Seattle and Northwest independent music.

A Jewish Bingo Parlor Becomes a Punk Showplace

The scene took a significant leap forward when four young men began promoting shows at a Jewish bingo hall that could hold more than a thousand patrons. The idea came from Jim Lightfoot, owner of a comic book/record store called Time Travelers, in late 1978.

Similar to Hubbard's experience the previous winter, Lightfoot found out that the Ramones were going to be playing

---

*Reid identified the band as the Thrown Ups, although they did not form until 1985. It may have been the Limp Richards or Mr. Epp and the Calculations. Both bands are discussed later in this chapter.

a show at the Rainbow Tavern in the U-District. Once again the punk community was frustrated since underage fans would be shut out. "I just remember thinking, 'That's fucked!' 'Cause [the Rainbow was] twenty-one and over. And I just knew that—I mean, I was over twenty-one—but I knew a lot of people who just couldn't go," Lightfoot remembers.

Like Hubbard, Lightfoot contacted the Ramones' management company. "[I] called them up. And, as it turned out," Lightfoot recalls, "the Ramones themselves were more than happy to play an all-ages show. And also 'cause they were workaholics, they were more than happy to have another show, period."

Lightfoot booked the all-ages show at the Norway Center just north of Belltown and had the Enemy open. It was a rousing success. More than six hundred people turned out. Clearly they were onto something.

In June 1979 Lightfoot and Mike Vraney, a Time Travelers employee, promoted a show for the following month featuring the Dead Kennedys, then an obscure San Francisco punk band. Unbeknownst to them, U-Dub alum Terry Morgan was promoting shows the same weekend featuring two local bands: the electronica-based Young Scientist and the dark, postpunk Blackouts. Both parties promoted their shows by the cheapest, most effective method available in 1979: stapling posters to telephone polls around town. Since the performances were on the same night, the two parties began tearing down each others' posters. Thus began Seattle's first poster war.

Given that the local music community was so small, both sides soon realized that such destructive behavior would hurt everyone. Thus, Lightfoot and Vraney asked Morgan to work with them. A fourth individual, Carlo Scandiuzzi, soon came on board, and Modern Productions was born. The partnership initially made total sense as each individual offered something different. Lightfoot brought a DIY spirit, as well as an

immense knowledge of underground music. Vraney had connections to Ian Copeland, Police drummer Stewart Copeland's
brother, who had founded a talent agency that brought British
punk and new wave acts to the United States. Morgan had business experience and connections to sound and lighting people,
and also managed the Blackouts and Young Scientist. Finally,
Scandiuzzi had roots within the local artistic community and
thus could help get the word out.

Modern Productions promoted its first show at a downtown Jewish bingo hall known as the Talmud-Torah, located
just south and across the street from the landmark Pike Place
Market. The venue, originally called the Showbox, dates back
to 1939 and hosted top-line talent such as Frank Sinatra, Nat
King Cole, and Harry James in its heyday. By 1979 the once ele-
gant hall had fallen into disrepair, although its thousand-person
capacity made it an ideal venue to host American and European
punk bands.

The Modern crew immediately began preparing the venue
for its first show. They had to clear out the bingo tables, trash
loads of bingo cards, and construct a stage by hand out of two-
by-fours.

The Modern Productions era began on September 8, 1979,
when Magazine, a postpunk descendant of the Buzzcocks,
headlined. Morgan's Blackouts opened. The show was a hit.
People came, and an institution was born. The Showbox name
was restored to the building later that month. Over the next
two years, Modern Productions would transform Seattle's punk
community on a number of levels.

First, punk fans of all ages would get to see some of the most
cutting-edge British and American punk and new wave bands
of the era. The British roster included the Police, the Specials,
XTC, Ultravox, the Psychedelic Furs, 999, Gang of Four, Public
Image Ltd., and Squeeze. In addition, Modern Productions

brought in a stable of American punk artists like Iggy Pop, Black Flag, X, the Ramones, and the Dead Kennedys.

This was music that most Seattle kids would not otherwise be exposed to, as it was rarely played on the radio. The records weren't even available at local stores, except perhaps in the U-District. So this experience—young people seeing these bands live—often constituted their entire exposure to contemporary punk rock and new wave.

Modern Productions' success is all the more amazing given its owners were in their twenties. How were these young people able to bring some of the most electrifying music of the late '70s and early '80s to Seattle? The answer is not quite so mystifying, given the context of the times. Large local promoters were simply not interested in booking these bands. Modern thus had little competition and even brought in legendary blues and R&B artists that other promoters ignored, like Willie Dixon, Muddy Waters, and James Brown.

In addition, the Showbox, more than any other venue of that era, created a sense of community and helped generate a valid local music scene. Punk and new wave music fans in that still-small punk community discovered each other. The Showbox became a shared experience. Young music fans helped out Modern Productions as they could, working security, cleaning up after shows, cleaning the bathrooms—all on a voluntary basis. "We were hanging flyers for the Showbox," says Blaine Cook of the hardcore Fartz, "and quote unquote doing security. We were actually just grunt workers. We'd get in for free. So we got to see pretty much all those bands that came through the Showbox."

The sense of bonding between musicians and fans is hard to fathom in today's era of corporate-sponsored events. Back then, the line between artist and fan almost did not exist—at least within the punk community. It was not unusual for members of bands like the Ramones and Devo to accompany fans to aftershow parties. For example, members of Devo came to an aftershow party at the Enemy's rehearsal space. "Devo came over," Enemy drummer Peter Barnes recalls, "and we were hanging out with 'em. And I'm sittin' on this couch next to the drummer in Devo. And these two chicks come up to *me*, and they go, 'Oh, we just love your band—Devo! So much!' Well, I'm sitting right fucking next to [Devo's] drummer. He and I are laughing our heads off."

The Showbox had its share of amazing events. Fans particularly remember Gang of Four introducing them to English post-punk and Devo offering the American version. But perhaps the most distinctive events involved two English bands, the Specials and Public Image Ltd. (PiL), and two local acts, the Heats and the Blackouts.

The Specials—the British band credited for creating the ska revival—opened for the Police. A logistics issue arose since the Showbox's small stage could not accommodate the Police's abundance of equipment. Running out of time, Lightfoot & Co. came up with an idea: extend the existing stage with bingo tables, duct-tape them together, duct-tape the tables to the existing stage, and throw a cloth over the entire contraption. This setup proved adequate for the Police since they tended to stay in one place while they played. The Specials, however, were quite another matter. The band was much more animated, highlighted by singer Terry Hall climbing up and jumping off amplifiers. "We could see this whole contraption we built just quivering, shaking," Lightfoot recalls. Fortunately, though, the bingo table–enhanced stage held and disaster was averted.

The PiL show witnessed another near-collapse of the stage, this time by design. PiL's lead singer, John Lydon—previously known as the Sex Pistols' Johnny Rotten—encouraged the audience to come up on stage. The bingo-table extension had been disassembled, but the stage still was not designed to hold the fifty to sixty people who were now pogo-ing on it. Lydon was standing on the drum riser, belting out the PiL anthem "Public Image! Public Image!" while Terry Morgan, standing next to Lydon, pleaded with him to stop the show before the stage collapsed. "He turns to me," says Morgan, "and winks in only the way that John Lydon can wink, hand[s] me the microphone, and walk[s] off the stage. And the chaos just ebbed—it just eased off. It was like the most out-of-control situation that I'd ever been in—but he was in full control."

The Heats/Blackouts show was decidedly the strangest pairing. Having these two local bands on the same bill was almost akin to Jimi Hendrix playing with the Monkees a decade and a half earlier. The Heats' upbeat pop sound and new wave haircuts made them popular with the college fraternity crowd. The Blackouts, on the other hand, represented the Heats' antithesis: a dark, postpunk sound. Naturally, the two bands and their fans despised one another.

The Heats had created a parallel world to the punk scene. While its members knew about and associated with some of the punk kids, the Heats early on ventured into the bars and embraced commercial opportunity by playing covers as well as originals. Furthermore, the Heats got to tour, opening for acts such as Heart and the Knack. Essentially, the band made a statement that would still resonate in Seattle years later: you can make original music and find an audience in the clubs, and you can take that act on the road.

The Showbox pairing with the Blackouts combined two very different mind-sets and, for the most part, two mutually exclusive fan bases. As expected, neither band won over the other's audience. While fans had a relatively mild reaction to the Heats/Blackouts gig at the Showbox, another gig shortly thereafter was not quite so innocuous.

Shortly after the Showbox gig, the Blackouts were scheduled to open for the Heats at Baby O's, a club located a few blocks from the original Bird. As the kings of dark punk rock, the Blackouts felt they had to make an anti-Heats statement. So when the lights came on, fans gasped as the Blackouts took the stage completely naked and covered in fresh pig's blood. The sight and smell of the spectacle elicited screams from the shocked audience.

Legend has it that the Heats themselves were similarly repulsed. But Steve Pearson, the band's guitarist and singer, recalls their reaction as one of indifference. "Nice statement," he remembers thinking, "[but] I don't know what it is you're stating. You hate the Heats? You hate the Heats' audience? You don't like pigs? I don't know."

The Heats and the power pop crowd were generally excluded from the Showbox and its audience. So the power pop thing pretty much ran in its own circles as Modern Productions continued to cultivate a young punk rock audience by bringing them British talent and providing opening slots for local bands.

The Showbox experience had an indelible effect on those still too young to form their own groups. Future members of bands like the Young Fresh Fellows, Green River, Mudhoney, Soundgarden, and Chemistry Set attended Showbox events, inspiring them to create their own version of punk rock, some of them mixing it with various genres to create grunge.

Upchuck and the Fags

The Showbox also helped usher in a small club scene favorable to the newer acts. In particular, Pioneer Square's Gorilla Room and Belltown's WREX provided additional forums for local punk and new wave bands.

The Gorilla Room opened as an all-ages venue in March 1980 but within a few months began serving alcohol. Previously a wino bar, the Gorilla Room was transformed into a true punk "palace," making the Showbox appear upscale by comparison. "Their idea of decorating the place was . . . they literally spray painted everything in the place black: the tables, the chairs, the vinyl booths, the posters on the wall, the beer advertising, the empty bottles that happened to be laying on the floor left over from the winos," artist Art Chantry remembers. "The only thing they didn't spray paint black was the mirror behind the bar—which was broken."

Up in Belltown, an even more vibrant scene began developing around WREX and Tug's, two clubs catering to a gay clientele. The Belltown piece of the Seattle scene included a mixture of straight and gay punks. The gay punk subculture was a natural evolution of the cross-dressing/makeup glam aesthetic. No single individual better represented the Seattle gay punk culture than the late Charles Gerra, better known as "Upchuck."

Referred to as plain "Chuck" by his friends, Upchuck was almost indescribable. He was a larger-than-life character, an openly in-your-face homosexual during a time when many straights were uncomfortable with that. Upchuck never dressed the same and never kept the same hairstyle. He was also an incredibly talented performance artist and singer. Love him or despise him, Upchuck would not be ignored. He gained notoriety within the scene fronting Clone, his first band. "I went and saw Clone . . . and [Upchuck] was wearing Converse tennis shoes, see-through plastic pants, and a T-shirt that said on the front, 'RAM IT DOWN MY THROAT,'" says drummer Ben Ireland. "On the back it said, 'CRAM IT UP MY ASS.' And he had short, punk, canary-yellow hair. He was just amazing. Just blew me away. That was the first time I saw anything like that live. And I said, 'I really wanna play in a band with that guy.'"

Ireland got his wish when Upchuck invited him and his sister, keyboardist Barbara Ireland (later bassist and vocalist), local guitar legend Paul Solger, and artist/poet Dahny Reed to form a punk/glam supergroup. Upchuck also asked Jane Brownson, a gorgeous, blue-haired punk chick, to round out the band at bass. The group had yet to name itself as it took the stage for its first gig at the Lincoln Arts Center in Belltown. Friend Steve Pritchard, waiting to announce the band to the audience, asked the members what they wanted to be called. "We just jokingly said, 'Upchuck and the Fags,' 'cause we hadn't decided yet," says Ben Ireland. "And he just grabbed the mike and said, 'Ladies and gentlemen, Upchuck and the Fags!'" The name quickly became shortened to just "the Fags," inciting derision from macho hardcore punks.

The Fags often attracted those same homophobic hardcore fans to their shows. The ensuing violence and destruction quickly got the group banned from WREX and the Gorilla Room. Fortunately, the Fags' manager rented a ballroom known as Danceland USA, just north of the Showbox.

The Danceland shows were events in every sense of the word. The Fags would perform, and Upchuck would wander around in the audience, typically only actually singing for two or three songs a set. It didn't matter, though—Upchuck's magic made the Fags his band. Fags shows were unpredictable, especially after the band began dabbling in MDA, a precursor to ecstasy. MDA had the impact of veering the band in a more psychedelic direction, with a nod to the Velvet Underground. Band members would take MDA either before or during a performance, and once the drug hit in full force, the entire band would collapse in the middle of the stage in a "Fag pile."

Some of the most notorious Fags shows revolved around food products, including one that involved spoiled vegetables. Members of the Fartz showed up, angered that Upchuck had lifted Solger from their band, and brought decayed vegetables to heave at the Fags. Now on MDA, the Fags could actually see the vegetables coming in slow motion and for the most part were able to avoid the rotten bell peppers and tomatoes. It was almost akin to Neo dodging bullets in *The Matrix*. "A vegetable *Matrix*," corrects Ben Ireland.

The Fags—other than from some of their hardcore detractors—represented a comfortable comingling between the straight and gay punk crowds. Furthermore, their use of MDA would lead others to venture along that path and would result in a psychedelic aesthetic that would have an influence on the punk and grunge scenes throughout the 1980s.

The Rocket

As the music community grew throughout downtown, Belltown, Pioneer Square, and Capitol Hill, the late '70s also saw the beginnings of lasting support from radio and print media. Other than articles by the *Seattle Times*' Patrick MacDonald and sporadic radio play, little media existed to support the early punk scene. Mostly, the scene had been driven by fanzines, posters on telephone poles, and word of mouth. In 1979 that all began to change with the first issue of the *Rocket* and radio support from KZAM-AM and KCMU-FM.

Prior to the *Rocket*'s existence, new music and local bands received scant coverage from the print media. Even MacDonald, who championed coverage of the 1976 TMT Show and the early scene, generally favored established bands over the upstarts. "I can't recall my having ever been in that position of discovering a band in some dark bar and leading people to them," MacDonald told the *Rocket*'s Bob Newman in a 1981 interview.

By the turn of the new decade, MacDonald was writing about bar bands like the Heats and Jr. Cadillac—the acts generally reviled by the punk community. In fact, his negative stance on newer punk bands was so commonplace that he became predictable. "Basically, if he really loved a record . . . you stayed away from it," says Chantry. "And if he really, really hated a record to the point where he wanted to pan it in print—that was the one you wanted. I mean it was that consistent."

The *Rocket* changed all that when it debuted as an insert in the October 1979 issue of the *Seattle Sun*. The monthly newspaper would quickly gain notoriety as Seattle's rock magazine, covering local and national music as well as visual arts and cinema. Furthermore, in December of that year, the *Rocket* began a free musicians' classified section. These classified ads would become a crucial way for bands to obtain musicians and vice versa.

During its life, the *Rocket* would boast an almost embarrassing array of talent, including music biographers Charles R. Cross and Gillian Gaar, renowned journalist and critic Karrie Jacobs, *The Simpsons* creator Matt Groening, Sub Pop Records founder Bruce Pavitt, musician Scott McCaughey (Young Fresh Fellows, Minus 5, R.E.M.), and punk graphic artist Art Chantry—and those are just the famous people. Without this critical media support, Seattle's music scene would likely have remained in obscurity.

Musicians would later complain that the *Rocket* focused too much on national acts, especially after Cross became editor in 1986. Still the newspaper spent considerable space covering local music throughout the '80s. In its early days, it reviewed records and live shows by local acts like the Enemy, the Blackouts, the Heats, the Beakers, Student Nurse, and the Cheaters. Finally, the local music community had serious journalistic support and a stable way of communicating through the musicians' classifieds.

KZAM's Rock of the '80s

Radio was another matter. Not only did Seattle radio stations avoid playing local bands, but they—like many stations around the country—avoided punk and new wave acts in favor of tired album-oriented rock or what was left of Top 40. In Seattle, that dinosaur attitude would begin to change when a young DJ named Stephen Rabow made his presence felt at KZAM in 1979, when that station switched to a "Rock of the '80s" format.

Rabow was a product of Olympia's Evergreen State College (see Chapter 2) and moved to Seattle in 1978 to pursue a career in medicine. He obtained an evening position at a Seattle hospital, but he also had a passion for radio that he had nurtured at KAOS, Evergreen's student-run radio station. Rabow wanted to apply KAOS' progressive and avant-garde leanings to a commercial station. In fact, he wanted to get on KZAM so badly that he even obtained his own sponsors.

Rabow was one of the first to infiltrate Seattle with the Evergreen experimental ethos. The Evergreen attitude not only embraced newer music, but championed independent and local artists. After convincing KZAM music director Jon Kertzer to expand the station's format, Rabow created a show called *House Party* that featured an eclectic mix of artists such as punk pioneers the Sex Pistols, postpunk bands Gang of Four and Throbbing Gristle, avant-garde musician Brian Eno, and even oldies like Elvis and Little Richard. The point was to expand the limits of what commercial radio could be. "The very first song I played," Rabow remembers, "was this unknown group—and I had [an] import recording—out of Ireland by a group called U2. And the second song I played was [by] a local group called Red Dress."

Soon Rabow spearheaded a *Local Tape Extravaganza* show where he encouraged anyone to send a tape in and he'd play it, record contract or not. He teamed up with the *Rocket*, who helped promote his show, and the tapes began coming in. The show would sometimes last as long as twelve hours and provided invaluable exposure for local bands.

Rabow also brought a twisted sense of humor to his radio shows. He made up a segment called "Driving Tips for Stupid People," which was sponsored by the Stupid Jean Company.

Rabow's fictional Stupid Jean Company offered "unique" styles that encouraged its customers to be hip while looking like everyone else. Rabow drove a Ford Pinto, which was notorious for having its gas tank explode upon a rear-end collision. He had flames painted on the car and a license plate that read "K-BOOOM!"

KZAM's support lasted until February 1981, when the owners decided to nix the new format. Everyone at the station, including Rabow, lost their jobs. Yet his impact was dramatic. He demonstrated that the newer music could attract an audience at a commercial station. Furthermore, Rabow's efforts were critical, along with the *Rocket*, in nurturing Seattle's underground music scene.

KCMU

Around the same time as the "Rock of the '80s" demise, rumblings were happening at U-Dub's KCMU. In 1981 it was a 10-watt station broadcasting from campus. The signal could barely be heard outside the U-District. The station had a split format at the time: during the day, it would play soft rock and jazz, with '70s-era album-oriented rock in the evenings. Playlists included artists like Molly Hatchet and Lynyrd Skynyrd and "new music" by bands like Aerosmith and Pink Floyd. With few exceptions, national and local punk and new wave acts were virtually ignored.

In 1981 U-Dub was undergoing a round of budget cuts that included funding for the station. If nothing was done, KCMU would cease to exist after the 1980/81 school year. A group of students, led by Mike Fuller, did not want that to happen and appealed to the university for help. U-Dub agreed to provide the station a one-time grant of $12,000 until it became self-funded. Fuller and his associates quickly scrambled to keep KCMU running into the next school year.

The budget was so tight that when the station organized its first promotional record giveaway, Fuller realized he had nothing to give away. So the staff got together and raided the library for any older records they knew they wouldn't play, like Carol Channing and the Royal Canadian Mounted Police marching band. "We told [listeners]," says Fuller, "'Seventh caller gets this mystery pack of records.' We didn't even have the money to mail it to them. They had to come to the station to get it."

The university agreed to the grant with a few stipulations, one of them being that journalism students would have to come in and do the news. U-Dub would provide an Associated Press teletype machine for this purpose. The machine was so loud and clunky that it made the floor shake. (If you've ever seen an old Walter Cronkite–era newscast and heard the constant chugging sound in the background—that's a teletype machine.) The teletype was free to KCMU as long as the station provided the paper. "We thought that was a great deal," Fuller recalls, "but what we didn't know is how expensive the paper was. And so, sometimes when times were tight what we would do is, in the night, we would go into the men's room and jimmy the lock on the paper towel dispenser, take out a roll of paper towels, and put that in the teletype machine."

Fuller believed that the station had to shift its focus away from its split format and concentrate entirely on newer music, since that's what callers were requesting. By the fall of 1981, KCMU's playlists included artists like Elvis Costello, the Ramones, Echo and the Bunnymen, and the Jam. In those early self-funding days, the station did not support local music as intensely as KZAM, but it was headed in that direction, playing music from Seattle bands like the Heats, Student Nurse, Visible Targets, 3 Swimmers, and Moving Parts. KCMU's role as an advocate for local music would continue to evolve and expand throughout the decade.

By 1980/81 Seattle had successfully developed a healthy, albeit small, original music scene and had arrived at its third punk wave. Musical styles were even more varied than the first two waves and included power pop, arty new wave, hardcore punk, metal, and noise. The power pop bands included the Heats, the Cowboys, and the Allies, who were popular among the college fraternity crowd and seemed to have the most reasonable possibility of commercial success.

Arty new wave bands were often the types that would play Reid's Rosco Louie and other galleries. These bands blurred the line between visual and audio art, as their shows were often accompanied by performance artists and projected visualizations. Their sounds ranged from the pop-punk of the Fastbacks (who lasted into the grunge era and beyond) to the offbeat and arty Student Nurse, the glam-edged Fags, the post-punk-influenced Beakers (and their successors, 3 Swimmers), the goth-sounding Red Masque, and the avant-garde, dissonant Blackouts.

Hardcore punk made its way up from Los Angeles, influenced by the likes of Black Flag and the Minutemen. Bands like the Fartz, the Refuzors, and the Rejectors played a hyper-fast one-two/one-two onslaught, driven by angry political lyrics. Like their hardcore brethren in other cities, the Fartz became energized by Ronald Reagan's 1980 election. Reagan became the symbol of rebellion for hardcore punks, just as he had for the hippies as governor of California in the '60s.

The hardcore shows—Fartz performances in particular—were often accompanied by fan violence, with hyped-up, testosterone-fueled males wreaking havoc. As such, these bands were often marginalized and became targets of the Seattle Police Department. "Back then, that's just what people did," says Fartz vocalist Blaine Cook (whose stage name was Blaine Fart). "You'd have a hall show and—inevitably—somebody's gonna break a window, somebody's gonna pull a toilet out, somebody's gonna break a sink." As a result, the city would begin to crack down on the all-ages scene and eventually close it down entirely.

The Suburban Metal Scene

East across Lake Washington sits Bellevue, today one of Seattle's most upscale suburbs. Back then, however, the town was more of a middle-class bedroom community, but it was still financially better off than urban Seattle. Bellevue is one of those "not cool to be from" places. It didn't have Seattle's cachet, Olympia's hipness, or the grittiness of working-class towns like Aberdeen. Bellevue, along with nearby Kirkland and Bothell (collectively referred to as the Eastside), represented everything antipunk. Let's face it: there is nothing cool about the suburbs. "There was a joke," recalls Bellevue native and drummer Mike Musburger (later with the Posies). "What do Bellevue housewives make for dinner? The answer would be: reservations."

The suburbs, including Bellevue, had a counterpoint metal scene that predated Seattle's punk community. Much of the suburban metal scene actually called West Seattle home, but Bellevue had an all-ages venue where everyone could play: the Lake Hills Roller Rink. The Lake Hills facility had been hosting musical acts of various genres since the early '60s, including performances by the legendary Sonics and Wailers. In the '70s, the venue began hosting shows headlined by Rail, an early Northwest hard rock/metal band. By the end of that decade, local promoter Craig Cooke began coordinating "Battle of the Bands" contests at Lake Hills to help rekindle interest in rock music during the disco craze.

Lake Hills attracted the "prettier side" of the metal scene, that is, the rich Eastside kids. The tougher West Seattle metal and hard rock crowd would usually avoid the venue. Thus, the few urban punks who did venture over to Lake Hills ended up observing a skewed version of the suburban metal community—rich boys with fancy equipment, who compared each other's teased-out hair and clothes, so they could see how many sleazy women they could sleep with. "You'd get yourself a Flying V instead of a beat-up Telecaster," says Steve van Liew, who played on the Eastside in Overlord.

"Everybody would just dress up in their most garish glam outfits," adds writer and metal fan Jeff Gilbert. "And these girls—their hair, [they] had to duck walking in the door half the time 'cause their hair was so poofed up."

The metal kids could really play, though, even if their repertoire rarely featured originality. Dawn Anderson was one of the few urban punks who attended Lake Hills shows. "Some of them were pretty damn good musicians," she recalls. "But . . . at the time, it didn't seem like very many of them were being very bold about originality. A lot of 'em went up there and played Judas Priest covers and Black Sabbath covers and shit."

At this point, metal kept itself in a distinct world from the downtown scene, and metalheads hated the punks—punks generally meaning anyone involved with the urban Seattle scene. At the time, metal meant long hair; loud, droning, cool-looking guitars; long solos; and pure testosterone. Punk meant short hair, shorter songs, and embracing the feminine. Women were in punk bands, and sometimes the men dressed like them. Metalheads and punkers held a healthy mutual disdain.

Occasionally, some metal kids would venture downtown to stir up trouble. A group of them would hang out with some other antipunk kids at a doughnut shop just north of the Showbox at 1st and Pike. These so-called Doughnut Holers would lie in wait for unsuspecting punks exiting the Showbox. The SPD, not wanting trouble, would sometimes warn punks leaving the Showbox to head in the opposite direction. "If a group of metalheads ran into some punks after dark," says Chantry, "they'd kick the shit out of 'em. And vice versa."

"At that point in time, you've got short hair, you know, you're a punk rock fag," adds Cook. "Then comes the mid-'80s— mid- to late-'80s—where everybody's growin' their hair out long. Now you're a long-haired fag. Somebody wants to beat your ass no matter what's goin' on. And they all seem to know what's gay, you know?"

Seattle's metal scene had always received the least amount of media coverage. The *Rocket* was pretty much an urban-centric paper. Overall, however, the Seattle region really was metal dominated and had been for over a decade. City and suburbs wouldn't mix musically for another couple of years.

The Blackouts

The Blackouts were one of those bands that come along maybe once a decade. They had an indefinable quality that not only sets a band apart from its peers, but creates a timeless appeal. Seattle had three of these bands during this book's time period: the U-Men (Chapter 3), Nirvana (Chapter 6), and the Blackouts. Unfortunately, Seattle had not yet developed a strong enough local support system to elevate the Blackouts to national status, as Nirvana would enjoy a decade later.

The Blackouts formed in 1979, a descendant of the Telepaths. The band's artistic center was singer Erich Werner, who also played guitar and wrote most of the lyrics. Supporting Werner were bassist Mike Davidson, synthesizer player Roland Barker, and drummer Bill Rieflin. Unlike their arch-nemesis the Heats, the Blackouts were not a happy band. Their music eschewed Reagan-era culture and painted a dark portrait of tortured art. Modern Productions' Terry Morgan was immediately struck by the band's presence and decided to manage them. "They just had an aggressive 'in-your-face' kind of [attitude] that wasn't just punk rock," says Morgan, "but it was very musical and intellectual. They as people were just challenging individuals who wanted to go out and do something spectacular."

The Blackouts' first single, 1979's synth-driven "Make No Mistake," did not fully capture the band's striking live shows, but the Seattle music community knew even then that it had something amazing on its hands.

This band is one of the very few in Seattle that musically transcend the local scene. Those who've seen one of the shows where their energy, intelligence and deeply felt emotionalism have sparked and fused together, know about the potential of the Blackouts.

—George Romansic, *The Rocket*, May 1980

The band possessed the kind of musical ability that was anathema to the typical punk band of that era. In particular, Rieflin provided the drum chops to drive the band to new heights. Rieflin's combination of power, finesse, and personality made him one of the rare spectacular drummers within the rock pantheon. His style is unmistakable, akin to how John Bonham was indispensable to Led Zeppelin or Keith Moon to the Who. Rieflin is arguably the greatest drummer in Seattle music history, and that is a significant statement given that the city has produced its share of amazing percussionists, including Soundgarden's Matt Cameron (later with Pearl Jam) and 10 Minute Warning's Greg Gilmore.

Initially, the band had a synthpop sound inspired by keyboardist Barker. Then, in 1980, bassist Davidson left the band, and Barker switched to saxophone after his synthesizer was stolen at a Showbox gig. Suddenly, the band transformed dramatically, becoming more stark and macabre. Rieflin stated in an interview with writer Clark Humphrey that the band's sound became more tribal and bare bones, and that Barker's switch to saxophone coincided with the Blackouts "becoming the Blackouts."

The band's new sound was heavier and even more rhythm-driven. In some ways, their new persona laid the basis for the heavier grunge music that would come later. "The Blackouts were probably *the* proto-grunge template," observes Reid, who hosted the band at Rosco Louie. "It was sort of a thick, heavy sound."

Because of the limitations of Seattle's music scene, the band moved to Boston in 1982 and proceeded to implode shortly thereafter. Rieflin and bassist Paul Barker—who replaced Davidson—joined Ministry, and Rieflin was later invited to tour with R.E.M. The Blackouts' recorded output can be heard on Olympia's K Records 2004 reissue *History in Reverse*. "Their recordings literally do not do them justice," says Jim Tillman, later with the U-Men. "Their live shows were about the most invigorating, visceral, and just wild-eyed experiences."

In retrospect, the conventional criticism of this era of Seattle music is that it was highly derivative of national and British acts. The Fartz were Black Flag wannabes, 3 Swimmers raided the Gang of Four's repertoire, the Heats sounded like the Knack, etc. Commentators in the documentary *hype!* refer to pregrunge Seattle as "lame" and imitative. Yet these criticisms are patently unfair and blatantly inaccurate.

Any local music scene at any point in time can be referred to as derivative of more well-known acts. The line separating influence from imitation is a blurry one. Very few artists are completely original; even great artists build upon what has occurred before, and add their personality and talent to create their own original expression. Seattle's third punk rock wave was no exception.

Additionally, referring to this era as "lame" is, well, lame. The Showbox under Modern Productions was a phenomenon that will likely never occur again. The DIY ethic of this era was critical to what came later. Furthermore, this period of Seattle music was unadulterated *fun*. The music, the attitudes, the venues—all of it had a certain naive innocence. Finally, if nothing else, the Blackouts proved that Seattle could create something timeless.

Noise Bands

In addition to the Blackouts, more originality can be found in an underground group of bands that simply played noise. The main proponents of this aesthetic were suburbanite transplants to downtown: the Limp Richerds and Mr. Epp and the Calculations. The Limp Richerds were the brainchild of Dave Middleton, a kid from Federal Way, a town about a half-hour drive south of Seattle. The band's name, an obvious sexual reference, was also kind of a tongue-in-cheek poke at Rolling Stones guitarist Keith Richards. The band purposely misspelled Richerds to avoid being lumped in with the hardcore bands. At the time, if a hardcore band had an *a* in its name, it pretty much had to be circled to create an anarchy symbol.

The Limps had little musical ability and made a hell of a racket, with Middleton playing clarinet and singing. The drummer, Ross Guffy, often used suitcases for percussion since the band couldn't afford a real drum kit. Guffy also played percussion on items found around the neighborhood, like real estate signs, garbage can lids, and a space heater. Writer Dawn Anderson vividly remembers her first Limp Richerds show. "Mark Arm [who played guitar for Mr. Epp] was in the audience," Anderson recalls, "and he kept on shouting out, 'Suitcase solo! Samsonite solo!'"

The band also exemplified the Seattle sense of humor, with songs such as "Death to Ivar," about the owner of a chain of Seattle-area seafood restaurants. The joke is that the band had no issues with Ivar—in fact, they thought of him as a pleasant enough fellow. "Death to Ivar" is totally Seattle: pick an innocuous target, spew totally meaningless venom about him, and sit back and laugh at the reactions.

Mr. Epp's story is perhaps even more exemplary of Seattle's sense of humor. Epp hailed from Bellevue, and was initially a fantasy creation by Bellevue Christian High School friends Jeff Smith, Darren Morey, Peter Wick, and Mark McLaughlin. Bored with math class, Smith thought it would be funny to create a fictional band named after his math teacher, and thus came the idea for Mr. Epp and the Calculations. "And we just kind of made it up," Smith recalls, "like as a thing that people [who] are nerdy [who] aren't into Dungeons and Dragons [might] do."

"And some of those guys like went off to study French in France for a semester—like in some kind of exchange program," says McLaughlin (later Mark Arm). "And, that was the Mr. Epp European tour."

Similar to the Limps' feelings about Ivar, Smith and his friends possessed no animosity toward their math teacher, unlike, say, '70s Southern rockers Lynyrd Skynyrd, whose moniker is a dig at a hated gym teacher named Leonard Skinner. They used the name Epp simply because it sounded funny. "People always thought it was like Lynyrd Skynyrd, like we hated [Mr. Epp]. He was actually a pretty cool guy," says Smith. "And I saw him as late as '86 or something, and he just seemed to think it was funny."

Smith & Co. created fake albums, fake tours, and started putting up posters on telephone poles around town about fictional Epp shows. Soon there was a buzz about Mr. Epp—a buzz about a band that didn't exist. Maire Masco, co-owner of a local label called Pravda Records, noticed the Mr. Epp posters around town and became interested in this "band." One day she observed Smith tacking a poster on a telephone pole and ran over to ask if his band would open a show she was promoting.

Assuming she was with the police, Smith fled. Eventually Masco caught up with him and convinced him to have Epp open her show. "So we were like, 'OK, well, we have some equipment. We can probably play a show,'" Smith recalls. "And that was pretty much how it began at first. And then we realized, 'Oh, we need to write some songs.'"

Epp changed personnel over its life, but its classic lineup—if you can use that term—included Smith on vocals (adopting the stage name Jo Smitty), McLaughlin on guitar (Mark Arm), Morey on drums (Darren Mor-X), and his brother Todd Morey (Todd Why?) on bass. The band purchased the cheapest equipment it could find, and the members found themselves unable to tune their guitars. "So it didn't take too long to realize," says Smith, "that it sounded like chords if you just moved your hands fast."

They also happily referred to themselves as the Worst Band in the World—the inverse of the Rolling Stones' status as the "World's Greatest Rock-and-Roll Band." The idea came from KZAM's Rabow, who introduced an Epp tape on the air by stating, "Let me . . . turn on the cassette player and you too, for yourself, can hear Mr. Epp and the Calculations, perhaps the world's worst rock-and-roll band." Rabow's exclamation was all in good fun, of course, and he and the band freely joked about it.

Pravda was intrigued enough to bankroll studio time for the band. Along with Masco, label co-owner Dennis White was struck by the concept of recording a band that didn't know how to play. "It sounds kind of like a concept thing. But it wasn't, really," says White. "It was partly put on and partly 'let's see what happens if we do this.' They put together a band that [didn't] really exist and they [became] a band. [We] put out a single that is probably the worst thing anybody ever heard but [we made] it work." Perhaps appropriately, the resultant single, "Mohawk Man," became a hit on KROQ, a hip LA radio station.

Mr. Epp and the Limp Richerds' noise rock certainly wasn't for everyone, and their commercial potential was severely limited. But as unstructured, as undisciplined, and as unmusical as those bands were, no one else sounded like them. They didn't copy English proto–industrial noise outlets like Throbbing Gristle or Whitehouse, who almost used their music as a weapon—a sonic assault of the senses meant to disrupt. Epp and the Limps did not have the same pretensions of those English groups or, for that matter, the New York no wave bands of that era. They weren't out to prove how grotesque life is by providing some "music to live your miserable life by." Rather, the Seattle bands were products of their suburban environments, groups of bored young men making music almost as a joke. "In retrospect," says writer Anderson, "I'd say probably Mr. Epp and the Limp Richerds and those guys were so completely pure and uninfluenced by anything."

The Seattle Syndrome

Epp's recording debut represented another step forward for local music: a burgeoning local record label scene. By 1980 small-scale local labels included Pravda, No Threes, Mr. Brown (out of Olympia), and Engram.

Engram was the creation of Neil Hubbard, Homer Spence, and Danny Eskenazi. Hubbard had been a key contributor to the 1976 TMT Show, as well as the 1978 opening of the Bird. Spence played in the Telepaths, and Eskenazi owned a vintage clothing store. Spence and Eskenazi also played together in a pre-punk experimental band called Lamar Harrington. The label began its existence by releasing the Blackouts' *Men in Motion* EP in 1980. From the start, Engram, like many of the small labels, never really made any money. It was strictly a labor of love for those involved.

As 1980 faded into 1981, Hubbard, Spence, and Eskenazi envisioned putting out an Engram compilation featuring Seattle's most important and influential third-wave punk bands. Today, compilations (or "comps") have become mostly obsolete, given the ability of the average music listener to download songs and create his or her own song lists. But with the rise of independent record labels in the '70s and '80s, comps became a critically important tool for small labels to introduce themselves, their bands, and their community to prospective buyers. Comps acted as samplers, a cereal variety pack if you will, to help discerning consumers decide whether to explore further. In addition, comp bands often couldn't afford to record enough of their own material to fill an EP or LP.

Engram released the *Seattle Syndrome, Vol. 1* comp in late 1981. Hubbard came up with the title, which reflected the frustration local bands had experienced up to that point. Typical Seattle groups of the era would get some momentum going and either disband or move out of town and disintegrate. The communal feeling was, despite the germination of a valid scene, Seattle remained a dead-end town. If your band wanted a serious musical career, you had to move somewhere else. As expected, the grass typically was not greener. Chinas Comidas moved to Los Angeles in 1980 and promptly fell apart. The Blackouts fled to Boston in 1982 and eventually disbanded in San Francisco. The Fags and Jim Basnight tried New York with little success. Some made permanent homes in their new haunts: the Screamers and Popdefect (an iteration of Seattle's Psychopop) in Los Angeles, and the Avengers in San Francisco. Regardless of the outcomes, the Seattle syndrome attitude permeated the music community.

Despite the negativity, *Seattle Syndrome* represents an important document of third-wave Seattle punk rock. Engram made a point of choosing bands that represented the diversity of talent within the scene, not necessarily the most popular artists. The comp includes selections by Student Nurse, the Blackouts, the Beakers, Jim Basnight, the Fastbacks, and the Fartz. Purposely left off were power pop bands like the Heats and the Cowboys. "Groups like the Heats," says Hubbard, " . . . were not [a part of] the creative scene that [later] blossomed into . . . the grunge scene."

Seattle Syndrome became a critical yardstick in the history of underground Seattle music. In fact, the scene would define key points in its existence through comps. In 1986 *Deep Six* documented the beginnings of grunge. *Sub Pop 200*, released in 1988, represented the moment when Seattle music had reached fruition and maturity, and at the same time received attention from cultural centers in the UK.

This compilation demonstrated to those outside the Seattle music community that a viable original music scene did in fact exist. For example, the record found its way into the hands of one Chris Hanzsek, then a budding recording engineer living in Boston. *Syndrome* helped convince him to move to Seattle and jump-start the grunge era when he opened Reciprocal Recording, the studio that gave Nirvana, Soundgarden, and Mudhoney to the world.

By 1982 Seattle's third punk rock wave had dissipated. Bands had either left town, broken up, or were splintering. The few venues that hosted punk shows were either forcibly shut down by the Seattle Police or had financially collapsed. Modern Productions was a financial casualty, and The Showbox's successors were less oriented toward new music. WREX and the Gorilla Room closed their doors. Even Rosco Louie came to an end that December.

As 1983 dawned, urban Seattle music entered a new era, one that began to distance itself from its punk and new wave forbearers. The scene started to shift toward a group of all-ages venues centering in Pioneer Square. Those that hadn't moved out of town began to forge a darker artistic statement, one that was more insular—one that became characteristically Seattle.

CHAPTER 2

KAOS in Olympia

From our perspective, it's really the Olympia scene that sort of exploded out into Seattle.

—John Foster, founder, *Op* magazine

Beat Happening at a warehouse party in Belltown, 1988. (Photo by Charles Peterson)

It's all about perspective. From the standpoint of the United States, Saigon fell to the Communists in 1975. From the Vietnamese perspective, Communist forces liberated Saigon from imperialist occupiers in 1975. If you examine baseball standings in an Eastern newspaper, the divisions are listed from east to west. On the West Coast, the divisions progress from west to east. So it goes with Olympia and Seattle. From Seattle's vantage point, Olympia added some interesting ideas and approaches to an already burgeoning local music scene. Viewed from Olympia, Seattle's music community merely extended Olympia's vitality and spirit.

As with most two-sided stories, each perspective has its merits and limitations. Comparatively small-town Olympia had no business telling big-city Seattle that it had been upstaged. Yet there is no denying that the development of Seattle's music scene would not have happened the way it did without an infusion of some outside forces, and in this case, Olympia's small size becomes irrelevant.

Olympia is Washington's state capital and lies about sixty miles southwest of Seattle. Two hours to the south sits Portland, Oregon—the next closest city. Olympia's minimal population (about twenty-seven thousand residents in 1980) makes it an unlikely candidate for an independent music mecca. In most circumstances, Olympia would be just another small town, except for one significant difference: Evergreen State College.

Evergreen: Olympia's Roosevelt High

Evergreen's freethinking philosophy encourages students to experiment with eclectic curricula. If Seattle's early scene drew from Roosevelt High School, Olympia's emerged from Evergreen. The college is located just south of the city and is surrounded by hundreds of acres of fir trees. Rainfall in the Olympia area tends to exceed Seattle's, creating a constant dampness on campus. "You had to look down when you walked from the dorms to the main buildings," recalls Evergreen alum George Romansic, who later drummed for Seattle's Beakers and 3 Swimmers, "because you [had] to be careful not to step on slugs with every other step."

Evergreen became a home for those looking to escape the typical big-college experience of Seattle's University of Washington, as well as for kids from other parts of the country searching for a more liberal education. The college's rural setting and creative atmosphere attracted those who would not only create a vibrant music scene in Olympia, but would also connect the region to independent music throughout the country.

In the '70s, KAOS, Evergreen's radio station, played a slightly offbeat mix of music, but otherwise ignored underground trends hitting American and British markets. That abruptly changed upon the arrival of John Foster and Stephen Rabow, who had roomed together at a Quaker high school in Poughkeepsie, New York.

In 1973, Rabow decided to travel west in search of a college that fit with his liberal view of the world. He visited over a dozen institutions before he settled on Evergreen. "I couldn't leave," Rabow recalls. "I just couldn't leave. It was the most amazing thing I've ever seen in my life. Everything was open. Everything was accessible. They had a Steinway grand piano in the library. They had video equipment you could take out with a library card."

Rabow initially studied pre-med, but quickly gravitated toward KAOS. He immediately shook things up at the somewhat staid station, playing everything from avant-garde vocal groups to early Bruce Springsteen and Mozart. That all changed in 1976, when the Ramones' single "Beat on the Brat" showed up at the station. "And I put it on the turntable . . . and I literally fell on the floor," says Rabow. "I just fell on the floor. I just couldn't believe it. I'd never heard anything like it before."

At Rabow's urging, Foster came out to Evergreen and joined KAOS. Like his former roommate, Foster had eclectic tastes and envisioned a radio station unbounded by format. "When you put Black Sabbath next to Abba," says Foster, "that would be called a train wreck. That's the kind of stuff I love. I love train wreck radio."

During this time, an aesthetic of independent music began to permeate KAOS' staff. By the mid-'70s, mainstream music had become stale and monotonous. Fortunately, an explosion of independent music labels occurred around the country as cheaper recording equipment allowed musicians to put out their own material. Without national distribution or the existence of the Internet, however, independent music remained a mostly disconnected phenomenon. Foster took the lead in discovering underground music and incorporated it into KAOS' programming.

Under Rabow and Foster's leadership, the station ventured into uncharted waters. Anything seemed open for on-air exploration—Gregorian chants, classical, free jazz, experimental noise—whatever direction the DJ decided to venture in. Show hosts pretty much got away with anything, partially because the low station wattage guaranteed a small audience beyond the campus. Romansic (then a DJ, later music director) found out at least one person was listening when he began playing a modern experimental string quartet late one evening. The double album consisted of four sides of a singular, annoying drone. "[It] would've made your cat's hair stand up. And, one night [at] about two in the morning I put on side one," says Romansic. "Played it. Followed it by side two. Followed it by side three. And about halfway through side four of just this long continuous . . . screech, [I] got a phone call. By then, it was like three, three-thirty in the morning. And a very sort of nonchalant, blasé voice on the other end said, 'Uh, yeah, hi, uh . . . I'm just wondering, you gonna be playing this much longer?'"

The Lost Music Network

The station experienced an important moment in 1976 when Foster embarked on a music journalism internship in New York City. He worked at a record store with an entire floor dedicated to independent music. Already intrigued with non-mainstream music, Foster made it his mission to create a database of independent labels and bands. He obtained his information from the backs of record albums, fanzines, specialty music magazines, libraries—anything he could get his hands on.

Despite his mere twenty years, Foster had already become a legendary, almost mythic figure at Evergreen. His return to the college became a transcendent moment within the KAOS community. "When I first [met] John," Romansic remembers, "it was in the CAB Building [student activities center]. . . . He was surrounded by girls. And it was like, 'Hail, the conquering hero!'"

Upon his return, Foster led a charge to switch KAOS' format to an independent label focus. After an extremely close vote, the station agreed to change its policy to 80 percent independent music in 1978. That is, at least 80 percent of the music played on KAOS had to come from independent record labels and distributors. This format became known as the "Green Line Policy" since independent records were designated with a green line. The Green Line Policy still holds at KAOS today.

Foster's vision led to his creation of the Lost Music Network, a foundation that sponsored an all independent-music periodical: *Op* magazine. *Op* began sending out record review requests to various independent labels and artists. The reaction from these labels was dramatic. Most were thrilled that someone was taking an interest in their music and artists, though of course, there were exceptions. Romansic had written a letter to a Michigan punk band called Half Japanese, requesting a free sample of their music to review. "And I got back a letter from [guitarist] Jad Fair," says Romansic, "that [began]: 'Dear Lowlife Scum.' That's verbatim. The rest of it—to paraphrase—was sort of, 'How dare you ask me for a free record!'"

Op grew quickly to the point where Foster had to focus on the venture full time, turning over the KAOS music director keys to Romansic. With his energies entirely focused on the magazine, Foster began to grapple with the sheer volume of music to review and, in particular, how to organize it: chronologically, by genre, by label, by location? It was Foster and co-hort Dana Squires who came up with an idea that was brilliant in its simplicity: organize the issues alphabetically. The first issue, for example, would cover all artists beginning with the letter *A*, such as Albert Ayler and Laurie Anderson. Thus in 1979, *Op* began the first of its 26 alphabetical issues.

The format fit Foster's vision perfectly since he did not believe in limiting his magazine to genre, region, or any other categorization. *Op* began taking subscriptions and commenced mailing issues to subscribers and the various independent labels. Eventually, the magazine found its way into hip record stores around the country.

Op's incarnation created a connection between Evergreen and independent musicians and fans throughout the country. In the pre-Internet world, London and New York media outlets drove the direction of popular culture. Any trends with any validity typically emanated from the two cities and, after several years, made their way to U.S. West Coast cities and the hinterlands. By the time most Americans learned about the latest trends in pop culture, London and New York had already moved on. *Op* changed all that. Perhaps for the first time, music fans around the country learned about underground trends as they were happening. For once, these fans were not beholden to London and New York. There actually were valid artists, bands, and scenes that existed everywhere. *Op* had opened up an entirely new and exciting world to an increasing audience.

Op also had an unintended consequence. Along with Evergreen and KAOS, the magazine created a magnet for offbeat music fans looking for a home. In particular, the *Op*/KAOS universe attracted three individuals who would help create a vibrant music scene in Olympia and beyond: Calvin Johnson, Steve Fisk (who would later produce Nirvana, Soundgarden, and Screaming Trees), and Bruce Pavitt.

Johnson, the son of a gubernatorial press secretary, started hanging around KAOS when he was just 15. Having already been to England, Johnson had developed a voracious appetite for punk rock. In 1978 he began taking a noncredit radio course at Evergreen that culminated in students getting their own KAOS show. "I'm reading about these bands like the Ramones and Blondie," Johnson recalls, "but I never heard the Ramones and Blondie. Because, they [didn't] even have them at the record store. . . . They certainly weren't being played on the radio, and there was no way for me to actually hear these bands. . . . Going to the [KAOS] record library, they had all these records that I had read about, but I never heard. After school I'd go out there on the bus, and hang out at the record library and listen to like all these records, and it was real exciting."

Johnson became the proverbial annoying kid, hanging around Foster and effectively becoming his protégé. So when Foster began focusing exclusively on *Op*, Johnson naturally went with him. Johnson began writing for *Op* right away and found himself rubbing elbows with Fisk and Pavitt, while at the same time noting that a local music scene was brewing in Olympia.

Under Foster's leadership, Johnson and his fellow *Op* music reviewers—called "elves"—effectively connected the Evergreen community to the cutting edge of independent music throughout the United States and beyond. Olympia had become aware of exciting new music that emanated from the Midwest, the South, the Southwest—places that hip publications like the *Village Voice* and *New York Rocker* did not necessarily know about.

Sub/Pop

Op and KAOS in effect created an aesthetic that would soon permeate from Evergreen north to Olympia. It was one of fierce independence and openness, a willingness to attempt anything. Surrounding all of it was an attitude that became prevalent in underground music throughout the 1980s: DIY, or do-it-yourself. Don't like mainstream music? Start your own band and record your own music. Don't like the media that publicizes only certain artists? Start your own fanzine and publicize your own bands. Angry that radio stations aren't playing music you like? Become a DJ and start your own radio show. DIY was not unique to Evergreen and Olympia. The difference from other regions was perhaps the degree of talent that Evergreen attracted, as well as the openness to attempt music-related ventures. This attitude created an incredibly creative and vibrant regional environment, which becomes all the more amazing given Olympia's size and relatively remote location.

Pavitt emerged from Foster's shadow to explore the regional aspect of independent rock music. Unlike Foster, who never believed provincial characteristics impacted artists' sounds, Pavitt pursued regionalism with a passion. "And I kept hearing about this Bruce [Pavitt] guy from people," Johnson recalls. "He was really focused on this idea of regional music, like the *Op* idea, except he narrowed it down to just rock music, 'cause *Op* was so broad-based . . . he wanted to focus on just underground rock music . . . from places that were just completely invisible to most people—which was the Northwest and the Midwest."

Pavitt's vision resulted in his own fanzine, called *Subterranean Pop*, shortened to *Sub/Pop* after the second issue. He also created an audio version of his fanzine on KAOS. *Sub/Pop* piggybacked off *Op*, even sharing its post office box, but Foster never viewed his protégé's zine as competition. In fact, he encouraged Pavitt to pursue his passion.

For his fifth issue, Pavitt's fanzine took the form of a cassette compilation. *Sub Pop 5* included twenty-one independent rock songs from the likes of Seattle's Beakers and Visible Targets, San Francisco's Pell Mell, and Steve Fisk. Fisk had migrated to Evergreen from Los Angeles by the way of Ellensburg, Washington. "We all lived in this house on the west side of [Olympia]," Fisk remembers. "Bruce lived downtown, and so he would go to the [*Op*] PO Box and find whatever had come in and would march up the hill to our place where we had tape machines and proper monitoring systems. And we'd listen to the people [who] were submitting things for *Sub/Pop*. That was always kind of interesting, kind of fun."

Sub Pop 5 became a surprisingly successful venture. The cassette sold about two thousand copies, a remarkable figure for an independent release. Furthermore, Pavitt's stature began to grow within the Evergreen community due in no small part to his oddly spacey charisma. "He was always a hard read," says music photographer and friend Charles Peterson, "and he still is, but that's sort of what made him so compelling to people, I think."

The Birth of the Olympia Scene

Meanwhile, Johnson launched a cassette-based label called K Records in the summer of 1982. Cassettes were coming into vogue in the early '80s, as fidelity continued to increase. Furthermore, the relative ease and lowered expense of recording and dubbing cassettes made the format preferable for small labels. K's emergence represented another significant moment in Olympia's music history. K symbolized the transfer of independent music from Evergreen to Olympia.

Before long, Olympia bands emerged, including the Supreme Cool Beings; Beat Happening; the Young Pioneers; Wild, Wild, Wild Spoons; and John Foster's Pop Philosophers. Unlike Seattle bands that often defined themselves stylistically, Olympia's artists delineated themselves by how they approached their craft more than by the music itself. Olympia music tended to be simple, and bands routinely featured male and female singers who rotated instruments. "It wasn't necessarily advancing music that people were trying to do," says Beat Happening's Bret Lunsford, "as much as advance their own . . . creative ideas."

Olympia's audiences welcomed these expressive ideas, as long as they were genuine. Be what you are. If you're a pop band, be a pop band. If you're a dance band, be a dance band. If you're a punk band, be a punk band. The quality of the playing became inconsequential. "I think [the] musicianship was sort of secondary. . . . Whether you could really play or not didn't matter all that much," says the Young Pioneers' Chris Pugh.

By 1983 Olympia's scene had outgrown Evergreen's confines. Like Seattle five years prior, Olympia needed a venue to house its growing music community. Enter Pugh and bandmate Scott Vanderpool.

In the fall of that year, Vanderpool wandered into downtown Olympia and stumbled upon an empty storefront. He tracked down the owner, who was willing to let it out for $150 a night. Vanderpool and Pugh organized a show featuring Portland's Wipers and the Young Pioneers. The pair's efforts resulted in Olympia's version of the TMT show.

The show's success led to the opening of the Tropicana, which became a home for Olympia's emerging scene. In addition, the connections between Seattle, San Francisco, and Los Angeles soon pulled Olympia into the underground orbit. The club soon hosted shows by Los Angeles' Black Flag and the Rain Parade, Austin's Butthole Surfers, Tacoma's Girl Trouble, and Seattle's Room Nine. "Things were ping-ponging back and forth between Seattle and Olympia and Portland," Vanderpool recalls. "There was a stop in between Seattle and Portland all of the sudden."

Olympia's proximity to Seattle created both a bond and a fissure between the two locales: Olympians believed Seattle was too hip for its own good, while being imitative of London and New York. Seattle thought of Olympia as snotty Evergreen kids who couldn't play. Yet the two towns mixed freely. They were only an hour apart, and Seattle's big brother status created a natural draw for Evergreeners outgrowing Olympia's confines.

Spreading Olympia's Ideals

Olympia's confines could not contain the vitality of its music community, whose collective confidence drove it north to Seattle. Rabow was one of the first Evergreeners to try his hand in Seattle. As mentioned in Chapter 1, Rabow's stint at KZAM helped support the growing Seattle punk community. He shared a house near the U-District with fellow Evergreener George Romansic. Romansic DJ'ed at KRAB, the only Seattle radio station other than KZAM that played newer music. He also drummed for two third-wave Seattle punk bands: the Beakers and 3 Swimmers.

1983 became a key year for Olympia's growing scene. Johnson formed Beat Happening with fellow Evergreeners Lunsford and the Supreme Cool Beings' Heather Lewis. In many ways, that band symbolized the early '80s Olympia approach. None of the players was particularly accomplished. Johnson and Lewis shared lead vocal duties, and the players rotated instruments. Beat Happening also played without a bass.* The band's songs were simple and repetitive, and often dealt with a loss of childhood innocence. All of these ingredients combined to create what became known as Olympia's "infantile rock" sound, even though all local bands didn't sound like that.

The following year, Johnson's K Records released a compilation called *Let's Together*, featuring Beat Happening, the Young Pioneers, the Melvins (from Montesano, Washington), and other independent artists from around the country and the world. The same year, K issued its first vinyl release, a Beat Happening single called "Our Secret." K had established itself as a hip label with its own identity, including its trademark *K* shield logo.

In the spring of 1984, Beat Happening decided to go to Japan and tour. The band had no promoter, no manager, and no infrastructure for conducting such a bold venture. It didn't matter. "It's just one of those dares that nobody backed down from," says Lunsford, "and all the sudden you're in Japan trying to find shows."

K's ascent and Beat Happening's Japanese tour exemplified an attitude that began to permeate north to Seattle. Independent punk rock bands simply didn't tour. Seattle underground bands up to that point had ventured up and down the West Coast, but going beyond that seemed akin to Europeans venturing across the Atlantic in the fifteenth century. No one had really done it before. Olympia demonstrated the possibilities.

---

*I made the mistake of asking Johnson why Beat Happening had no bass. His response, via a 2007 phone interview: "There *was* no bass. We didn't eliminate the bass. We didn't *have* a bass. And I don't understand where that question comes from because have you ever heard of a band called the Cramps? Well, there's the answer to your question. If they didn't need one, why would we?"

Within a year of Beat Happening's visit to Japan, that "what the fuck" attitude invaded Seattle. In 1985, Seattle's Young Fresh Fellows, Green River, and the U-Men all embarked on nationwide touring adventures (Chapter 3). Random happenstance? Perhaps. But at least subconsciously, Olympia's spirit soon found itself present in its neighbor to the north.

Johnson's friend and fellow KAOS/*Op* worker Pavitt finished up at Evergreen in 1981. He moved to Seattle thereafter and not only helped forge a connection between the two towns, but synthesized a number of influences that helped inject Seattle with a fresh energy. Pavitt took with him Evergreen's creative approach and a focus on regionalism he developed at KAOS and his *Sub/Pop* fanzine.

Addendum: Pop Lust for Life* (Rob Morgan and the Squirrels)

The Squirrels and front man Morgan are virtually indescribable. Put simply, the Squirrels are not just a rock band. Various tags can and may apply to parts of their repertoire: Performance artists. Mashup makers. Comedy-rockers. '60s aficionados. Pop culture lovers. Parody band. So for us writers who love labels, none of them do the Squirrels justice, except for perhaps one: entertainers.

Rob Morgan is a Seattle institution. He arrived in town just as the U-District punk rock crowd got going in the mid-'70s, working the door at the Bird, enjoying a minor hit that showed up on the first *Seattle Syndrome* compilation, witnessing the seminal U-Men (Chapter 3) form in his basement, then starting the Squirrels and far outlasting the rock stars of the grunge era. In short, he's pretty much done and seen it all: the lean times; the growth of the scene from nothing; the detonation of Nirvana

---

*Title per Rob Morgan, based on his on-again, off-again fanzine called *Pop Lust*.

and legions of Pearl Jam wannabes coming to town; the resultant grunge backlash; and Seattle's arrival as a big city.

He began hanging out in the U-District in 1975, meeting up with people like Lee Lumsden and Paul Hood of the Meyce and becoming part of the *Chatterbox* crowd. Out of high school and unimpressed with Edmonds's cultural offerings, the nineteen-year-old Morgan found a rental house on the Ave in 1977. Morgan's house quickly became a party headquarters; guests of note included members of the Ramones, the Tubes, and Blondie. "It was just one of those things," Morgan recalls, "where somebody came up to me after [a] show: 'Hey dude, we wanna go to a party. We're all going to your house.' So half the town shows up at my house."

Falling in with the burgeoning punk crowd, Morgan brought not only an appreciation for glam and punk rock, but also an obsession with '60s music. His tastes ran anywhere from Northwest icons like Paul Revere & the Raiders to bubblegum pop like the Monkees to cult bands like Sparks.

Morgan's first serious band, the Pudz, successfully debuted at a 1980 house party attended by about three hundred people. The Pudz' height of success, in a manner of speaking, came in 1981 when the band released a 45 with a cover of R. B. Greaves's "Take a Letter, Maria" on one side and the original "Take Me to Your (Leader)" on the other. "Maria" was supposed to the hit, but the interminably catchy original enjoyed major airplay on KZAM. Soon, passersby of U-Dub's frat row regularly heard "Take me to your . . . leaderleaderleader, take me to your . . . scenescenescene" blasting from windows. The same year, "Leader" became a standout track on *Seattle Syndrome Vol. 1.* "I refer to it as the two-and-a-half minutes that refuses to die," says Morgan.

The Pudz lasted another year before the guitar player split town and they called it a day. After a short stint in the Pamona Boners, Morgan found himself sans band in 1984.

That year, he accompanied the Young Fresh Fellows (Chapter 3) to shows, which only increased his itch to get in a band again. He offered to front the Fellows, but instead the band decided to create their own opening act, with Morgan as the singer. Taking the name Ernest Anyway & the Mighty Mighty Squirrels, the Fellows donned wigs and opened for themselves. "They'd come out with wigs on and open for themselves doing covers," Morgan recalls. "And I'd hop all around, and half the time the [audience was] so distracted by me hopping around, they wouldn't figure out it was the same band."

"At first maybe, some people [watching the Squirrels] might have been like, 'Oh, this band's kinda cool,'" the Fellows' Scott McCaughey recalls. "And then, the Fellows were playing later, [and] they must have been like, 'Hey, wait a minute!'"

This version of the Squirrels lasted about six months, when Morgan decided he wanted a real band. With himself on vocals, high school buddy Eric Erickson on guitar, and Tad Hutchison on drums, Morgan located guitarist Joey Kline, who at the time was playing with Prudence Dredge. Morgan and Kline hit it off and a new Squirrels was born: the New Age Urban Squirrels. For bass, Morgan asked Tower Records coworker and former Bay Area native Craig Ferguson to join. "And so it turned out that I was the new guy that nobody in town knew," Ferguson remembers. "That's how I started off being listed in the band as 'the mystery bassist.'"

Morgan's love of '60s covers kept the band rooted there initially, but over time, the musicians' tastes and sense of humor led to something completely different. Morgan and Kline's nearly limitless knowledge of pop culture and music minutia pushed the Squirrels into a different realm. Today, we might call it mashup. Back then, however, no one used that term.

Morgan and Kline (who became the Squirrels' "copilot") thought about combining songs and lyrics that have something in common, but not necessarily in an obvious sense. For example, how about combining jazz legend Dave Brubeck's "Take Five" with the *Hawaii Five-0* theme song and calling it "Hawaii Take Five-0"? Or maybe combining the lyrics to Patsy Cline's "Walkin' After Midnight" with the music of Judas Priest's "Living After Midnight"? Ridiculous on its surface—yet somehow it worked.

Originally a guitar player, Ferguson switched to bass upon joining the Squirrels. The new bass player found himself enveloped by the Squirrels' offbeat world during their early rehearsals. Ferguson recalls, "It was like, 'OK, we're gonna play the Who song "Baba O'Reilly," but right when it gets to the part where he's supposed to start singing, we're gonna switch it into "Just the Way You Are" by Billy Joel.' And I'm like, 'Ohhhh-kay . . . '"

The Squirrels would become Morgan and Kline's near-lifetime passion. In addition to those two, the band would feature Jimmy "J. T." Thomas on lead guitar, and John Fleischman (aka Hollis the Bug) on drums. They would serve as regular players, but the band acquired a cast of guest musicians, including members of Prudence Dredge, the Posies, the Frazz, the Fastbacks, Flop, and Pure Joy. "It wound up being more of a men's club with instruments than a band," says Morgan.

In addition to the musicians who drifted in and out, the Squirrels took on as many names as their varied lineups, including Ernest Anyway & the Mighty Mighty Squirrels, Squirrels for a Day (one gig only), New Age Urban Squirrels, Squirrels Group '87 (which included bassist Kevin Crosby and drummer Nate Johnson, also billed as Crosby, Squirrels & Nate), Squirrels Group 2000 (aka Red Lobster Cult), and the Old Age Urban Squirrels.* And that's not all of them. Local insurance agency Vern Fonk's slogan—"Remember to honk, when you drive by Vern Fonk"—

---

*Obtained from thesquirrels.com/poplust/lineups.htm under the caption "Through the Past, Dorkly."

also inspired a potential band name: "We wanted to be Vern Fonk Railroad for a while," says Kline.

Squirrels gigs occurred infrequently, perhaps three times a year, and the band's touring was rather limited. Yet as they progressed, the Squirrels began to develop an incredibly dedicated, if small, cult following. Soon stage props arrived, with Morgan and the band wearing ever-more-elaborate getups. Between the odd mashups, off-the-wall humor, and intricate props, fans began to expect the unexpected at Squirrels shows. Morgan soon found himself dragging more stuff to gigs than his drummer.

As far as recordings went, the Squirrels kept quite busy with twenty-seven EPs, LPs, and singles. A highlight was a 2000 parody of Pink Floyd's *The Dark Side of the Moon*, called *The Not-So-Bright Side of the Moon*. Guest musicians included guitarist Kurt Bloch of the Fastbacks and Tortelvis and Ed Zeppelin from Dread Zeppelin. The record is classic Squirrels, combining clever and often hilarious satire with top-notch musicianship. The original Pink Floyd record opens with the sound of a heartbeat accompanied by nonsensical lyrics, a ticking clock, a cash register, a laughing lunatic, and menacing industrial sounds. The Squirrels use a hiccup in place of the heartbeat, and in addition to a ticking clock, they add random effects like a kazoo, a cow, and a telephone dialing into a fax machine with the resultant *eeeaaahhhh* connection.

As the band worked through its various incarnations, its live act began to feature nonmusical guests. For a while, Morgan was accompanied by Secret Service–like "bodyguards," who inexplicably shadowed him during performances. "We'd be playing at like, the Mural Amphitheatre—the Seattle Center—[and] I'd be out on the lawn," says Morgan. "This guy would be like, following me around—you know, about six feet away, like [a Secret Service agent] would do. And just follow me around and never say anything."

Audience reactions often consisted of bewilderment and/ or puzzled looks. That was part of the deal. Either you got the Squirrels or you didn't. "It was pretty interesting how severely the Squirrels could polarize an audience," says Ferguson. "What I tend to find was, people who took themselves really seriously did not like the Squirrels whatsoever, [whereas] people who would like to have fun—we can win those people over fairly easily."

Regardless of the band's onstage antics, its level of musicianship remained at a higher level than most other acts in town. Certainly, the Squirrels did not subscribe to the "less competence is more" aesthetic emanating out of Olympia. Band members had to prepare themselves for anything—including on-the-spot improvisation, often initiated by Kline. "And all [of] the sudden Joey would just launch off on something. It'd be like something from the '60s or something," Ferguson recalls. "It's like, 'Uh oh, where's Joey going with this? OK, shit. Watch his hands. Here we go.' And try to remember that song, and hopefully, Joey remembers it the same way. And actually a lot of the stuff that turned [out] to be regular Squirrels shtick—that's how that stuff would start."

"I remember thinking that the Squirrels must be one of the best bands in Seattle, when I [first] saw them," producer Jack Endino recalls. "I mean they were kind of a ridiculous band, but they were also extremely impressive on a technical level."

In 1991 the Squirrels came across a popular kids' doll, and history—as well as the very fabric of the universe—was about to change. Prior to a Vancouver gig, the band members were sitting around backstage, collecting themselves before their performance. As they relaxed, Morgan looked over and noticed a Cabbage Patch doll sort of sitting up. Suddenly, the doll sprang to life and spoke in a weird baby voice. Kline laughed and for some reason blurted out "Baby Cheevers" in a childlike voice, and a legend was born. "So we decided," says Morgan, "'Well, that was really stupid. Let's just use that [doll] during the show.'"

The Squirrels used Baby Cheevers as a prop on that brief tour, and it ended up becoming a permanent appendage. During a set Morgan would hold Cheevers up in front of a microphone, and the doll appeared to talk to the audience. Just a few feet away, Kline would speak into a mike, shielding his mouth from the audience with his hat. The world's worst ventriloquism act worked quite well for the Squirrels. "It was just such a gloriously polarizing thing," recalls Morgan. "I mean, there were people that truly, truly, truly loved Baby Cheevers. And then there were people that would get really upset and actually run on stage all drunk and try to tear him away from me."

The Squirrels' all-ages gigs drew amusing reactions from younger music fans as well. Periodically, the band would play street fairs attended by families with their children. Kids would look up at Morgan holding Baby Cheevers in front of the mike, not noticing Kline chatting in the baby voice a few feet away. "And Joey's just over there talking, you know what I mean? So the kids are staring at me," says Morgan. "They're like, 'Whoa! That thing's talkin'!'"

In 1989, the band began an annual tradition that would last for twenty years: the Squirrels' Christmas show. The annual holiday event quickly became a reunion of sorts for fans, some of whom flew in from Canada and California just for the show. It also became an annual touchstone for those feeling disenfranchised during the holiday season. The Christmas version of the Squirrels, just like the band itself, defies description.

Take a "regular" Squirrels show—and I use that adjective rather loosely—add irreverently mashed-up Christmas songs and yet more elaborate stage costumes, and you get . . . ? For example, the band would combine the traditional "Silent Night" with Black Sabbath's "Black Sabbath." Seems ridiculous, doesn't it? "You wouldn't think of it until you saw it," says longtime fan Ned Raggett. "Then you're like, 'Of course!'"

Over time, the Christmas shows became ever more elaborate. Santa would make his appearance and often have rather inappropriate conversations with Baby Cheevers. Cheap toy soldiers and Christmas trinkets would come to the fore. Then came the Fallen Angels, who were played by the Secret Service actors.

The Angels donned white T-shirts, tinsel halos, wings, and short robes. Similar to the Secret Service, the Angels had nothing to do with the band. They would stand on opposite sides of the stage completely ignoring what the Squirrels were doing.

Sometimes, an Angel would—again, for no particular reason—level a death stare at various audience members during the performance. "And it was the weirdest thing," Raggett remembers. "'cause you'd be up there groovin' along, and every so often you'd just catch him out of the corner of your eye. And you're just going like, 'AHHH!'"

As with all things of value, the band and Morgan's passion for it began to run its course. The Christmas shows would take weeks of planning, and the whole thing just became tired. "I'm a big enough Alice Cooper fan to know that if I go see Alice Cooper, he'd better damn well chop his head off," says Morgan. "And I knew if people went to see the Squirrels, they wanted bubbles, and they wanted a bunch of goofy costumes, and they wanted this and that and the other thing. And my heart wasn't really into doing that anymore."

The Squirrels ended things on a high note in December 2009, completing their "Death with Dignity" twenty-fifth anniversary tour. Fans of the band, long known for bringing various artifacts to gigs, lavished the Squirrels with parting gifts at that final show. "Somebody put like a big . . . plastic plaque thing that says, 'Thank you, Rob Morgan, for 25 years of the Squirrels,' and stuff in my prop bag . . . that I didn't even find till the next day," he says.

The end of the Squirrels brought with it an appreciation from many corners of town. The band had regularly played gigs at the annual SeafoodFest in Ballard (a neighborhood northwest of downtown). During the summer of 2010, Morgan roamed around during the event—his first post-Squirrels attendance—when he heard someone shouting at him. He turned around and noticed a homeless man about half a block back screaming, "We miss the Squirrels, man!" "And I turned around," says Morgan, "and I [said], 'Hey, thank you. We did it as long as we could.' And he literally went—and this really meant a lot to me—'I just wanna tell ya that you entertained me for years and years and years. And you had bubbles and Santa Claus and all kinds of crazy shit. And I just wanna let you know that we really appreciate it, man.'"

In the end, the Squirrels tapped into the depths of why human beings like music, perhaps better than any other band in Seattle. Not only did their fans have fun at gigs, but clearly the musicians enjoyed themselves as much, if not more, than their audience. "If I could roll that clock back twenty-five years," says Ferguson, "I would do it all over again for sure. And I don't think you would find any Squirrels that wouldn't say that."

CHAPTER 3

We Must Be Musicians

They were definitely, um . . . oh God, there are no words.

—Dawn Anderson describing the U-Men

Metropolis audience at a 10 Minute Warning/Replacements show, 1983.
Fans include Mark Arm (front left) and Steve Turner (front right).
(Photo by Charles Peterson)

If one band symbolized musical evolution in Seattle, it would have to be the U-Men. The U-Men created a bridge between late '70s/early '80s punk/new wave and late '80s grunge. The fact is, though, they were neither. The band was too arty for the hardcore punks and too punky for the art rockers. The U-Men were their own thing.

The band formed in 1980 in the basement of Rob Morgan's U-District house with Tom Price on guitar, Charlie Ryan on drums, and Robin Buchan on bass. Practices were primitive at first. Nobody had any money. Price and Buchan plugged their cheap Japanese, hollow-bodied electric guitars into one cheap thirty-watt amplifier. They channeled their vocals through a cassette-era microphone, plugging into the same amp. Ryan owned about half a drum kit with no cymbal stands. He attached his cymbals to the ceiling using rope. If he broke a drumstick, he had to raid Morgan's kitchen for a wooden spoon or similar substitute. The tiny amplifier would typically begin to crackle after just a few songs. "And they would practice in my basement," Morgan recalls, "and . . . drive me crazy 'cause they'd play the same song for hours."

The band began to write some offbeat songs, and their rudimentary practices soon evolved into rudimentary shows. The U-Men's growing audience rewarded the band by dropping off beer at performances.

The U-Men's inception may seem fairly unremarkable, somewhat typical for a young impoverished punk rock band, yet there was something a little off about them from the start. Their name, for one. The members were big fans of Ohio's arty postpunk Pere Ubu and named themselves after an Ubu bootleg.* Furthermore, like Pere Ubu, the U-Men became fascinated with French surrealism, thus displaying a sophistication beyond the range of typical teenage punks.

Price, who had played bass in the Showbox-era Psychopop, switched to guitar for his new band. He drew from early Northwest garage rock—especially the Sonics. He also added offbeat jazz chord progressions to the mix. He had taken guitar lessons for a few months, and his teacher forced him to learn complex jazz fingering. "And then when I started playing with the U-Men," Price explains, "I was just kinda like, 'Well, I know all this shit. I might as well use it.'"

Up to this point, the band had no full-time vocalist. That changed when Price met John Bigley, who turned out to be an important piece of the puzzle. Bigley became the band's shamanic leader. His growling vocals and intense stage presence often left audiences in a trancelike state.

Bassist Jim Tillman completed the picture. Replacing Buchan, Tillman contributed a high level of musical professionalism. The U-Men intrigued him, but Tillman immediately began upgrading the band, like a new coach rebuilding a team. "He [looked] at Charlie's drum kit and [said], 'Dude, you can't have cymbals with big chunks missing from 'em,'" Price recalls. "'Tom, you can't have a guitar that's completely impossible to tune.'" In exchange for his band-parenting skills, the rest of the U-Men forced Tillman to cut his long locks and exchange his glasses for contacts. (Note: Tillman disputes this.)

---

*Tom Price believes the band's name was also inspired by a World War II–era photograph showing German U-boat sailors. The photograph's caption was "The U-Men." So who knows?

With the lineup set, the U-Men began to develop their per-sonality. Most great rock bands have one, perhaps two members at their artistic center. The U-Men had four, yet somehow they coalesced. Bigley became the consummate front man, typically roaming the stage in black, leading the audience with his growl-ing/shrieking, barely intelligible mantras, creating a feeling of danger at shows. Like all great punk rock singers, Bigley's onstage charisma left the audience wondering down which path he was leading them: to destruction or salvation? "John Bigley . . . [had the] ability to get himself into a trance . . . he [was] having fits up there," remembers Stone Gossard, later with Green River and Pearl Jam.

Charlie Ryan was not just a drummer. He synthesized the band's varied musical personalities and made the U-Men swing. Price referred to him as a traffic cop, because he would direct the other players during gigs. If things didn't sound right to him, he would sometimes force his bandmates to stop and start over. Perhaps more than anyone in the U-Men, Ryan created the band's swagger. "Charlie was a really innovative drummer," says Mark Arm, later with Green River and Mudhoney. "And he was able to play a whole show and keep his top hat on the whole time."

Bigley and Ryan developed a bond and a shared musical experience. Both explored postpunk pioneers like Joy Division, but it was Nick Cave's Birthday Party that most intrigued the pair. Following the Birthday Party's 1981 seminal "Release the Bats" single, Bigley and Ryan immediately drew on Cave's dark, shrieking vocals and avant-garde dissonance. In retrospect, the U-Men have been compared to the Birthday Party—sometimes even accused of imitation. Yet, while Bigley and Ryan were responsible for moving the U-Men in that direction, the band had a much different perspective and approach.

Price and Tillman provided the contrast to Bigley and Ryan's eccentricities. Price in particular was rooted in punk rock and

'60s garage rock. Because of him, the band would play Sonics covers at almost every show. But it wasn't just the covers: the U-Men had an older vibe about them. "There was just something about 'em that was unique," recalls James Burdyshaw, later in the grungy 64 Spiders, "that made 'em seem like, if the Doors were a punk rock band, they'd be the U-Men."

At that point, punk nationally (and in Seattle) was dominated by hardcore bands. Hardcore punk required its adherents to play loud and fast, and typically limited lyrics to anti-Reagan rants. Shows turned into slam fests laced with violence, making the earlier Showbox era seem tame by comparison. The U-Men had a foot in that world, sharing bills with some of the local hardcore acts.

U-Men shows, like the band itself, were inconsistent. Sometimes the band played tight and grooved together seamlessly. Other times Ryan and Bigley would veer off into uncharted waters, leaving Price and Tillman to pick up the pieces. Occasionally, as is typical with any punk show, amplifiers blew and PA systems didn't work. The U-Men were forced to adjust on the fly. The band quickly adapted to inevitable equipment maladies by turning a musical presentation into performance art. "We [became] used to the fact that any piece of equipment could crap out at any time," Price explains. "John could crap out at any time. . . . Any of us could be too drunk to play at any time. And so, you have to be prepared to deal with that. And how you deal with that is by going avant-garde. If the music isn't actually happening, do something crazy. Turn your amps up louder and set your hair on fire or something. And it generally worked."

The band slowly built a cult following based entirely on their live act. Their performances could be chaotic, tight, or horrible, but they were never boring. Audience members often left shows with their collective mouths open.

The U-Men remained a self-managed act until June 1982, when Bigley attended a Fastbacks show at Larry Reid's Rosco Louie gallery in Pioneer Square. Bigley urged Reid to see a U-Men performance. "And then I kinda went to see 'em," says Reid, "and all hell broke loose. Oh man, it was great. It was just utterly chaotic. I don't even know if they performed. It was just kinda this riot going on. That totally appealed to me."

Reid was sufficiently impressed and decided to manage the band. His first show was that August, at the Oddfellows Hall. The U-Men opened for the Blackouts, who were playing their last Seattle show. Having reached a level of preeminence in Seattle, the Blackouts felt they had outgrown the region and had decided to move to Boston. No one realized it at the time, but in a sense this show symbolized a transfer of power between the Seattle syndrome era and a new musical age. The U-Men had effectively become the harbingers of Seattle's next wave.

Reid was also in charge of rehabilitating the band's image. By the time he took over, the U-Men had had thirteen shows in a row canceled due to fan violence and damage.

The New Pioneer Square All-Ages Scene

Reid and the U-Men helped forge a connection between the Pioneer Square and Capitol Hill music communities. This neighborhood link would prove important as Pioneer Square developed a rich all-ages scene over the next two years.

At one end of the Pioneer Square scene lay the Graven Image gallery, Reid's successor to Rosco Louie. Opening in the fall of 1983, Graven Image had a smaller gallery space than its predecessor, but compensated with a large basement that became a place for bands to perform. It also became the U-Men's rehearsal space. There was one small issue, however: the only escape route from the basement was one stairwell up into Reid's gallery. "It was a total fire hazard," Tillman recalls. "There was one way out. And that was it."

Graven Image became the U-Men's unofficial headquarters. The gallery also symbolized Pioneer Square's comfortable marriage of the visual and performing arts, becoming one of four clubs/rehearsal spaces located within a square mile of each other. Punk fans could see bands at Graven Image and then catch shows at the all-ages Metropolis, Ground Zero, and Grey Door. The clubs occasionally would host shows in common, featuring two dozen bands for maybe a five dollar cover charge. "It was just a sea of black leather down there," Reid remembers. "It was so much fun."

Of the four facilities, the Grey Door was the most clandestine. The venue existed behind an unmarked grey door—hence the name. Punks found out about its existence through word of mouth. It also became home to a skate/punk gang called the Bopo Boys. The Bopos (pronounced *Bop-poes*) weren't all skaters nor were they a gang in a Los Angeles gangsta way. Think of the Jets and the Sharks, just slightly more annoying. Yet despite their role as constant irritants, the Bopos have an endearing appeal.

In short, the Bopos existed to fuck things up. The gang enjoyed creating havoc at shows and beating up U-Dub frat boys. Ultimately, though, they had a definitive goal: "The whole idea was just to have as much beer as possible," says ex-Bopo Lance Mercer.

So if you got the Boys their beer, you could perhaps avoid their direct wrath. That of course would not necessarily protect a party house from property damage. "I remember one party," recalls Leighton Beezer (later with the Thrown Ups), "where someone said, 'Oh, fuck! The Bopo Boys are coming!' And so, everybody turned off the lights and hid. They're like pounding on the door. 'I know there's a party here, man!' Eventually, they went away. They showed up at another party, and they fuckin' threw the TV in the fireplace."

"If you went to a Bopo party, there was always a point at about three o'clock in the morning," remembers Max Godsil, later with My Eye, "when somebody would put on Black Sabbath, and everybody would start fighting."

In their quest for beer, the Bopos would sometimes pound on the back door of clubs, then bull rush their way in for free. Usually a handful of them would make it in before the bouncers stopped them. Unfortunately, that tactic was destined to fail. "The problem," says Mercer, "[was] that we became pretty recognizable 'cause we were wearing vests that said 'Bopo Boys' on [the back]."

With the Bopos calling the Grey Door home and the U-Men residing at Graven Image, the Metropolis became the center of the punk community. The Metropolis opened in March 1983 and symbolically received the baton passed from the Showbox during the Modern Productions era. The Metropolis acted more as a community hub than a club. As at the Showbox, people throughout the Pioneer Square community volunteered to work the door, do lighting, and clean up afterward. The one difference was that the Metropolis spotlighted local bands, while the Showbox emphasized national or British acts.

The Metropolis sprang to life primarily as a result of the efforts of Gordon Doucette, a local musician, and Hugues Piottin, a transplanted Frenchman.

Piottin (pronounced *Pee-oh-tah*), who then went by "Hugo," hails from Lyon, France. Prior to his arrival in Seattle, he spent several years fishing in Alaska. Hugo and Doucette located a space in Pioneer Square. Immediately, the pair began renovating, using money Hugo had made as a fisherman. By March, the Metropolis was ready. It was a beautiful location for musical presentations.

Patrons entered the three-thousand-square-foot facility via a long corridor, its walls coated with galvanized steel. The hall then opened up into a handsome space with brick walls. In the middle of the main floor stood a support beam surrounded by benches. The area surrounding the beam was filled with sand, and artists displayed sculptures and other items there. Music fans would stand on the benches to better see the bands. The Metropolis had the feel of an old tavern.

Since Hugo was unfamiliar with punk rock, he relied on Doucette and his then girlfriend, Susan Silver, to book bands. Despite its status as a punk rock palace, shows rarely got out of control. With no security per se, Hugo personally kept a tight rein on those attempting to incite violence, and that included the Bopo Boys, who characteristically tried to get in for free. He wasn't afraid to physically engage them if necessary. "After fishing [in Alaska] for four years," says Hugo, "I tell ya, I didn't have much fear of any of these guys."

Unfortunately, the Metropolis lost its lease in March 1984, and the Pioneer Square all-ages scene soon followed.

The Metropolis' demise symbolized the transfer of Seattle's music scene to a deeper underground stage—specifically to parties in the U-District. This underground interlude, beginning in the fall of 1983 through early 1985, became an incubator, in effect, a period when musicians who chose to stay in Seattle could perfect their craft, free from expectation.

Interlude Underground

One particular U-District party stands out as an example of what was to come from this deep underground phase. In November 1983, with the weather especially dreary even for Seattle, word got around about a massive party with a Hawaiian theme, held at a U-District abode called the Big House. In addition to the usual beer intake, mushrooms were consumed, adding to the surreal atmosphere.

The party also featured the debut* of a new band, one that would demonstrate to all the potential musical possibilities amid the gloom: the Young Fresh Fellows.

The Fellows originated as a partnership between Bay Area natives Scott McCaughey and Chuck Carroll. A contributing writer to the *Rocket*, McCaughey brought a gift for songwriting as well as such varied influences as garage rock, surf music, punk rock, and the Beatles. Three years prior, the two had self-released a homemade cassette called *The Fabulous Sounds of the Pacific Northwest* to entertain their friends. At that point, no band existed per se, so they recorded two songs based on potential names: the Power Mowers and the Young Fresh Fellows. Eventually, the pair went with the Fellows moniker since it better represented their offbeat sense of humor.

The Fellows killed at the party. "I remember thinkin', 'Wow, you know, we can do this. We're pretty good,'" McCaughey recalls. "'Cause people were lovin' it, you know? It was totally rockin'. It was loud and fast. And I was goin', 'Man. This is it. We're a band now.' It was cool. It was very cool."

That confidence permeated throughout the crowd, and would continue to grow within the music community over the next few years. Party attendees had the "if they can do it, why can't we?" reaction.

The Fellows played until about 10 p.m., leaving their instruments set up. Leighton Beezer, who lived in the basement and owned some of the equipment, saw an opening. He picked up the guitar and started jamming. Soon joining him were Ed

---

*This may have been their second show. Another gig, at Jeff Ament's (Deranged Diction, Green River, Pearl Jam) house in the Fremont neighborhood occurred around the same time and may have been the actual Fellows debut show.

Fotheringham on vocals, Jeff Ament on bass, and Mark Arm on drums. "It was drunken. It was insane. And it was really surprisingly good," recalls Beezer. "Then Ed, I think, said, 'That sounded like throwup looks.'"

The Thrown Ups became Beezer's vision: a loud, sloppy punk band of a completely improvisational nature, somewhat on the order of San Francisco's Flipper.

The band debuted at the Gorilla Gardens in 1985, opening for Hüsker Dü. Sensing the audience might react negatively to an improvisational punk rock act, band members brought raw oysters to heave into the crowd if necessary. "That was our first real show," says Beezer, "and I was convinced that we were gonna get booed off the stage and people were gonna spit at us. It was going to be an ordeal. And so, my attitude was, 'Well, I'm not going in unarmed. If they start spitting at us, I'm gonna throw these giant fist-sized loogies back at them.'"

To everyone's surprise, the crowd reacted favorably, but the band tossed the oysters at the audience anyway. "And they liked us! But," Beezer continues, "it was kind of like, 'Well, I've still got these oysters. So, um, here you go.' [Laughs.] The rest was history."

Throughout this underground party period, the U-Men often led the way, whether consciously or not. The band's connection to the '60s permeated Seattle's music community in 1984, not in terms of attempting to re-create that decade, but rather reimagining it from the lens of twenty years later. Seattle's '60s revival appeared in a number of forms: Sonics-inspired garage rock that the U-Men tapped into, California-influenced psychedelia, and Bob Dylan–inspired folk rock.

The psychedelic revival drew directly from Los Angeles's early-'80s Paisley Underground movement. Ron Rudzitis's Room Nine became this movement's Seattle representative. Like '60s San Francisco performances, Room Nine shows were accompanied by offbeat projections designed to create a certain mood. The drug of choice was different, however. Instead of acid, Seattle psychedelic musicians and fans imbibed MDMA (ecstasy), the successor to the MDA the Fags had been taking. MDMA created a heightened sense of awareness, a connectedness between fans and musicians. Like acid, ecstasy and the light projections altered reality.

Seattle psychedelia had significant distinctions from California's version. Local music reflected the Northwest attitude and culture, which was darker than Los Angeles or San Francisco. Michael Laton had a strong perspective on both regions. Laton was an integral part of the '60s San Francisco underground, performing lighting projections for the Grateful Dead and Big Brother & the Holding Company. He was even a minor character in Tom Wolfe's seminal book *The Electric Kool-Aid Acid Test*. He moved to Seattle in 1980 and eventually became Room Nine's projection person, creating presentations to alter moods at shows. "In relationship to San Francisco it was . . . the whole cowboy thing," Laton says. "You can look at the clothing that everybody was affecting in the '60s and into the '70s, whether you're looking at Crosby, Stills, Nash & Young on the cover of *Déjà Vu*, where they're all dressed as gunslingers. . . . [but] up here [in Seattle] . . . it all had that Valhalla Viking warrior kind of thing. It was a whole other kind of folklore in everybody's head."

Along with Room Nine, a new band called the Green Pajamas quietly appeared on the scene in 1984. Tapping into the psychedelic revival but also adding a late-era Beatles–inspired element, the Pajamas self-released a cassette that year called *Summer of Lust*, featuring a cover with the band name displayed in a paisley shape. Recorded in the band members' houses, *Summer of Lust* showed up on consignment at Cellophane Square in the U-District. Tom Dyer, who had a recording studio and a small label called Green Monkey, walked into Cellophane Square and bought the cassette on sight knowing nothing about the band. He brought it home, listened to it, fell in love with it, and decided to contact the musicians. "And I just thought it was cool as hell," Dyer remembers. "And so [I thought], I gotta get ahold of these guys [but] there [was] exactly no contact information on the tape of any sort."

Eventually, Dyer did find the Pajamas' founding members Joe Ross and Jeff Kelly, and persuaded them to record with him. While the Pajamas would never become a major player in the Seattle scene due to their dearth of gigs, they effectively became a bridge between Room Nine psychedelia and a revival of Dylanesque folk rock.

Seattle's two main proponents of the folk rock genre, the Walkabouts and Terry Lee Hale and the Ones, also set up shop in Seattle in 1984. Formed that year when guitarists/vocalists Chris Eckman and Carla Torgerson met at an Alaskan cannery, the Walkabouts played a varied mixture of folk, blues, rock, and punk—mostly reflecting Eckman and Torgerson's musical tastes. Unlike the Pajamas, the Walkabouts quickly made a name for themselves within the punk community, even though they didn't technically play punk rock. "We always had acoustic guitars on stage," says Eckman. "It was pretty loud. . . . We were listening to *Highway 61* [*Revisited*] by Dylan and even British folk rock like Fairport Convention. We were sort of all over the place, and sounded like it too."

Along with the Walkabouts, Terry Lee Hale and the Ones, originally playing without a bassist, offered an electric folk alternative within the punk rock community. A young musician offered his services and helped complete the Ones' lineup. The bassist, Jack Endino, later became the "grunge producer," recording Nirvana, Soundgarden, and Mudhoney.

Regardless of the form urban music was taking, it all loosely fit under the label of punk rock, even if it wasn't, as in the case of the Green Pajamas, the Walkabouts, and Terry Lee Hale and the Ones. Urban punk, regardless of whether it was punk rock or not, sharply separated itself from music eminating from Seattle's wealthier suburbs.

Eastside Metal

Suburban metalheads and urban punks had long sneered at each other from across the lake, but by 1983 the ice began to crack—at least a little. The Trids, a Capitol Hill glam-rock band of high school age, decided to venture out and enter an Eastside battle of the bands competition. They walked into the Lake Hills skating rink and stepped into another world: the audience and the bands sporting big, teased-out hair and spandex, with band names like Archangel and Sentinel. Yet within all that, the Trids found people they had something in common with—in particular, two metal bands that were not there just to look cool and get laid: Overlord, which later contributed two members to My Eye, and Shadow, featuring future Pearl Jam guitarist Mike McCready.

The Trids found themselves out on an island. Nearly all of the competing acts fit within the metal genre, while the Trids played originals, as well as New York Dolls and Ramones covers. The band would take the stage in women's clothing and makeup. "We kinda looked like Twisted Sister on a bad night," says Trids drummer Duff Drew.

Perhaps surprisingly, the Trids fared well. One night, the band made it all the way to the semifinals, competing against three metal acts. The irony of an urban glam band stealing the show from suburban metal acts was somewhat lost on the audience. "People [threw] explosives on the stage—at us. We're not talking a firecracker. It was like an M-80 or a cherry bomb. Like the full-on deal," Drew remembers. "And the show stops. And at this point, we are now being protected by the members of the band Overlord."

Despite these setbacks, Drew & Co. did expose suburban rock fans to glam, inspiring kids to venture into the city in the coming years. Some of those metalheads would eventually become Alice in Chains.

Overlord represented another subtle connection between Seattle and the Eastside. Even though Overlord played the suburbs, its roots lay in the North End. Overlord began gigging in 1982. The band's metal sound found little opportunity in the developing Pioneer Square all-ages scene, however. Instead, it dared to venture to the Eastside skating rinks and discovered an audience playing for suburban metal teenagers.

After a couple of years playing the Eastside, Overlord's singer Steve van Liew and guitarist Kurtiss Lofstrom decided they had enough of the skating rink scene and its teen metal fans. In 1985 the pair quit Overlord and the Eastside. Their new band, My Eye, added ex-Trid Duff Drew and Max Godsil on drums and bass, respectively. (Godsil hailed from Seattle, and grew up with Pearl Jam's Stone Gossard, playing on basketball and floor hockey teams with him.) Unlike Overlord, My Eye would not be mistaken for a metal band. They really weren't a punk band, either. Van Liew and Lofstrom's new venture had more of a psychedelic element, perhaps playing off Room Nine on some level. Yet while Room Nine's version of psychedelic had a mystical, playful element, My Eye's was definitely darker. The band was heavy. How much of that heaviness drew from the Eastside is subject to debate, but at least subconsciously, Overlord's metal experience pervaded My Eye's music.

The Trids and Overlord weren't the only punk kids venturing to the Eastside. By 1983 a glam band called Malfunkshun became curious about the suburban metal scene. Like the Trids, Malfunkshun drew from the glam rock of Iggy Pop, T-Rex, and Kiss. Malfunkshun became one of the early bands to slow their music down to a dirgelike tempo, and guitarist Kevin Wood's solos, then taboo in punk, often placed the band outside the inner sanctum of the urban punk community.

Malfunkshun's vision came in the form of its lead singer, front man, and keyboardist: the late Andrew Wood. Andrew, Kevin's brother, helped create an unusual personality for his band, one that was equal parts glam rock, cartoon metal, and punk rock. The singer—adopting the stage name Landrew, after a villain from the original *Star Trek* television show—often wore white-face makeup and typically donned costumes on stage. He also had fun playing the role of rock star. Landrew performed as if he were in an arena singing to the third balcony, when only twenty people were in attendance.

He was also insanely funny, and his humor and warmth rubbed off on the audience. He loved cereal and sometimes brought a bowl on stage. He might then heave half of the contents at the audience. The crowd would usually enjoy the singer's high jinks, realizing he intended no provocation. He was simply celebrating cereal. "The first time I ever met him . . . I was down in Pioneer Square. I was at this party," recalled the late Ben McMillan, singer with the grunge-era Skin Yard. "And I was just sitting there, and [Wood said], 'You know what, hey, let's start charging 'em for going out.' I said, 'What?' [He said], 'Let's start charging 'em for going out.' So as people tried to leave the party, we told 'em they had to pay $5 to leave."

It was Landrew's idea to take Malfunkshun on a trek across Lake Washington. Unlike the Trids, Malfunkshun had no intention of playing there. They were just curious what the metal scene was all about. The Wood brothers lived on Bainbridge Island at the time, a 35-minute ferry ride across Puget Sound west of Seattle. So, with no car and very little money, the band embarked across the Sound, then got themselves through Seattle on foot and by bus, then eventually across Lake Washington to the Eastside.

Like the Trids, Malfunkshun found themselves in another realm. Yet after looking beneath the surface, the band discovered something beyond cock rock posing. Some of the metal bands could really play; it was as if they were in another league technically. Malfunkshun was particularly impressed by a band called Myth, which eventually evolved into Queensryche. Myth's drummer actually wrote his parts out, a practice anathema to a punk band.

Malfunkshun took that metal experience and it inspired them to play better, while at the same time infusing a heaviness into their sound. The band was one of the few that refused to sneer at the suburban metal community, but rather drew from it to eventually inspire their fellow city punk brethren.

Around that time, the Fartz had evolved into a band called 10 Minute Warning. The name change represented the band's insistence on moving beyond straight hardcore. 10 Minute Warning was born of somewhat heightened expectations. Originally featuring the Fartz' Blaine Cook on vocals, the band quickly expanded its musical palette. Cook was forced out to make room for his replacement, Steve Verwolf. In addition, the band acquired bassist Duff McKagan, who had previously played in several Seattle bands, including the Vains, the Fastbacks, and the Living. McKagan later took his musical gifts to Los Angeles and joined Guns N' Roses. Anchoring 10 Minute Warning was virtuoso percussionist Greg Gilmore, but perhaps its most inspired player was guitarist Paul Solger.

Solger is a mythical figure in Seattle, but few outsiders know who he is. A gifted guitarist, Solger had a magnetism that drew others into his fold through his talent, presence, and unusual approach to the instrument. He had previously been in the glam rock Fags and the hardcore Solger. "I found [his playing] really appealing," remembers Stone Gossard, "in terms of finding strange little figures . . . and strange note combinations that weren't typical. They sounded a little sort of out there, maybe a little bit like in the way that Jimmy Page approached the guitar."

Propelled by Gilmore's intricate drumming, 10 Minute Warning blasted out of hardcore into uncharted territory. "You could tell, it was kind of bringing together these sort of different sort of elements," Gossard continues, "that wasn't just like, 'Oh, I know what this is. It sounds like heavy metal. I know what this is. It sounds like punk.' It sounded like something brand new . . . they definitely were experimenting and letting their art rock side sort of shine."

In fact, there was nothing punk rock about 10 Minute Warning. During its short life, (1983–1984) the band stylistically redefined urban Seattle's musical possibilities. Ultimately, the band's lack of direction and use of hard drugs doomed its chances for influence beyond Seattle. "People would call [10 Minute Warning] a punk rock band," says Gilmore. "It was a hard rock band that played real fast sometimes, but [it] never seemed like a punk rock band to me."

The urban punk/suburban metal connection, while still in its infancy, found support in a short-lived fanzine called *Backfire*. A local college kid made it her mission in life to combine the two worlds. Dawn Anderson grew up in Seattle and began writing about music for the Seattle University student newspaper. Her interests ran toward punk rock and metal. That didn't exactly sit well with her fellow students. "So I was writing rock music reviews," Anderson remembers, "and slamming people like Styx and Foreigner. . . . and, God, the whole school would just get up in arms, [and I received] nasty death threats in my mailbox."

In 1983 she openly comingled her two loves by launching *Backfire*. The magazine featured articles on mainstream metal bands like Kiss and Mötley Crüe, as well as underground punk heroes like the Fastbacks and Vancouver's D.O.A. What Anderson was doing wasn't totally unheard of: the previous year, the *Rocket* ran a cover combining the hardcore punk Fartz with the suburban metal band Culprit. Anderson, however, remained ahead of the curve, in tune with the notion that it's OK to admit to liking different styles of music, that one can like both Kiss and Sonic Youth. Perhaps, in a way, *Backfire* planted the seed for grunge. "I don't know if it planted the seed," Anderson counters, "but it was part of something that was sort of going on. Yeah, I'd like to think it had a bit of an influence."

KCMU and Bruce Pavitt

Print media and radio support remained somewhat small scale, but continued to evolve during this period. In particular, the University of Washington's KCMU began to change its focus and more actively engage itself within the developing music scene.

In 1984 UW student Faith Henschel became music director. During her tenure, the station began to shift its focus toward an increasingly eclectic format, as well as provide more on-air support for local bands. The station also began to pay attention to production values. Henschel's beginnings at KCMU belied her future accomplishments. Initially trained by Mike Fuller, the station's first music director when it became self-funded, Henschel panicked during her first on-air appearance when she yelled, "Shit! Fuck!" with the mike on. Despite her inauspicious beginnings, Henschel would have a significant impact on the station's future and, by extension, the local music scene.

Henschel, along with DJ and promotions director Jonathan Poneman, began to promote local shows at the Vogue in Belltown (formerly WREX) and the Rainbow Tavern in the U-District. The shows were typically on Tuesday and Wednesday nights. Both clubs either featured cover bands or became dance-oriented on the weekends, since that was where the money was. Midweek audiences were small and usually consisted of members of other bands.

In addition to those local promotions, KCMU began to encourage its DJs to expand their musical vocabularies, while at the same time providing an environment for on-air exploration. It was during this time that the station became flooded with talent that would make significant contributions to the music scene. KCMU DJs included Mark Arm (from Mr. Epp and the Calculations, later Green River and Mudhoney), Kim Thayil (Soundgarden), Ben McMillan (Skin Yard), music photographer Charles Peterson, and Poneman. The station also featured ex-Evergreeners Scott Vanderpool (Room Nine, Chemistry Set) and Bruce Pavitt.

The Most Eccentric DJ award, if there were one, would have to go to Pavitt. Pavitt's show, called *Sub Pop USA*, became a natural extension of the fanzines he had been doing at Evergreen. He continued to focus on independent music throughout the world. "I met [Pavitt] while I was DJ'ing at KCMU," Peterson remembers. "He had the Sub Pop show before me, his sort of little syndicated half-hour show. So, I would go in and listen to his show and was just totally blown away by the stuff that he was playing.

"He was always like one step ahead of everybody else," Peterson continues, "Well you thought you were cool playing the thing he was playing like the next thing. Just stuff like Shonen Knife. I mean here's like this totally obscure all-girl Japanese band kind of thing. You're just like, 'My God! Where did that come from?'"

Pavitt's personality also impacted his fellow DJs and listeners. He was, well, kind of a space cadet. But his goofy personality belied a quiet charisma. Pavitt would do shows after staying out late the night before, and sometimes listeners knew about it. "We used to love to listen to him because he was the only DJ we ever heard yawn on the air," Art Chantry says as he laughs. "We'd all wait for his yawn. It was hilarious."

In at least one instance, Pavitt took his fatigue to its logical conclusion. "I was on after Sub Pop," Fuller recalls. "And I remember I came in one night, and Bruce had fallen asleep at the controls. I think he'd been out DJ'ing or something really late the night before. . . . And the record was going, *k-chunk* . . . *k-chunk* . . . *k-chunk*—in the inner groove, the needle was stuck. And God only knows how long it had been doing that."

At the same time he was doing his KCMU radio show, Pavitt began writing a column in the *Rocket*, also called "Sub Pop USA." Pavitt's column became the written version of his radio show and also continued the independent music focus he had at Evergreen. His early columns focused on specific American underground communities: Pavitt's first three columns, for example, featured bands from Portland, Boston, and DC.

In the summer of 1984, Pavitt and partner Russ Battaglia opened a record store on Capitol Hill called Fallout Records & Skateboards. Shortly thereafter, he began his first venture into the record label business. A huge fan of the U-Men, Pavitt championed their cause by releasing an eponymous, four-track EP on his new Bombshelter Records label. While Pavitt didn't have the marketing muscle or distribution channels to drive national or even regional exposure, the local reaction was overwhelmingly positive.

The two standout songs were the explosive "Gila" and the offbeat "Shoot 'em Down." In some ways, "Gila" is the quintessential U-Men track: frenetic with strange jazz chords, and a swinging beat, topped off with John Bigley's unmistakable and unintelligible vocals. Its genesis came from guitarist Tom Price. He began playing a dissonant, jagged, frenetic chord progression that jerked to sudden stops and starts. "Tom was doing this classic sort of fuzzed-out guitar," Tillman remembers. "His hands were just moving back and forth on the fret board. And these bizarre sort of sludgy chords are coming out, with a lot of sevenths that he likes to use."

"Shoot 'em Down" is even more bizarre. It opens menacingly with an offbeat note sequence punctuated by Bigley's yowls and then ventures into Price's jazz-infused chord playing, all driven by Tillman's rolling bass line and drummer Charlie Ryan's swinging beat. "Shoot 'em Down" came into being when Price and Tillman switched instruments. Price started playing a bass line, while Tillman found chords on the guitar to match. "And within three minutes—literally—that song had been written. 'Cause he had the bass line in his head," Tillman recalls, "and within three minutes I had written the guitar part for the whole song . . . and once we had figured out the chords, Charlie just picked up the drum sticks and started playing along with it and putting it in this really swingy sort of stripper kind of beat. And John, I think he came up with the lyrics on the spot as well. The whole song just sort of appeared out of thin air."

Both "Gila" and "Shoot 'em Down" exemplify that magic that was the U-Men. By the summer of 1984, the U-Men had become kings of the Seattle underground. But where were they going from there? National touring was still unheard of to most independent bands, particularly those in Seattle. The U-Men attempted a small tour down to Los Angeles in 1984, but found few places to play and ended up doing shows for free. With scant national interest and no Seattle label with national connections, the U-Men were forced to toil in relative anonymity.

Popllama

Fortunately, a small but significant local music platform was beginning to emerge that would provide Northwest musicians with some access to the world: the record label Popllama Products. Popllama was the brainchild of musician/producer Conrad Uno, who had played bass in Uncle Cookie, a first-wave '70s Seattle punk band. After Cookie fizzled, he found himself doing sound for live shows throughout the city. His love for recording would eventually turn into a studio and a record label, albeit on a small scale. His label and recording career were so under the radar that he had to cut lawns for little old ladies to get by.

The name's origins are a bit muddled, but it seems to be a combination of pop music and a rather humorous animal. Uno recalls Chuck Carroll of the Young Fresh Fellows coming up with the name at a party. "Somebody came up and said, 'Hey, [Chuck] said this word: Popllama,'" says Uno.

Through his sound engineering gigs, Uno had became acquainted with a band called the Dynette Set, who had achieved some local recognition by 1983. Scott McCaughey, who then wrote songs and played backing musician for the Dynette Set, befriended him. By 1984 McCaughey was ready to turn his Young Fresh Fellows loose in the recording studio, and Uno offered him free studio time if Popllama could put out the record. For the sessions, McCaughey sang and played bass with Carroll manning the guitar. For drums, the pair added Tad Hutchinson, who had been living in the U-District at the Big House—"Tad was living there on the porch in a tent for a while," McCaughey recalls—and had played at the Fellows' debut the previous November.

The three-piece recorded the album at Uno's Egg Studios. Uno's fledgling label had not yet set roots, although he had previously released records for two of his favorite local bands: Red Dress and Moving Parts. The Fellows record transformed Popllama into a going concern. "The Fellows wanted to do this album," says Uno, "and I was kinda like, 'Well, is this a record label?' And one day, we just decided that it was."

With Uno producing, Popllama released *The Fabulous Sounds of the Pacific Northwest* as an LP in 1984. The record sounded like nothing Seattle bands had done up to that point: simple, surf-influenced, hook-oriented pop/punk songs. The record's authenticity and humor made it special. In fact, the Fellows' practice of incorporating humor into their music made them somewhat unusual among Seattle's bands. Their local brethren certainly possessed the requisite wit, but the music didn't always reflect that. In contrast, Fellows' songs could make the listener laugh out loud. "[It was] just an effort to entertain the other guys in the band, really," says McCaughey. "It was a very insular thing. I wasn't thinking about whether other people would think it was funny. I think that we developed this sense of humor within the band and I wanted to crack them up."

The title for the *Fabulous Sounds*—and the basis for its lightheartedness—came from a Pacific Northwest Bell promotional record Carroll found. The Bell recording had the feel of a corny old-time documentary. The Fellows felt it perfectly juxtaposed with their songs and wove portions of it throughout their album. It works seamlessly and perfectly fit the band's self-effacing personality.

Fabulous Sounds opens with a snippet from the Bell record. Birds chirp, a foghorn sounds, and the listener hears what appears to be local Native American spiritual music. A standard male baritone emerges: "Been thinking about a vacation trip to the Pacific Northwest? Well those are just a few of the sounds of this big country. We think sounds are about the best way of communicating there is. So, we've assembled a collection of typical sounds of the Pacific Northwest. Now sit back and listen." The record then launches into its opening track, the Kinks/surf-inspired "Rock 'n' Roll Pest Control." The contrast between the intro and music works so well that it easily could have led into Nirvana's "Smells Like Teen Spirit."

Uno's recording job was admittedly rudimentary. For some reason—and no one knows exactly why—McCaughey's bass

guitar was eliminated during mixdown. Yet somehow it works—
perfectly. "What you call the corny sound of that record," says
Uno, " . . . was the best we could do—which is why it's so great.
I had no monitors to speak of. That's why there's no bass on the
damn thing. Scott's playing away there, but the speakers must
have been showing way too much bass. I didn't know about mas-
tering. We didn't know what we were doing."

"Somehow we managed to mix the entire record without
thinking about turning the bass up," McCaughey adds. "I don't
know how we did it, but we managed—which is really funny
'cause Uno's a bass player too, and a very good bass player."

For publicity, Uno and the band scrawled "Please listen to our
record!" on pie plates and sent them out to about eighty college
radio stations. Soon, the band's music blared from radios around
the country. Although this publicity didn't translate into major
record sales, the Fellows had achieved more national recognition than any independent Seattle band up to that point. Local
reaction was also positive.

---

*What makes this record even more refreshing, is that it comes at
a time when I thought the Seattle music scene was dead in the
water. This is undeniably the worst period in the last 10 years
for Seattle music (with the exception of heavy metal)—there
are fewer bands, fewer clubs and there are almost no bands in
the area now making a living off music. Almost in spite of that
I sense a resurgence in an underground movement of bands and
the Fellows are the best of the lot.*

—Charles R. Cross, *The Rocket*, June 1984

Cross was correct in a visible sense. That is, the Fellows were
perhaps the most overt underground Seattle band in the summer

of 1984. While his comments do not reflect the vibrancy of the underground scene, he did pick up on the beginnings of something interesting happening in the city. For one, local bands began to have the audacity to do national tours. The Fellows were among the first to make that effort, venturing forth based more on sheer bluster than practical economic sense. Their tours took them all the way to Eastern hotbeds like Boston and New York City. The response was somewhat muted, but the Fellows proved it could be done.

The Fellows' early output was recorded at Egg, named for the egg cartons on the wall used to shield neighbors from the sound—which rarely worked. Although small-scale, Egg provided an important piece of the puzzle: an inexpensive place for local bands to record their music.

Soon, other independent, musician-friendly studios began popping up around town. These recording spaces would become critical incubators in taking local music to another level. Reciprocal Recording became one of those studios.

Chris Hanzsek, Reciprocal Recording, and Green River

Reciprocal was the creation of Chris Hanzsek, who came to Seattle in 1983 from Pennsylvania by way of Boston. A theater major at Penn State University, he grew restless with rural Pennsylvania and moved to Boston after graduation. Boston hooked him when, along with girlfriend Tina Casale, he saw Mission of Burma open for Gang of Four. Sufficiently blown away, Hanzsek began spending time with local bands and toyed around with the idea of recording them.

By the early '80s, however, Boston had become saturated with bands and studios, and its cost of living had spiked upward. Hanzsek thought of moving to a place where he could get in on the proverbial ground floor. That place turned out to be Seattle.

Some friends encouraged him to move there, but he was concerned that he was abandoning a rich musical city in Boston for a poor one in Seattle. So before he moved, he asked his buddies to send him a sampler of Seattle music. His friends obliged by forwarding the *Seattle Syndrome* compilation as well as singles by 3 Swimmers and the Blackouts. Impressed with what he heard, Hanzsek moved to Seattle in February 1983.

He found menial jobs to get by on while saving money toward his dream of opening a recording studio. Meanwhile, Casale soon joined him in Seattle, and the two began taking in the local scene. In particular, a pair of new bands struck them: Soundgarden and Green River. Soundgarden, fronted by singer Chris Cornell, drew heavily from metal as well as Led Zeppelin. Green River had an unusual Iggy Pop/Aerosmith mixture going. Little did anyone know at the time—these two bands would help lay the basis for a new heavier aesthetic that would sweep into town.

Green River took its moniker from a local serial killer and the name was characteristically Seattle: possibly offensive, possibly ambiguous, totally dark humor. "Green River was really a genius name," comments the Thrown Ups' Beezer, "because if you were in Seattle and you knew about what it meant, then it was just shockingly callous. If you were outside of Seattle, you thought they were a Creedence cover band."

Green River melded veterans of the noise scene with graduates of hardcore punk. Guitar player Steve Turner spent some time in both Mr. Epp and the Calculations and the Limp Richards. Drummer Alex Shumway hailed from the hardcore Spluii Numa. Mark Arm, guitarist with Mr. Epp, inherited vocal duties by default since his guitar crapped out.

For bass, Turner took notice of Jeff Ament, who had migrated from Montana with his hardcore band Deranged Diction. Ament played bass through a distortion box and jumped really high and that was enough for Turner. Unfortunately, nobody really knew him particularly well. "So Steve went on this sort of underhanded campaign [to get Ament in Green River]," says Arm, "to the point where he even got a job at the same place that Jeff worked just to kind of get to know him better." He succeeded.

In many circles, Green River gets the credit for becoming the first "grunge" band, even though nobody was using that term yet. Like Soundgarden, Green River began to slow the beat down compared to their frenetic hardcore contemporaries, and acknowledged their prepunk and classic rock forebearers. "During the last days of Deranged Diction, Jeff had brought a song called 'Possession' to the table," DD vocalist/guitarist Rod Moody (later in Swallow) states in an e-mail, "which was very slow and very heavy. We played it at a few shows and it definitely threw people for a loop. In my memory this was the first indication of what was to come. After we broke up, I went to see Jeff's new band, Green River, and they took the sound of that song and expanded on it."

Hanzsek crossed paths with Green River when he opened Reciprocal Recording in January 1984. He had placed flyers around town advertising his space as a musician-friendly independent studio. Reciprocal was located in Seattle's Interbay industrial district. The building literally sat adjacent to railroad tracks. Green River began recording demos for its first EP, *Come on Down*, that spring. The location created some interesting issues. During the sessions, the band had to stop periodically since the whole studio shook each time a train passed.

Shortly after the demos*, the band added a second guitar player, Stone Gossard, a schoolmate of Shumway and Turner's at the private, college prep Northwest School. Gossard's addition

---

*Gossard may have shown up during the tail end of the demos, per Chris Hanzsek's recollection.

changed the dynamic within the band, as he was one of those young punks who ventured over to Eastside metal shows. He added to Ament's hard rock and metal aesthetic, and began to tilt the band away from Arm, Turner, and Shumway's punk leanings. Green River was almost like an unstable chemical compound since each "camp" had an indelible power. "Right away I could tell that there was a kind of a controversy inside that band," Hanzsek remembers. "I even sat there during a couple of arguments between the one side [Ament and Gossard] that wanted the band to sound more polished, more commercial, more mainstream . . . more like an arena rock band. And then the other side [Arm, Turner, and Shumway] wanted to just be . . . silly and goofy and unexpected and not at all predictable, and free to screw up anything that they wanted to do . . . just complete silliness."

Turner quickly became a standout artistic presence. A voracious record collector, he tapped into the most obscure music he could find and possessed a charisma that drew others into his offbeat world. He also brought a "less competence is more" aesthetic from his time in Mr. Epp. Finally, Turner added an edge to the band, similar to how John Lennon impacted the Beatles. He had an immense self-confidence, coupled with a freewheeling defiance. "I think Steve tended to be contrarian," says Gossard. "God bless his soul, and thank God for it. . . . He just hears music just completely differently."

Given the eclectic nature of the players, Green River had little idea where to head musically. The band sometimes veered toward a raw Stooges-esque sound, with Arm playing the part of Iggy Pop, and sometimes took on a mainstream arena rock sound. "[Green River] were basically punks saying, 'Wouldn't it be hysterical if we could be Aerosmith?' And I don't think they expected it to work. You know, it was like 'What kind of train wreck will we get if we all decide to be Aerosmith now?' And the answer was no, it's not a train wreck at all. Everyone loved it," recalls Beezer, who later played with Arm and Turner in the Thrown Ups.

There was something else, however, that separated this band from its punk peers. The players clearly strove toward commercial success, a goal most Seattle bands had eschewed up to that point. "There was, especially in the case of Green River . . . definitely a different attitude with a lot of those bands that started around that time," Fastbacks guitarist Kurt Bloch recalls. "And they definitely had a little bit more drive to be successful. It's not like we tried not to be successful in the Fastbacks, but probably everything we did, we probably went about it the wrong way."

Gossard and Ament drove the band's business aspirations, and Green River soon inked a deal with New York's Homestead Records, then a hip indie label that boasted Sonic Youth on its roster. In anticipation of releasing *Come on Down*'s final version (recorded for Homestead in late 1984), the band scheduled a sixteen-city national tour in 1985. Like the Fellows, Green River had broken the mold of what a Seattle band could do.

Unfortunately, the band soon found out about Homestead's notorious unreliability. The record's release date was set prior to the band heading out on the road, but it didn't show up in stores until two months after the tour's completion. As a result, venues began canceling shows since no one had heard of them. The tour quickly shrank to just a few shows.

More tumult awaited. Just before Green River hit the road, Turner quit, concerned the band was headed in too much of a hard rock/metal direction. He was quickly replaced by Bruce Fairweather, also from Deranged Diction, further pushing the band toward a heavier aesthetic.

Come On Down, in some ways, melds the two worlds. The title track is arguably grunge's opening salvo beginning with thirty seconds of noise and feedback. Suddenly, Arm screams

"Whoa!" and the band launches into a distorted descending two-chord progression. The record sounds like something other than punk rock.

In Doug Pray's *hype!*, a 1996 documentary of Seattle music, Leighton Beezer plays a melodic two-chord progression that ascends up the neck of the guitar. He describes it as punk rock. He then plays a dissonant two-chord progression that descends down the neck. He describes that as grunge. Turns out the initial riff comes from the Ramones' "Rockaway Beach," and the second is Green River's "Come on Down." "And when I noticed [Green River] playing 'Come on Down' for the first time . . . that hook, I really liked it," says Beezer. "I was watching them play it, so I could do the same thing myself, and [I] immediately went, 'God, they're just playing punk rock backwards. Awesome!'"

He continues, "It is basically a tribute to Black Sabbath. The augmented fifth [note used in "Come on Down"] is the classic Black Sabbath sort of 'ominous, slightly discordant but also gets the adrenaline going in a strange way' kind of note. It's a very cool note—and it's not in punk rock."

I'm having a Black Sabbath flashback.

—Anonymous KCMU DJ review of *Come On Down*, 1985*

While the band delved into metal influences, the Black Sabbath connection did not arise consciously. "I think that I probably just tried to make a song that kind of was heavy as it could possibly be," says Gossard. "So, if it sounded like Sabbath, great. . . . So

---

*Used with permission from KEXP, formerly known as KCMU.

much of it was like visual for me in terms of like, you look at a guitar neck and go . . . 'Where's a weird note to go to?'"

Following the recording, Green River embarked on their truncated tour. Despite Homestead's shortcomings, the band made it all the way to New York City's notorious CBGB's, the punk palace that launched the Ramones, Blondie, and Talking Heads. The show itself was memorable, at least from the band's perspective. By the time Green River took the stage after midnight, only a handful of Japanese businessmen remained in the audience. "And we just ripped the place apart. . . . got paid nothing, but the only people [that] were there to see us I believe were [the] Japanese businessmen and the staff," says Shumway. "And the staff thought that we were great, so they gave us all the free beer we wanted. 'Hey, you guys are great. Here. You're not getting paid shit, but you can have beer.'"

Soundgarden started up around the same time as Green River. The band's impact was immediate, given the presence of Chris Cornell, its sexually charged lead singer (and sometimes drummer), and as well as the dynamic Kim Thayil and Hiro Yamamoto, guitarist and bassist, respectively. "From the very beginning," says Milton Garrison of Vexed (see Chapter 4), "Soundgarden was getting a ton of attention, which was no surprise because of the talent wrapped up in that group: great singer, great guitar player, great bass player."

Gorilla Gardens

Green River and Soundgarden's emergence symbolized a heavier aesthetic that was beginning to permeate the scene. Further assisting in that endeavor was the Gorilla Gardens, an all-ages club that opened its doors in February 1985. Succeeding the earlier Gorilla Room, the new venue was located in the International District, just east of Pioneer Square. The Gardens would turn out to be the last of Seattle's "great" all-ages venues, even though it lasted less than a year. The city began cracking down on all-ages clubs, citing public disturbances and fire department violations. By the following year, however, a generation of punk kids began turning twenty-one, making the all-ages format obsolete.

The Gardens' distinctive structure contributed to its musical format. Carved out of an old two-screen movie theater, it became two clubs in one. One theater, the Omni Room, featured Eastside metal bands, while the other, Gorilla Gardens, offered up urban punk bands. While the owner advertised the entire building as the Rock Theater, mostly people referred to the whole venue as the Gorilla Gardens. Patrons entered via a common lobby, forcing punk and metal fans to brush up against each other.

For the most part, the punk rockers and metalheads kept to themselves. Backstage in the old projection room, musicians did comingle, however. Furthermore, the projection room had two holes cut out where the old movie projectors resided. The openings allowed punk bands to spy on metal bands and vice versa. The club attracted national punk/alternative acts like Sonic Youth and Hüsker Dü, as well as local bands like the U-Men, Soundgarden, and Green River. On the metal side, the Gardens brought in national acts as well as Eastside bands like Shadow. One of those acts was a new Los Angeles band called Guns and Roses, later shortened to Guns N' Roses. The band's bass player, Duff McKagan, enjoyed a homecoming, having played in 10 Minute Warning, the Fastbacks, and several other Seattle-area bands.

The Gorilla Gardens' mixing of punk and metal did not produce any tangible results, however. The punk and metal bands continued to sneer at one another. Punk fans saw their bands in the punk room, and the metal fans caught their acts at the metal club. Metal kids would sometimes show up at punk parties in the U-District but would make little headway with that crowd.

Beezer specifically remembers a party at his house where two Eastside metal kids stopped by. The pair sported the look: spandex and long, teased-out hair and makeup. They marched past Beezer and fellow Thrown Up Ed Fotheringham, shooting them a look of derision. Five minutes later, the two emerged dejected, apparently having endured a mocking by punks at the party. "And Ed says, 'Wow! They must be musicians!' in a tone of contempt," Beezer recalls. "And what was funny is the guy turned around like he knew he'd been insulted. But he thought being a musician was a compliment. He didn't have a comeback. He turned around like he was gonna say something like, 'Fuck you too!' but it was [as if he thought] 'All he did was call me a musician. And, goddamn it, I am a musician!'"

Perhaps the biggest accomplishment of the Gorilla Gardens, besides providing an all-ages venue, was that the punk and metal kids refrained from doing violence to one another. In addition, the punk kids intermingled enough with the metal crowd to at least acknowledge what bands like Malfunkshun already knew: the metal kids could really play. Finally, on a superficial level, around this time punks began to grow their hair long, effectively creating the signature look for what would become known as grunge over the next few years.

A Gorilla Gardens highlight show, a not atypical Seattle event, occurred in January 1985. Hugo and Susan Silver's Metropolis Productions (formed after the Metropolis club closed) sponsored the Violent Femmes. The event was also promoted by KCMU. Metropolis took the financial risk of guaranteeing the Femmes' payout. The venue oversold its 300-person legal capacity, and patrons clamored to get in. Some kids had discovered a hole in the roof and made their way down through the rafters to catch the show. Ceiling tiles began falling into the crowd, alerting Hugo. He climbed up into the rafters to chase the kids out of the club. By the time Hugo escorted the uninvited guests to the street, he was met by the police department.

The police had been called since the overflow crowd had spilled onto the street. The fire department soon followed to make sure the club was up to code—which of course it wasn't. The fire exits were boarded up, making the club an absolute fire hazard. The fire chief informed Hugo that the venue had to be evacuated immediately, literally in the middle of the Femmes' set. "And I was just on my knees," says Hugo, "basically saying, 'If you shut me down, I'm bankrupt.'"

Out of desperation, Metropolis staffers took a chainsaw and cut a hole in the side of the building and, voilà! The building had enough exits. "I mean, how can you argue with that shit? It was like perfect," says Art Chantry. "'You want a fire exit? We'll give you a fuckin' fire exit!'"

Deep Six

Regardless of whether the Gorilla Gardens or the Eastside was responsible, a sonic heaviness had begun to infect the punk scene. Bands like Green River and Soundgarden represented the progenitors of the new sound. Hanzsek decided to document this as yet un-named musical genre with a record compilation. He had lost his original studio lease and started up a record label called C/Z Records with his girlfriend, Tina Casale. (C/Z is an abbreviation for Casale and HanZsek.)

Arm and Ament assisted Hanzsek in choosing bands for the compilation. Green River and Soundgarden were shoo-ins. Malfunkshun was another obvious choice, since that band also had hard rock and metal leanings. The Melvins, a dirge band from Montesano (near Nirvana's hometown of Aberdeen), became the fourth band. The progressive rock–leaning Skin Yard made five. For the sixth band, Daniel House of Skin Yard suggested the U-Men, then at the pinnacle of Seattle's underground scene, to give the comp instant street cred. After House made a number of calls to U-Men manager Larry Reid, the band agreed to contribute one song.* The other acts contributed two each.

C/Z would entitle the record *Deep Six*. The "Six" represented the number of bands. The "Deep" perhaps alluded to the bands' collective sound, although the people involved are not entirely sure.

Recording sessions for *Deep Six* took place in August and September 1985. Since Hanzsek was without a recording space, he found a studio called Ironwood. With Casale providing $2,500 to fund the entire project, the sessions were understandably rough-shod. "I think we recorded it in like two sessions," says Hanzsek, "where we had three bands come in, one right after the other. We would just leave the microphones set up. We'd get the first band in, record their songs. They'd load back out. Next band would come in. So it was just kind of a rapid-fire recording process."

Deep Six represented a symbolic transition between eras, a passing of the torch from the U-Men to the beginning of what would become known as grunge. The record, C/Z's first release, would not come out until January 1986.

Shortly after the recording sessions, the U-Men were scheduled to play at Bumbershoot, Seattle's annual Labor Day outdoor music festival. The show would become legendary in the annals of underground Seattle music.

Bumbershoot didn't seem like a good fit for punk rock in 1985. The festival was outdoors, as opposed to a dark club. Families typically wander around outside, replete with baby strollers. The U-Men were to perform at the Mural Amphitheatre, which had the unusual feature of a moat separating the stage from the audience. The moat stuck out a few feet from the stage, which was made of fire-retardant wood.

---

*According to Rob Morgan, the U-Men song on *Deep Six*, "They," is identical to the riff the nascent band was annoying him with in his basement back in 1980.

U-Men drummer Charlie Ryan came up with an idea. For the finale, the band would pour lighter fluid into the moat and set it ablaze.

To test Ryan's idea, the band retreated to Reid's apartment. They filled up his bathtub with water, pouring lighter fluid into the tub. Upon ignition, the results were spectacular—towering flames leapt up to the ceiling and began to consume the bathroom. The fire department arrived and fortunately extinguished the blaze before Reid lost his apartment. The reaction was typical U-Men. "We just kinda looked at each other," says Reid, "and just went, 'Alright. This is great! It'll work!'"

With their "plan" ready, the U-Men took the stage in front of about three thousand fans at Bumbershoot that weekend. The entire punk community packed the front rows, excited to see one of their own at the festival.

For the finale, the U-Men launched into "10 After 1," a noisy number with varying tempos, exploding at its conclusion. As the band played, two roadies walked to the front of the stage, emptying a half gallon each of lighter fluid from vodka bottles. To the audience, the liquid appeared to be vodka. Meanwhile, Bigley hid behind the PA and soaked the tip of a broom with lighter fluid, then set it aflame. He emerged onto the stage dancing around with his broom-torch. As Bigley pranced to the band's tribal-like incantations, the roadies motioned fans close to the stage to get back.

Bigley made his way forward and touched the flaming broom to the moat soaked in lighter fluid. A wall of flame, nearly ten feet high, instantly erupted. Time seemed to stop. James Burdyshaw, later with the grungy 64 Spiders and Cat Butt, was in the audience that day. "I just stood there with my mouth open," he says.

The view from the stage was just as spectacular. As the flames surged skyward, they began to part in the middle, allowing the band a unique view of the awestruck audience. "All of the sudden," Tillman remembers, "the whole crowd just like surged to the front of the stage—towards the moat—which isn't really where you want them to be."

The audience literally went crazy, and the handful of police officers was completely unequipped to deal with the sudden mayhem. Bopo Boy Lance Mercer stood in the front, his eyebrows nearly singed off as the flames leapt upward. "We just started dancing like crazy," says Mercer. "And this cop all the sudden ran into the crowd . . . he was gonna arrest somebody. And he ended up just getting bounced around."

Meanwhile, on stage, the band had another issue to deal with. "Here's what we failed to take into consideration. The stage was built out over the pond," says Reid. "The water actually went under the stage [so] the flames went under the stage."

The band continued to play on, unfazed by the potentially serious danger. The soundman, fearing for his equipment, cut the PA. Fortunately for everyone involved, the lighter fluid burned off rather quickly, and the fire burned itself out after about 30 seconds.

As the audience and police confrontation began to escalate, Reid remembered he was already on probation for fire department violations, and in Three Stooges–like fashion, he ran away. The band similarly packed up its equipment as quickly as possible and loaded it onto a bus idling by the side of the stage, vacating before any arrests could be made.

The entire incident lasted only a few minutes, but afterward the city filled the trench with concrete to prevent future flaming moats. Not surprisingly, the U-Men themselves were never invited back to Bumbershoot. "And that's the best thing that's ever happened at Bumbershoot," says Green River's Mark Arm, also in attendance. "I can guarantee you."

While the U-Men continued to make music over the next three years, the Bumbershoot show and *Deep Six* symbolized the changing of the guard, from the U-Men era to the heavier grunge period. In retrospect, some have argued that the U-Men's singular combination of avant-jazz garage rock/punk laid the basis for grunge. Perhaps, but the U-Men were too inventive to simply be a foundation for something else. "I'd be happy to *not* be credited with inventing grunge," says U-Men guitarist Price.

CHAPTER 4

The Deep Six Generation

Have you been to the Cleveland Rock and Roll Hall of Fame? I went [there] a fair amount of time ago, and in the basement they have . . . this grunge section. And my husband at the time pointed, tapped me on the back—and what's in there but the Deep Six album, along with the Seattle grunge thing. [Laughs.] It's just kind of interesting to see my album in the Rock and Roll Hall of Fame.

—Tina Casale, *Deep Six* backer and coproducer

The Young Fresh Fellows' first ever club performance, the Rainbow Tavern, 1983.
(Photo by Marty Perez)

A pivotal year for local musical creativity, 1986 was also the coming of age of a new generation of musicians and their fans. These young people brought with them a shared formative life experience quite distinctive from their Seattle predecessors. This new group of kids was born around 1965, attended Modern Productions–era Showbox events, participated in the 1983 and '84 Pioneer Square all-ages scene, and went to every U-Men show. In 1986, they built upon the music they'd grown up watching and responded by starting bands of their own.

Previous generations were not necessarily lacking in confidence, but they had to create their own raw materials in a sense. If musicians wanted to put on a show in those pre-grunge days, halls typically had to be rented, posters had to be stapled to telephone poles, and fanzines had to be created. Further, documenting their work often became problematic due to the lack of low budget, musician-friendly recording studios in town. By 1986, however, this new generation found clubs to play at, radio support from U-Dub's KCMU, print media coverage in the *Rocket*, and more low cost recording options. All of that combined to give the "grunge kids" more of a platform to make music, even if it was just for their own enjoyment.

The Out-of-Townies

Some of these kids came from out-of-town, and thus brought with them a broader perspective than the Seattle natives of previous generations. This group of transplants, arriving in the late '70s through the mid-'80s, came to a place that, from the outset, seemed ill-suited for a major music scene expansion. Seattle was still viewed by most outsiders with little interest, as a sleepy, rainy town tucked away in a remote corner of the country. Guitarist Kevin Whitworth moved to Seattle from New England and expected a city similar in size to Boston. "And in 1984, when I moved to Seattle," Whitworth remembers, "I was shocked. It didn't have half of the buildings [that Boston had]. It was raining. It was . . . boring. It was really, really boring and drab. It was like a Soviet city."

Despite Seattle's apparent lack of appeal, a number of major players came from all over the country including Kim Thayil (Soundgarden), Jack Endino (Skin Yard, producer), Jeff Ament (Green River, later Pearl Jam), Bruce Fairweather (Green River), Chris Hanzsek (producer), Tad Doyle (H-Hour, later in TAD), Terry Lee Hale (musician and booking agent), Whitworth (later in Love Battery), Jonathan Poneman (KCMU DJ, later co-owned Sub Pop Records), and Bruce Pavitt (founded Sub Pop Records).

This generation possessed a confidence that perhaps previous ones lacked. It wasn't a straight confidence, however. Rather, this generation's hubris was born of the previous' frustrations. Many of these kids grew up watching some of the more popular local bands leave town, only to disintegrate. They knew the major record labels weren't coming up from Los Angeles to check them out. They saw a once vibrant all-ages scene die out, and they cut their musical teeth playing shows at house parties. This generation felt it had little technical prowess and no national exposure, so why not make music for its own sake? In effect, this confidence emanated from a kind of inferiority complex-driven naïveté, resulting in a pervasive "we have nothing to lose" attitude. "The general feeling was that we were all too cruddy—that if anyone was really interested in our bands, they would come sign us up," remembers Rusty Willoughby of Pure Joy (discussed later in this chapter.) "And everyone was pretty naive. So our feeling was that, 'Ah, you know, we kinda suck, and we're not good enough to make records,' but it was a blast playing music."

These folks also represented Generation X, post-Baby Boomers who did not necessarily see the United States as the "land of opportunity." They came of age during Reagan's America, when the term "yuppie" described energetic and enterprising young college-educated professionals basking in the glow of the new materialism.

These Gen Xers consciously rejected Reagan and consumerism, at a time when local software behemoth Microsoft was just beginning to expand, laying the basis for the coming '90s dot-com boom. Many of them were college-educated, but instead of taking the professional job and venturing toward an upwardly mobile career path, they started bands without any prospect of commercial success. Since they had little money, they moved into group houses on Capitol Hill and in the U-District. "And a lot of us, I think, that were in the music scene [thought] 'Hey, you only get to go through this life once,'" says Laura Weller-Vanderpool, later in the harmonic ballad-oriented Capping Day. "'Let's not focus so much on the career thing. Let's just get in a van and go on the road and play music and see what happens.' If we're all living in a crappy little house in the University District or whatever, and just barely getting by, it didn't really matter. Because, it was more important that we were doing something that mattered. And I think we were all really afraid of just steppin' on that escalator to kind of a boring, secure future."

Everybody Lived in Group Houses

"Everybody lived in group houses," says the Thrown Ups' Leighton Beezer. "I remember my budget was $400 a month: $80 for rent, $50 a week for food, and the rest went to beer. It was not a bad life."

"I moved into a house with five people—well, four people at the time," says Jack Endino. "It was like a five-bedroom house, with a couple of rehearsal rooms in the basement—a classic band house. My share of the rent was like $150 a month. . . . I'm living in this punk rock house. Everybody's splitting the bills five ways. There [were] rehearsal rooms in the basement, so we didn't have to pay for that. I was just living on nothing—living on chicken livers, for crying out loud. [Laughs.] I'm not joking. I don't know what I was thinking."

"That's part of that whole generation thing," adds drummer Scott Vanderpool. "See, we all grew up on the Monkees and the Banana Splits and all this other crap. And that's just what you did. You know, when you grow up, you're in a band and you live with your bandmates in a big house."

"When I was a little kid," Vanderpool continues, "we were watching the Beatles' *Help* and the Monkees. You know, every damn cartoon seems like was about a band somehow . . . *Josie and the Pussycats*, and *The Bugaloos*—all that shit. We were trained."

Some of the punk rock houses had names, either after the band that occupied them or for other reasons: the Monster House, the Chem Set House, the Walkabouts House. Perhaps the most famous (or notorious) was the Room Nine House, located behind the Rainbow Tavern. The house was the headquarters for the band, but it also became the scene's unofficial party haven. "Room Nine House was a little weirder than most [because] they had all kinds of weird Pier One Imports tapestries hanging off the ceiling," Vanderpool says, "and Indian hunks of cloth hanging off the ceiling in a lot of the parts of that house—kinda covered shit up. In fact, I remember one time sitting in the living room gettin' baked, and hearing a weird scratching noise and the whole thing kinda came tumbling down when a rat fell out of the ceiling."

Capitol Hill's counterpart to the Room Nine House was the House of Squalor. Kevin Whitworth lived there, along with

U-Men roadie Tommy Bonehead and drummer Jason Finn (who played at various times with Endino's Skin Yard, Love Battery, and the Presidents of the United States of America). "Why our house was 'squalored,'" says Whitworth, "was because Daniel House, I don't know if he was promoting shows or what he was doing, but people would come by and be playing at the Vogue or different places and he'd always say, 'You can go stay at Kevin's house.'"

This new generation of scenesters not only lived together, but worked together in crappy day jobs so they could pursue their band interests at night, which of course didn't make any money either. They had shitty, low-paying jobs—the kind of work where musicians could return after a three-week tour and still have a job waiting for them. These were the dirty jobs. "I was . . . working part-time as a journeyman butcher," Tad Doyle recalls, "trying to get into the union. And, you just do whatever you can to make it happen, you know? I mean, the music was the goal. And working was just a vehicle to let us do that goal.

"This guy I did landscaping for . . . he basically just let me come and go—at will," says Chris Eckman of the Walkabouts. "He had a very small landscaping company and he was like, 'OK, you got a three-week tour. Fine. You know, I'm not rich enough to donate to the symphony or to the art museum, so you're my arts donation. So, [I'll] just let you come and go when you want to come and go. You always have a job here when you come back from tour.' So, I mean, this was a lifesaver of course."

"Steve [Wied, TAD drummer]," bassist Kurt Danielson adds, "he worked at a string of really strange jobs. . . . He worked at a gas station once. [Laughs.] He filled a bus up with regular gasoline instead of diesel. And [his boss] was so pissed off. Steve was flustered. They drained the gas tank right there, so the gas poured down the street. And they were on a hill, so it just plunged down this hill. There could have been an explosion very easily. He got fired for that. [Laughs loudly.]"

"There [were] a whole lot of people working in one or another capacity in the food industry," says Endino, "a whole lot of people working at restaurants as cooks or dishwashers. You know, that was what people did.

"Musicians, by and large, don't get the best jobs," continues Endino. "You have to get a job flexible enough that you can like take some time off if you need to drive out of town and play a gig for a few days. So, food service jobs are usually good for that because you can sort of set your schedule a little bit."

A small clique began working in the warehouse at Yesco/ Muzak, consisting of Doyle, Room Nine's Ron Rudzitis, the Young Pioneers' Chris Pugh, Bruce Pavitt, Mark Arm, and Chris Eckman's brother Grant, who also played in the Walkabouts. There is something ironically humorous about rock musicians working at a company that created insipid versions of pop songs for doctors' offices and elevators. "[I was] working at Muzak," says Doyle, "And that's where I met a lot of the, uh, suspects and characters in this Seattle rock thing."

All of this communal living, playing, and working menial jobs created an equalizing force within the music scene. A person's background or economic status meant little in this musical mini-world. For example, Jack Endino, an engineer, hung out with Tad Doyle, a butcher, and Doyle befriended Kurt Danielson, who studied poetry, and—you get the idea. "There were no such false barriers, false notions of class that separated anybody," says Danielson. "I mean, everybody knew—from the get-go—that it was music and that was the important thing. Nobody talked about it. It was a tacit understanding, and it would have been considered totally uncool to speak of it. Therefore, nobody even considered it."

"And I think the proof of that," says Chris Eckman, "is I can't remember anybody ever talking about their day jobs. Really. It was like, when work was done—you were at a club—it was just like you existed in the here and now. I don't remember anybody talking about what they did to make money outside of [music], or even what their education was, or for the most part, where they came from."

There was one other element present in this generation, one that got little play later when Sub Pop Records perpetrated the grunge myth: intellectualism. The caveman stereotype has enveloped all perception of grunge musicians. In reality, many of these young people drew from the U-Men idea that it's OK to weave intellectual elements into punk rock. This intellectual bent could perhaps be viewed as arrogance, but that's only if you take it literally. For example, one such college kid, guitarist Jamie Lane, expresses this confidence when describing his band, Bundle of Hiss: "Kurt [Danielson, Bundle of Hiss bassist] used to like to say that we were a Dionysian band. I always liked that. You know Dionysus, the Greek god Dionysus? He's like the Greek version of Bacchus, he's the god of frenzy . . . anyway, look it up. . . . We were intellectuals," Lane recalls. "We were really into all that stuff, thinking about how we could link [the music] up to our academic work. . . . We were that really frenzied—not a lot of thought, more of the spirit. You think about Apollonian art versus Dionysian art. Apollonian art is thoughtful and intentional and controlled and all that. Dionysian [art] . . . is frenzied, based on inspiration. And we were like that."

To further this community's musical ambitions, the local club scene began to offer additional possibilities for local bands. In particular, Belltown's Ditto Tavern, and Pioneer Square's Central Tavern became friendly confines to newer bands.

Central Tavern

By 1986, the Central began to struggle to fill its weeknight bills. The venue had traditionally booked what were then known as the old school bar bands like Jr. Cadillac (dating back to the early '70s), and the Rangehoods (Steve Pearson's successor to the Heats). Acoustic rocker and booking agent Terry Lee Hale stepped in. Hale had played with the Ones and befriended a number of the younger bands, some of whom he booked at the tiny 5-0 Tavern up on Capitol Hill. In 1986, he offered to help Central owner Mike Downing fill his place with burgeoning local rock talent.

"I booked all the local acts," says Hale. "Soundgarden had a show there, Skin Yard, the Walkabouts, Pure Joy, Danger Bunny. Those were like the bigger indie bands. I [call] them indie bands to separate them from bands like the Rangehoods, who were well established. These guys like went on tours. These were bands—Jr. Cadillac—they were big [locally]. They had guaranteed draws. They always did well for Mike at the Central. And these other bands had to prove themselves. And that's kind of what happened."

Within a few months, once small audiences swelled to over a hundred. The Walkabouts and other younger bands began to get weekend gigs. Soon, nationally known alternative rock bands like Faith No More, the Meat Puppets, and the Butthole Surfers began to headline at the Central, with local acts like Soundgarden and 64 Spiders opening. Seattle's Central, like the Bird and the Metropolis before it, became a connection for bands heading up from California on their way to Canada or as a stopping point before heading east.

KCMU, continuing its support for the still-small scene's increasing vitality, promoted future Sub Pop Records co-owner Jonathan Poneman to promotions director. Around the same time, the station moved its transmitter from the U-Dub campus to Capitol Hill and doubled its wattage, thus expanding its range beyond the U-District to the rest of the city.

Reciprocal Recording II

With increasing opportunities to play live, a music scene also requires recorded documentation to flourish. Other than Conrad Uno's Egg Studios, the city had few inexpensive recording options. That changed when Endino and Chris Hanzsek reopened Reciprocal Recording together in July. Hanzsek originally started Reciprocal in 1984 in Seattle's industrial Interbay district, but lost his lease the following year. He then crossed paths with Endino, and the two decided to go into the studio business together. "Chris, in the meantime, he was looking for a studio building," Endino recalls, "and he had a whole eight-track rig in his basement and nowhere to set it up. And, as it happened, I knew where there was a studio that was just about to go out of business. And I said, 'Hey, I know the guys who have this building. . . . You're looking for a place to set up a studio. I'm looking for a studio to work in, and I know all these bands.'"

The new Reciprocal would locate in Ballard, a neighborhood northwest of downtown. Endino and Hanzsek found an odd, triangular-shaped building in a nondescript section of the neighborhood. The previous tenant had called itself Triangle Studios.

Hanzsek bought out his partner shortly thereafter, leaving Endino as the primary recording engineer. Reciprocal, using Hanzsek's affordable pricing approach, would become a preeminent Seattle indie rock studio into the '90s. Green River, Soundgarden, and later TAD, Nirvana, and Mudhoney would all make seminal recordings there.

With the newer generation and its bands receiving more support, and the scene moving out of the underground and into the clubs, the music demanded documentation on vinyl. That notion would come to fruition with C/Z Records' release of *Deep Six* in January 1986. As discussed in Chapter 3, the compilation featured six bands: Green River, Soundgarden, the U-Men, Malfunkshun, the Melvins, and Skin Yard.

Soundgarden

By 1986, Soundgarden began to develop its own personality, combining elements of Led Zeppelin–like cock rock posing, Black Sabbath dissonance, and the darkness of postpunk bands like Bauhaus. Chris Cornell became the consummate front man. Tall, lanky, with flowing dark hair and blue eyes, he quickly became a "rock star" within the still formative scene. "I could never be Chris," said Skin Yard's Ben McMillan. "Men wanted to fuck Chris, and [so did] women. Nobody wanted to fuck me."

Soundgarden began to openly break the urban punk rules with the use of minor riff progressions, extended solos, and open-ended jams. Perhaps more than any other urban band, Soundgarden drew metal fans in from the suburbs. They weren't just a punk/metal hybrid. They had the chops to play as well as the Eastside metal kids, including mixing strange time signatures with their thrash. At the same time, Soundgarden had that genuine urban vibe in that they clearly weren't posers. "Kim [Thayil], he brought that monster punk/metal guitar—equal parts Black Flag/Black Sabbath," says metal fan and writer Jeff Gilbert. "And all the sudden, it made sense. Everything just made sense after Soundgarden.

"When they came out on stage," Gilbert continues, "they started out sometimes kinda slow and drony, and kinda swirly hippie, psychedelic. Then, all of a sudden—*Bam!* It would detonate. And the whole place would just erupt."

The Melvins

The Melvins drew from Kiss, Black Sabbath, Scratch Acid, and Flipper. The band hailed from Montesano, a small logging town about two hours southwest of Seattle. The Melvins were the only non-Seattle band on *Deep Six*, and were one of the first groups to slow things down to a crawl. Their sense of danger, sludginess, musicianship, and sheer volume kept their audience on edge despite the slow tempo. "I remember seeing them play in Boise [Idaho] a long time ago," Doyle recalls, "and I remember thinking, 'Damn! This band's heavy,' and it would scare away a lot of the people, which is what I really liked. I stayed through the whole set, and by the end of the set, there was probably like, eight people [left], and I was one of 'em."

Led by singer Buzz Osborne (sporting a hairstyle perhaps best described as a cross between Don King and *Seinfeld*'s Kramer), bassist Matt Lukin, and the intensely hard-hitting drummer Dale Crover, the Melvins became masters of creating tension during performances. Crover was one of the few drummers who would routinely blow people away. The only other local percussionists arguably in his class were the Blackouts' Bill Rieflin, 10 Minute Warning's Greg Gilmore, and Soundgarden's Matt Cameron. The band's incredible skill created an intense live set. "They could do something with incredible amounts of slowness and space," says Endino, "and still maintain the tension, and just have you on the edge of your chair just like, looking at the stage, just not knowing what they're gonna do next."

Skin Yard

Of all the *Deep Six* bands, Skin Yard was arguably the least punk. Formed in 1985 by guitarist Jack Endino and bassist Daniel House, Skin Yard initially used progressive rock as a basis, with each member adding his own influences. Endino's guitar drew from prog as well as heavy rock in the Zeppelin/Sabbath vein, as well as Motorhead. In contrast, House's bass lines reflected influences from postpunk bands like Joy Division and Killing Joke. Finally, Matt Cameron anchored the band with a prodigious drumming style, displaying almost limitless ability. "And

Matt . . . is absolutely one of the best drummers ever, even then," says Endino. "People would just watch us play and they would just stare at the drummer. He completely upstaged us. [Laughs.] He was, by far, the best musician in the band. We played a King Crimson cover at one point, and he played all the drum parts note-for-note perfect. That's how good he was."

Ben McMillan, a KCMU DJ, took on the vocal duties. "I dared myself and tried out for Skin Yard," remembered McMillan, who passed away in 2008. "And they said, 'You're in,' and I said, 'Oh, no!' And they said, 'We have a show in two weeks and its gonna be with the U-Men at the Oddfellows Hall up on Capitol Hill.' I had no lyrics. . . . and so I just ad-libbed."

Skin Yard recorded its eponymous debut LP in 1985 and 1986. The record reflected the band's eclectic nature at that point. Jazzy, yet metalesque, *Skin Yard* sounds like a band still searching for an identity, led by a melodic vocalist who could sing like David Bowie or Ozzy Osbourne. "People couldn't fig-ure out what the hell we were trying to do," says Endino. "Are we trying to be heavy and loud? There was nothing punk rock about Skin Yard on our first record at all. . . . It was a weird, proggy, strange heavy-rock record. Our singer [McMillan] had sort of a Bowie fixation at the time. No one could quite figure that out. . . . [But] it's a musically coherent vision, the first record. It's just a completely different vision [from] what we ended up turning into."

Deep Six's Impact

The release of *Deep Six* represents a seminal moment in Seattle music history, both contemporaneously and in retrospect. The record signified not only the existence, but the viability of this generation of urban punk bands playing heavy, metal-infused music. For urban punks who were closet metal fans, *Deep Six* was a coming-out party. It became cool to be punk and admit liking metal. "There was this group of bands—and the *Deep Six* bands were some of them—that just took anything from everything that they liked at all, and just threw it together and threw it in a blender," says writer Dawn Anderson, "with absolutely no thought to whether it was cool or not. And it really got some people's heads spinning. . . . It was just fucking great watching snobs squirm like that."

In effect, *Deep Six* documents the beginning of what would later be referred to as the "Seattle sound." Yet, unlike the media manipulations of the grunge phenomenon in the early '90s, *Deep Six* was the real deal. Its raw authenticity validates the arrival of the new sound in Seattle. The record was mere happenstance: it didn't set out to document the arrival of grunge. It just came out that way. Yet for all its retrospective cachet, *Deep Six* is far from a finished product. The record displayed a murkiness, a forming of something beyond previous eras. For whatever grunge was, the record had not arrived there yet.

Deep Six did not sell particularly well. C/Z's Tina Casale and Hanzsek had no plan to seriously promote the record. (Last I checked, Hanzsek had a box full of them in his garage.) Furthermore, Casale, the primary backer, left the project for personal reasons and over alleged conflicts with Green River. So, with little money, Hanzsek promoted *Deep Six* as best he could. The record went nowhere commercially and generated some resentment from the bands. "There were big expectations," says Hanzsek. "I didn't expect it. And I sort of blame myself now for being a little naive."

"I think he always kind of felt bad about that. . . . Really, we never promised anybody anything," says Casale. "I mean, we paid for everything. All they had to do was show up and record. And for people like Soundgarden, they were just starting. . . . But for us to approach them and say, 'Hey, we're gonna put a record out. We'll pay for everything. You just show up.' I think they saw that as a good opportunity, because then they used the record for their promotion."

Regardless of *Deep Six*'s lack of commercial success, the record did create a local buzz.

Deep Six LP. You got it. It's slow SLOW and heavy HEAVY and it's THE predominant sound of underground Seattle in '86. Green River, Sound Garden [sic], The Melvins, Malfunkshun and even Skin Yard prove that you don't have to live in the suburbs and have a low I.Q. to do some SERIOUS head banging. As an extra bonus you also get one cut by local sex gods the U-Men. They is one of their mega-hits but sounds quirky and out of context (a fat slab from skull thumpers My Eye would've made more sense). But enough slack, THIS RECORD ROCKS.

—Bruce Pavitt review of *Deep Six*, *The Rocket*, April 1986

Near *Deep Six* Bands

Four other bands didn't make the *Deep Six* cut, but nonetheless represented significant contributors to the scene's heavier aspect: Feast, 64 Spiders, My Eye, and the Thrown Ups.

Feast* was one of those "coulda been" groups that never broke out of the underground. Originally called Feast of Friends after a William Blake poem, the band showcased Tom Mick on vocals, Dan Blossom on guitar, Jane Higgins on bass, and Dan Peters on drums.

---

*Green River's Jeff Ament and Mark Arm ultimately decided on the *Deep Six* bands per producer Chris Hanzsek. According to an e-mail from Green River's Stone Gossard: "Jeff said we all just told Chris our [favorite] bands. Jeff said Feast shoulda been on it."

Feast was extremely charismatic live, with Mick playing the active front man. The band's sound combined the *Deep Six* punk/metal hybrid with postpunk. In 1986 Feast had become a top draw at the Central. "Feast was always one of my favorite bands," promoter Claudia Gehrke states in an e-mail. " . . . they had a very heavy sound. I remember when I [booked a show with] Soundgarden and Feast together. Feast was the headliner at the time, and then we found out that Soundgarden was getting scoped out for a record deal. We had to switch the lineup to Soundgarden playing at the headliner time. It was a huge night. Both bands were great. Feast was a guaranteed heavy hitter. [They had] great posters, stepping out into their own brand of art and music. I wish I had seen them get signed. They always had a great crowd."

64 Spiders were guitarist James Burdyshaw's vision. An unabashed fan of the '60s, Burdyshaw loved the early mods like the Who and the Small Faces, as well as successors like the Jam. He also drew from psychedelic influences as well as garage rock. For Burdyshaw, the U-Men drew the blueprint. "I think the U-Men made me believe that [combination] made sense," he says. "And I could be in a band just like them that would play songs that sounded like psychedelic weird effects-driven tunes . . . and then turn around and play a song by the Chocolate Watchband."

My Eye came together from the ashes of the Trids and Overlord, two bands that had played on the Eastside. The new band would create a metal sound combined with a dark, psychedelic influence.

Finally, the Thrown Ups arguably best represented Seattle's new musical aesthetic. By 1986 the band consisted of vocalist Ed Fotheringham, Steve Turner (from Green River) on guitar, Leighton Beezer on bass, and Mark Arm on drums. As per Beezer's ethos, the band rarely practiced, and avoided playing rehearsed songs live. The band took the stage with no idea what was going to happen. While the Thrown Ups championed the improvisational format, their loosey-goosey approach quickly permeated their brethren. "It was not necessary to finely polish your stage act," says Beezer. "To whatever extent you felt was necessary to have structure, go for it, but don't overdo it. Get out. Have fun. Make contacts with people. And so, the scene was much healthier. The bands weren't all isolated and focused on their careers. They were practicing maybe once a week, and they weren't too uptight if they didn't have it right. And in fact everybody knew full well that a show that turned into a train wreck was probably better than one that didn't. It's OK to get up and forget your song.

"So," Beezer continues, "instead of a bunch of mathematicians on stage going, 'Is this the third verse or the fourth verse? Is it time for the chorus or the bridge?' [Rather] there are people on stage who are just going, 'AAAAHHHHHHHH!!!!!!!!!!!!!!'"

Terry Lee Hale booked the Thrown Ups, and the band provided the Central with one of its most notorious shows. Some detractors had begun referring to Beezer & Co. as "the dirtiest band in the world." In response, Beezer and Fotheringham decided to rub dirt on themselves before a Central performance. "I figured we would rub dirt on our faces and clothes and call it a day," Beezer states in an e-mail. "But Mark or Steve went out to the median strip and filled a guitar case with beauty bark and bought a six-pack of Coke. Mark told me to go into the restroom before the show, where I found that Steve had shaken up the whole six-pack and was opening the cans one at a time, getting us (and the bathroom) all covered in sticky liquid. Then the beauty bark came out. It was definitely a mess."

Hale got a firsthand view of the mayhem. "I just remember walking into the bathroom," he says, "and . . . [the band] had brought buckets of dirt in there and they were standing at the sink. . . . They were making mud. And the bathroom was caked—I mean, it looked like a tornado had gone in there. The whole place was just . . .

"And those guys are sheepish," Hale adds. "Mark was like, 'Uhhhhhh . . . I'm really sorry, man.' But they were kinda laughing too. And Mark's a really nice guy. I mean, he's a gentleman."

The Thrown Ups, covered in beauty bark mixed with mud and Coke, took the stage with Beezer playing the bass riff from the Stooges' "Dirt" for about twenty minutes. "Man, that [was] not comfortable," Arm remarks. "But, you know, you gotta suffer for your art."

Sub Pop 100

With the scene continuing to heat up, Pavitt decided to turn his old Sub/Pop cassette-based fanzine, the *Rocket* column, and KCMU show into a record label. In July, he released *Sub Pop 100*, a compilation of national alternative rock acts he liked, such as Scratch Acid, Steve Albini (from Big Black), and Sonic Youth. He also included the U-Men's "Gila" (originally released on Pavitt's Bombshelter Records in 1984), as well as tracks from Portland's Wipers and Olympia's Steve Fisk. At this point, Sub Pop Records didn't even have an office yet. That didn't stop him from announcing the arrival of his label to the world in classic Seattle ironic fashion.

Sub Pop: The new thing; the God thing; a mighty multinational entertainment conglomerate based in the Pacific Northwest.

—Printed on the spine of *Sub Pop 100*

Despite the tongue-in-cheek nature of Sub Pop's claim, Pavitt had serious ambitions to make his new label successful. He used his *Rocket* column to promote the record, beginning with the October 1986 issue. Furthermore, around the same time, Hanzsek gave Pavitt a Melvins EP he recorded (called *6 Songs*) to review in his column. After Pavitt's glowing assessment of *Deep Six*, Hanzsek fully expected another favorable write-up of the Melvins record.

Local boys the Melvins finally put out their own record. They are a good band. They practice a lot. They are slow and heavy, but sometimes they thrash. They are great live. But the sound on their six song seven-inch record is weak and thin and lame. The Melvins need to put out a good recording before they put out a good record.

—Bruce Pavitt review of the Melvins' *6 Songs, The Rocket,*
November 1986

"And I just thought, 'Well that's odd,'" says Hanzsek. "'Why would he do that?' And then . . . I heard from someone, 'Hey did you hear Bruce is starting a record label?'"

Other Comps
Despite the increasing prominence of the *Deep Six* bands and their brethren, the scene continued to maintain a healthy musical diversity, much of that born out of the U-District incubation period discussed in Chapter 3. Producer Paul Scoles decided to document the "non-grunge" side of the scene. He would do everything he could to distinguish his comp from its predecessor: no *Deep Six* bands, no singular sound, no lo-fi recording.

Instead, his comp would feature professional twenty-four-track recording. Despite Scoles' preference, Soundgarden wanted to appear on the record. "I wanted [Soundgarden] on the record," recalls drummer Ben Thompson, who assisted Scoles, "and Paul said, 'Absolutely not. I don't want any of the bands that were on the *Deep Six* compilation on my record.'"

Recorded in the summer of 1986, *Lowlife*—the title an ironic reference to Seattle's punks—also displayed a subtitle, *The Seattle Underground Rock Album*, in obvious defiance of *Deep Six*. One touchy issue remained, however: the cover.

Feast's Jane Higgins designed the cover art, beginning with a Ben Thompson photograph of Soundgarden's Chris Cornell. By the time she learned that Soundgarden would not appear on the record, it was too late to change the cover design. So Higgins distorted the image to disguise Cornell's likeness. Despite her efforts, the Soundgarden front man's distinctive portrait was apparent to those who bought the record. "The photo . . . was supposed to be so altered as to be unrecognizable as Chris per se," says Thompson. "And that just didn't happen."

Yet despite the cover embarrassment, *Lowlife* did accomplish its objective. The record does a nice job of documenting the non-grunge part of the music scene, featuring artists like Room Nine, the Walkabouts, Terry Lee Hale and the Ones, Pure Joy, Vexed, and Bundle of Hiss.

Room Nine represented the psychedelic wing of the scene, with the Walkabouts and Hale's Ones providing a folk/rock element. Pure Joy contributed a psychedelic/postpunk effort with "Ocean." Vexed offered up a completely different aesthetic with their mostly instrumental "Sixes and Sevens."

Formed two years prior, by 1986 Vexed had evolved into a three-piece featuring drummer David Lapp, bassist Alfred

Butler, and guitarist/vocalist Milton Garrison. Vexed drew from varied sources, including postpunk bands Wire and Gang of Four, progressive rock, and world music. The combination created a mixed jumble that exhibited offbeat, dissonant, rhythm section-driven songs in odd time signatures. Vexed's closest approximation within Seattle was Skin Yard, the only other band that openly tapped into prog rock. "We didn't hear people really incorporating world music and punk rock—hardcore punk—and prog," says Garrison.

On the continuum between tight and loose, the Thrown Ups would sit at the open end—completely devoid of song structure and arrangement. The Thrown Ups minimized practice time and effectively abandoned the song format, while Vexed went in the completely opposite direction with precise song structures and impeccable stop/start dynamics. Vexed actually storyboarded their songs. One could even argue that Vexed helped create the modern phenomenon known as math rock. The band's precision tended to set it apart from the scene's sloppier artists. Vexed's oddball status kept it outside of the coming grunge scene, but at the same time allowed the band to venture into more creative musical territory.

Finally, Conrad Uno's Popllama Products put out another key 1986 compilation: *12" Combo Deluxe*. The record included the comedy rock of Rob Morgan's Squirrels (then called the New Age Urban Squirrels), the R&B funk of Red Dress (Uno's favorite band), and the surf/pop/tongue-in-cheek punk of the Young Fresh Fellows.

Red Dress began life in the early '70s and operated in a parallel world to the underground punk scene. Instead of coming from a punk rock angle, however, Red Dress' core players: vocalist Gary Minkler and guitarists John Olufs and Peter Pendras, tapped into R&B and the avant-garde. "They were like Captain Beefheart meets James Brown," Uno says.

Rolling Stone Reviews the Young Fresh Fellows

Despite the scene's continued vitality, few outside Seattle's confines took notice. But while the scene was percolating with no apparent interest from the outside world, something quite unexpected happened, and it involved the Young Fresh Fellows.

In 1985 the Fellows had followed up their *Fabulous Sounds* debut with a second record, *Topsy Turvy*. In contrast to *Fab Sounds*, producer Uno and the band had figured out how to bring up the bass during the mixing process. Furthermore, the new record showcased the Fellows' ever-expanding musical vocabulary without losing their trademark sense of humor. *Turvy*'s humor begins right away with opening track, "Searchin' USA."

The song starts out in an upbeat, country manner, as singer and now guitarist Scott McCaughey intones:

> I've been to Pauline's Café in Bellingham
> Jack said he'd be with me in a minute
> I asked him for a glass of water
> He said, "What for? You wanna put some LSD in it?
> There's already speed and marijuana in the hash browns."
> Pauline always gets a kick out of that crap
> That kind of service brings the customers back

According to McCaughey, the description is pretty accurate. "The Fellows started going up to play in Bellingham," he recalls, "and we'd spend the night. And we'd go to Pauline's Café. We stumbled upon it one time for breakfast, and it was so fucking weird. Of course, we would try to go back there every time. And yeah, that verse pretty much reports exactly what happened."

The Fellows followed the record with a tour, eventually ending up in New York, and *Rolling Stone* took notice. In the summer of 1986, Seattle music fans opened up the national music magazine to read a favorable review of the record.

You've had a long hard day in the alternative-rock trenches,
fighting the good fight with Hüsker Dü, the Replacements,
Live Skull, and R.E.M. Now it's Topsy Turvy time. After all
that underground apocalypse, the Seattle good-humor men
Young Fresh Fellows are the perfect refresher, a bracing bop
cocktail of daffy comic relief, canny pop songwriting, and
punk-rock drive.

—David Fricke review of the Young Fresh Fellows' *Topsy*
Turvy, *Rolling Stone*, July 17, 1986*

The review didn't deliver an earth-shattering explosion to
turn Seattle into a major phenomenon, but the record did provide a glimmer of hope to local musicians. The scene, however,
remained underground and intrinsically creative. "Everybody
in Seattle thought we were a really big deal because we got a
review in *Rolling Stone*," says McCaughey. "Everybody I think
thought that we just completely made it. They didn't know—as
far as we were concerned, we were still going on playing shitty
shows for $150."

Thus as the year came to a close, the music continued to per-
colate. Unfortunately, the U-District's Rainbow Tavern closed
its doors, again adding to the city's dearth of decent clubs. Yet
despite the pessimism, this new generation had started something. No one knew where it would head, but as 1986 passed
into history, local musicians could begin to revel in their art as
an end in itself.

CHAPTER 5

What's Your Heavy?

*You wanted to be heavy for sure. But, heavy and what . . .
what's **your** heavy?*

—Stone Gossard, Green River

*Green River at the Ditto Tavern, 1986. Audience members include James
Burdyshaw (bottom, center), and Jack Endino (bottom, far right).*
(Photo by Charles Peterson)

As 1987 dawned, the *Deep Six* slow/heavy aesthetic began to expand and evolve. Bands that hadn't previously worked that territory became sonically darker. No band better exemplified this musical shift more than Bundle of Hiss. In 1987, Hiss made a rather abrupt shift from postpunk to grunge.

Begun in 1980 in Stanwood, Washington, Hiss first gigged in Seattle that year, playing in early punk-friendly venues like WREX and Baby O's. The band delved into postpunk due to the influences of vocalist Russ Bartlett and bassist Kurt Danielson. By 1984, Bundle of Hiss included guitarist Jamie Lane and drummer Dan Peters and sounded like a speeded-up version of Joy Division. "Like Joy Division on crystal meth," Lane clarifies.

In 1987, Bartlett left the band, Lane took over lead vocals and Bundle of Hiss became a three-piece. Around the same time, Lane ventured into the Central to catch a Meat Puppets concert. One of the first things he noticed was the Puppets' combination of Les Paul guitar and Marshall amplifier, creating a deep, sludgy sound. "I went from playing a Fender guitar and amp to a Les Paul and a Marshall," says Lane. "So that completely changed our sound. We decided we wanted to be heavy and sexy. We wanted to be like Led Zeppelin. We wanted that vibe of rock, but we wanted to add the sludginess to it."

At the time, Hiss—like many of their Seattle brethren—had been listening to a lot of Big Black and Scratch Acid. Those influences, plus Lane's Meat Puppets concert experience, helped change Bundle of Hiss from a postpunk group into a grunge band. "Russ, in fact, had been a bit resistant to this heavy stuff,"

Danielson continues. "And so, now that he was out, it was sort of a shifting—like a tectonic shift—towards this heavier stuff instantly. You can hear it in the recordings. . . . You could tell the difference between the songs where Jamie is singing and where Russ is singing. The whole aesthetic is different. That's where the postpunk sort of permutates into the more blues-inflected hard rock–influenced [sound].

"The band changed—and began to really soak up the heavier aesthetic that was coming," Danielson says, "that we could feel coming like a locomotive, a black locomotive, or maybe a black sailboat with red sails, over the water, over the horizon."

As in 1986, Green River led the way. In June, the band's second EP, *Dry as a Bone*, began showing up around town. The record represented Bruce Pavitt's first noncompilation release on his fledgling Sub Pop label. Unlike the band's Black Sabbath–influenced debut, *Come on Down*, the new EP explored a number of musical styles. The opening track, "This Town," has a '70s riff-rock stamp on it, albeit speeded up. "Unwind" begins with an electrified Delta Blues riff, and "Queen Bitch,"* a David Bowie cover, sounds like the Buzzcocks. In other words, the record is all over the place, reflecting the band's collective state of mind. "I think, already we were sort of moving past this pure super-slow heaviness for heaviness' sake," says guitarist Stone Gossard. "I think we were moving into more up-tempos and trying to figure out what we were doing."

Dry as a Bone featured a sound that would become commonplace among local recordings: raw, bleeding, and guitar dominated. Produced by Jack Endino at Chris Hanzsek's Reciprocal Recording, Endino's lo-fi eight-track recording system became ground zero for the grunge scene. "I barely knew what I was

---

*"Queen Bitch" was recorded in July 1987, after the original *Dry as a Bone* EP was released, but was included on CD in 1988, as part of a double EP set.

doing," says Endino. "I mean, I was really working by the seat of my pants and by instinct. Technically speaking, as [a recording] engineer, I wasn't that experienced. At that point, I'd only been working in a studio for a couple years." Despite his lack of experience, Endino had a vision of how he wanted to record a rock band. "[My] recording philosophy has never changed much," he adds. "I'm anti-perfection."

In essence, *Dry as a Bone* alerted other Seattle musicians that they could create their own kind of heavy. Some bands, like Skin Yard and Vexed, wove progressive rock and world music into the mix. And then there was TAD.

TAD, the band, evolved from Tad Doyle, the person, in 1987. Doyle had moved to Seattle in 1986 from Boise, Idaho, along with his postpunk-inspired band H-Hour. Doyle played drums and stood about at five-foot-ten and weighed three-hundred-plus pounds.

Upon relocating to Seattle, H-Hour soon found itself gigging locally, at venues like Belltown's Ditto, Eastlake's Scoundrel's Lair, and Tacoma's Community World Theater. "The first time I saw [H-Hour] was a picture in the *Rocket*, and I saw the picture of the drummer," Danielson recalls. "It was this big guy. It was like, 'Wow! The guy must be a powerful drummer. I'd like to see these guys play.' Watching Tad play the drums was incredible. He didn't have to put new drum heads on his drums, because he hit them so hard he made even a dead drum sound alive. You couldn't believe his drum set could withstand such pressures—such a beating—a thunderous pummeling, unlike anything I'd ever seen before. And [he performed] with great, light-fingered finesse, like a jazz player." Doyle and Danielson hit it off right away.

Around the same time, the members of H-Hour began to tire of playing together, while Doyle envisioned switching from drums to guitar. "And I had dreams where I was playing guitar on stage and knew how to play it," Doyle remembers. "And I'd wake up and I'd go, 'Holy crap, I know how to play guitar!' And then I'd go grab one of my friend's guitars and pick it up, and it wasn't the same, but I had that vision, you know?"

As a result, Doyle taught himself to play guitar. In June he took his $500 1986 federal income tax refund and bought some studio time at Reciprocal. There he recorded three songs, singing and playing all the instrumental parts. Two of those recordings, "Daisy" and "Ritual Device," would end up as a Sub Pop single. Doyle's new music took the heaviness aesthetic to a new level. Take the distortion and volume of Green River, add a touch of the Melvins, some heavy metal, and top off with Doyle's guttural vocals, and you get something bigger than Tad. You get TAD. TAD would come to fruition in 1988, when Doyle would join forces with Bundle of Hiss' Danielson, the Treeclimbers' guitarist Gary Thorstensen (Jon Poneman's band), and drummer Steve Wied.

Alice 'N' Chains

As the heavier bands began to predominate downtown, an Eastside hair metal band quietly made its urban presence known. Calling themselves Alice 'N' Chains, its members were inspired by urban-originating bands they had seen in the suburbs like the Trids, Overlord, and Shadow. The band sent a demo tape to the *Rocket*, which offered reviews in its "Mass Tapes" section for anyone who wanted to submit a tape, regardless if they had a record deal or not. At the time, AIC's music and image differed dramatically from the hard-edged flannel shirt motif Alice *in* Chains would project in the '90s (1992's *Dirt*, for example, has song titles like "Them Bones," "Rain When I Die," and "Down in a Hole"). The 1987 version of the band was much different. "[My girlfriend] had a bunch of heavy metal chick friends," drummer Scott Vanderpool remembers, "and they dragged us one night to this glam-metal night at the Golden Crown [down-town]. And there was this band, Alice 'N' Chains. And they were all big hair and spandex."

Alice 'N' Chains play glam rock with a definite pop streak. The first-time out effort, if anything, is above all else fun. Party highlights are undoubtedly "Lip Lock Rock" with an interesting use of horns to punch up the ending, and "Fat Girls," the irresistible ode to the overweight. Non-offensive hard rock with eyeliner.

—"Mass Tapes" review, *The Rocket*, June 1987

The Young Fresh Fellows continued to flourish in their own way amidst the rise of the heavier aesthetic. That year, the band put out their third full-length record: *The Men Who Loved Music*. Co-released in 1987 by Popllama and Los Angeles's Frontier, the album continued to expand the band's musical horizons with tracks like the garage-y "Three Sides to This Story," the humorous "Why I Oughta" (so named for drummer Tad Hutchison's oft use of the classic Ralph Kramden line), and the funky hypocrisy-exposing "Amy Grant" (named after the Christian-turned-mainstream singer). In all, the record may represent the early Fellows at their finest. "For me, that record was really just about us being . . . a live band," says McCaughey. "We just went in and played our songs that we'd been playing live, and captured them."

Furthermore, the record continued to showcase the Fellows' special emphasis (at least within Seattle) on lyrics. Seattle bands of this era tended to focus on their sound over lyrics. With the Fellows, the words came first. "That's the way I write—especially back then," says McCaughey. "I mean, I would just think of words. I didn't really think that much about melody or anything. . . . Sometimes, by accident, I guess I would get something that was fairly catchy, but most of the time it was just about getting the words—words into a song."

The Squid Row

Despite the music community's burgeoning new sound and varieties of talent, Seattle's club scene remained dicey for new music. Some of the younger bands got shots at Pioneer Square's Central and Belltown's Vogue and Ditto. Until 1987, Capitol Hill had few places to hear new music, other than self-promoted shows at the Oddfellows Hall or the 5-0 Tavern. That changed when guitarist/booking agent Terry Lee Hale began scheduling shows at the Squid Row, a tiny venue on Capitol Hill. Despite its small size, Squid Row would provide a needed outlet for the increasing number of musicians taking up residence in the neighborhood. "I liked Squid Row a lot," says Rob Skinner, who began playing bass in a new band called Coffin Break. "It was small. It was my neighborhood bar. I lived two blocks away from it. I saw a lot of great bands there. It was just fun times—dollar pitchers on Wednesday, free pool on Tuesday."

Dan Trager, who later worked in A&R at Sub Pop, was then a college student who ventured with his girlfriend from Detroit to Seattle in the summer of 1987. He stayed in Seattle for about a month, soaking up the music scene. He was immediately taken with Squid Row and the sense of community that pervaded Capitol Hill. "You never knew who . . . was gonna be in there [Squid Row]," Trager recalls. "I remember there was a big Ethiopian refugee population coming into Seattle at that time. And the Ethiopians would show up and get drunk, and just like point at the guitar player, 'Look at him! Look what he's doing!' It was just like a really freewheeling time."

"That was a fun club to play," recalls Coffin Break's guitarist Pete Litwin. "Really small. The stage—and I'm not exaggerating—was probably two inches tall. So, you were literally right in the face of the audience. So it was really fun. Although, it kinda can get out of control a little, because people could be slamming into you while you're playing."

The Female Presence

While the younger bands began to find more opportunities to play, Seattle's tight-knit music scene remained heavily male-oriented. The bands and their friends were, for the most part, men. "We used to make a joke," says guitarist Laura Weller-Vanderpool, "that if you go to a Skin Yard show, it was great because there was no line at the girls' bathroom."

Male domination in rock music is nothing new, and Seattle is no exception. Photos of the period confirm the perception, with men swinging their long hair on stage and frenetic male audience members slamming along with the music. However, painting the grunge era as entirely male is an oversimplification that overlooks powerful female characters. Women did in fact have prominent roles in bands like the Fastbacks, Clay Alien, Feast, Pure Joy, and the Walkabouts.

Kim Warnick and Lulu Gargiulo represented two-thirds of the Fastbacks' core. Along with Kurt Bloch, the pair would create a lasting testament of Seattle punk. (The Fastbacks are discussed further following Chapter 7). Carla Torgerson of the Walkabouts sang and co-wrote her band's songs. Feast's Jane Higgins played bass and designed album covers.

"I think [the male] musicians thought what we were doing was great," says Weller-Vanderpool, who played in an acoustic duo called Capping Day (see Chapter 6). "In fact, I think they appreciated that we weren't trying to be *girls*. . . . I always kinda thought it was dumb when girls would form a band . . . and be like hot, slut, punk girls. 'Cause to me, it's like, well, you're puttin' the sex before the music. And the music needs to be good. It can't be like, 'Oh, they suck but they're hot.' I [didn't] wanna be [in a] 'they suck but they're hot' band."

In addition, women also played significant roles in the community behind the scenes. For example, Susan Silver promoted shows at the Metropolis and managed Soundgarden and later, Alice in Chains. Claudia Gehrke, a promoter, booked shows at the Vogue and the Central and various other clubs in the latter '80s. She handled a number of bands including Feast, the Fags, Nirvana, Soundgarden, the U-Men, and Green River. Dawn Anderson supported the scene with her *Backfire* fanzine (and its later iteration, *Backlash*, discussed at the end of this chapter) and also wrote for the *Rocket*. While men tended to predominate in the audiences, women did not feel excluded from shows or the scene in general. "I don't think I ever really felt like, 'Oh this is totally male dominated,' though," says Courtney Miller, a *Rocket* marketing staffer who regularly attended shows, "'and there's not a place for women to be a spectator or to be in a band if they want.'"

Soundgarden Changes Seattle's World

Susan Silver's Soundgarden inadvertently raised the scene's commercial aspirations. Soundgarden guitarist Kim Thayil convinced his friend Pavitt to work with Jonathan Poneman, then promotions director at KCMU, to put out a Soundgarden single and EP. Thayil's actions would push Bruce Pavitt's Sub Pop Records toward becoming Seattle's preeminent independent label. From that point on, Pavitt and Poneman would work together. The oddly spacey and charismatic Pavitt matched up well with the affable and supremely confident Poneman.

Soundgarden's recording sessions took place at Reciprocal with Endino manning the controls. The resultant EP, *Screaming Life*, yielded a Sub Pop single: "Hunted Down"/"Nothing to Say." The single in particular made others within the scene sit up and take notice: it just didn't sound like a local band anymore. The sheer power of Chris Cornell's vocals, along with Thayil's dynamic guitar playing and talented rhythm section, made Soundgarden seem larger than Seattle. "I think my first feeling that something significant was gonna happen," Stone Gossard recalls, "was when Soundgarden did 'Hunted Down.' . . . That's when I heard something and [it] made me go, 'Wow. That's actually professional fuckin'—that's *heavy ass shit*.'"

"At the time, ['Nothing to Say'] just seemed amazingly heavy," Endino stated in *hype!* "I thought, 'These guys can't possibly be really playing this song. This sounds insane. It sounds way too good for eight-track, and it sounds way too good for a crappy little Seattle band.'"

"Hunted Down," the A-side, showcases a strange minor note progression and sounds like it could almost serve as a James Bond villain theme song. "Nothing to Say," well, that's Black Sabbath meets Led Zeppelin. The single and EP created an excitement surrounding Soundgarden, an excitement that could translate into a major-label deal— something that seemed unheard of for a "crappy little Seattle band." In April, the *Rocket* reported that major-label A&R reps had attended a Soundgarden show at the Vogue, based solely on *Screaming Life* demos. "Soundgarden's strong visual image won't hurt either," Dawn Anderson wrote in the *Rocket*, "and it doesn't end with the singer. 'Is there any way to tastefully point out the fact that we're multi-racial?' they ask. Sure: [bassist Hiro] Yamamoto's Japanese, Thayil's Indian, and Cornell and [drummer Matt] Cameron are Caucasian though Cornell is often mistaken for a Latin American and doesn't seem to mind. This would all be irrelevant if it weren't so unusual in a genre traditionally ruled by white boys."

The Soundgarden single and EP proved that quality players existed within the Seattle punk scene. Certainly, the U-Men could play. 10 Minute Warning had a virtuoso guitar player, bass player, and drummer. But Soundgarden was the complete set, featuring immensely talented players in every role, and it showed in the recordings. Cameron anchored the band with an intricate yet heavy drumming style.

Yamamoto played a bass that combined finesse with depth. Thayil showcased a free-form style of guitar that could adapt nicely to jazz. Out front, singer Cornell always had a seductive presence, and by 1987 he could really sing too. "Chris Cornell learned how to sing . . . overnight," says Gossard. "He took the magic singing pill."

Word leaked out that Cornell was taking singing lessons. The stakes had been raised: Seattle could generate future rock stars. In some ways, the rise of Soundgarden led to the demise of Green River, led by the charismatic Mark Arm, who couldn't—at least in conventional terms—really sing. Cornell's success motivated Green River's Gossard and Jeff Ament to suggest that Arm take singing lessons as well. "Because Chris Cornell was taking singing lessons," says Green River drummer Alex Shumway, "and everybody knows how well Chris can sing. . . . Chris Cornell was being taught how to sing. And so they [said that] Mark should learn how to sing. There wasn't really so much pressure put on that, but I know it pissed Mark off to no end."

Green River's Demise

Green River—as they had done almost since their inception—not only led the way musically, but foreshadowed the ramifications of Seattle music's increasingly commercial potential. Tensions among the band members, present from the beginning, began to escalate as they watched their friends in Soundgarden rise to prominence. Gossard and Ament could taste mainstream rock success, while Arm in particular insisted on maintaining a strong punk rock ethic. "You could see . . . that there was a conflict," says Dan Trager, "between some of the members [Ament and Gossard] of the band wanting more to—ironically or not—dress up like in a classic Aerosmith style of rock star: you know, with scarves and bandanas and things like that. And [Arm had] more of a strident underground anti–rock star posing element going on there."

The splintering Green River entered the studio one final time in the late summer. Forgoing the Reciprocal/Endino lo-fi approach, Ament and Gossard moved the band into Steve Lawson's professional twenty-four-track studio. *Rehab Doll* represented Green River's final transformation from punk rock band to arena rock act. The record's centerpiece is the self-covered "Swallow My Pride," which originally appeared on 1985's *Come on Down.* Compared to the lo-fi sludge of Chris Hanzsek's eight-track system, the new recording sounded much more polished. Substitute Eddie Vedder for Mark Arm's Iggy-like vocals, and you effectively have Pearl Jam. "At that point, Stoney and Jeff, and Bruce [Fairweather] to a good extent, really, really wanted to become rock stars. [They] were just goin' for it. So, to do it, we needed something that sounded really, really pro," Shumway recalls.

Viewing *Rehab Doll* two decades later, after worldwide success with Pearl Jam, Gossard is less impressed with Green River's final product. "It sucked," he says. "We were gettin' ahead of ourselves. We were excited about recording in all these different ways and doing all this arranging."

The conflict within the band had grown to an irreconcilable level by the fall. Green River called it quits on Halloween Day, 1987. Shumway and Arm were down in their practice space, waiting for the rest of the band. Ament, Gossard, and

Fairweather strode in, announcing that Green River had come to a close. Arm reacted nonchalantly, since he had already been exploring options with ex-bandmate Steve Turner in the Thrown Ups. Shumway was dismayed, but quickly recovered and moved to Japan to attend graduate school.

The split had happened. Green River, two bands within one during most of its existence—had permanently fractured.

Ament, Gossard, and Fairweather moved on to form a more professional-sounding band, enlisting Malfunkshun's lead vocalist, Andrew Wood. The new group initially called itself Lords of the Wasteland, but eventually changed the name to Mother Love Bone.

Both Mother Love Bone and Soundgarden became Seattle's poster children for national success in 1988. Those bands' answer to "What's your heavy?" meant something loud and metal infused, yet accessible to the mainstream.

For others, the answer meant something far less commercial. For Green River's Arm and Turner, that meant forming a new band that remained true to its punk rock roots. In 1988 the pair would enlist the services of Bundle of Hiss' trapmeister Dan Peters and the Melvins' bassist Matt Lukin. The four-piece eschewed taking a "big" name like Mother Love Bone and instead opted for something more Seattle, naming their new band after a 1965 Russ Meyer film called *Mudhoney*. Meyer was known for creating softcore flicks with large-breasted women. Mudhoney became the ultimate expression of all things Seattle within a band name that was possibly offensive—like Green River—but in a more playful way. Furthermore, the "mud" part of the name appropriately reflected the new band's sound.

Dawn Anderson's Backlash

By the end of the year, the scene's continued percolation combined with the *Rocket*'s increased coverage of national acts, led

Dawn Anderson to create her own fanzine focused entirely on local music. *Backlash* debuted in December, featuring a suburban metal band, Q5, on the cover. As its title suggests, *Backlash* reacted to the *Rocket*'s changing focus, just when the local music scene was growing by leaps and bounds. "[The *Rocket*] covered local music," says Anderson, "but it seemed like they were just missing out on a lot. So, I sort of saw my advantage. And that's why I decided to focus 100 percent on local music and nothing else, just 'cause I didn't want it to be diluted at all.

"It's not like I started this magazine just to have a reaction against the *Rocket* or anything like that," Anderson continues. "I started a magazine because I wanted to start a magazine. And because there was a certain dissatisfaction with the direction the *Rocket* was going at the time, I sort of played up to that and capitalized on it."

Backlash would play a key role over the next four years, supporting Seattle's growing music community as it gained notoriety in Europe and then later throughout the United States.

As the year came to a close, Green River were not the only casualties. Feast called it a day as well, and the Melvins split for San Francisco. The scene had not entered a period of decline, however. Rather, as 1988 approached, the music community would reach a level of creativity and excitement not seen since the '60s Sonics era.

CHAPTER 6

Wasted Landlords

Some of us were still basically having fun and playing the same stupid music, but it dawned on everybody that maybe, maybe, we should scale it back a little—and play the game a little—and maybe we will get insanely rich.

—Leighton Beezer, the Thrown Ups

Central Tavern promotional poster, 1988.

Despite the demise of several key bands, 1988 was a magical year for Seattle music. Musicians, writers, DJs, and fans all displayed an increasing confidence and vitality. Green River, though, became the first local example of the inevitable conflict between artistic expression and commercial gain.

Green River had essentially played the role of adolescent attempting to find an identity during its three-year life. As the band migrated further away from punk toward mainstream arena rock, internal fissures became ever more pronounced, ultimately leading to a clean break in the fall of 1987.

Guitarists Stone Gossard and Bruce Fairweather, along with bassist Jeff Ament, desired mainstream success, particularly in light of the buzz surrounding Soundgarden. So, they took their hard rock and metal leanings with them when they left Green River. They wanted an upgrade, a more professional singer than the punk rock Mark Arm, and a more sophisticated drummer than Alex Shumway.

Gossard and Ament quickly tapped Malfunkshun's Andrew Wood and Regan Hagar as their charismatic front man, and drummer, respectively. The new act, initially called Lords of the Wasteland (later Mother Love Bone) was built for mainstream stardom, with an attractive frontman, and big rock sound. Unlike Soundgarden, who had garnered so much attention, that they could afford to play major labels against each other while recording with indies, Lords had little street cred. The local pushback was almost immediate. In reaction to the band's somewhat pretentious moniker, Arm formed a side project called the

Wasted Landlords (which also included H-Hour's Tad Doyle, Room Nine's Ron Rudzitis, and drummer Scott Vanderpool). "It's not important to me that I be a 'rock star,'" Arm told Dawn Anderson in *Backlash*. "If it happens, fine. But [Gossard and Ament] were serious about calling on major labels and stuff, which I didn't really care about."

Mudhoney

Meanwhile, on the other side of postmortem Green River sat Arm, who had been playing drums in Leighton Beezer's Thrown Ups. The Thrown Ups also included guitarist Steve Turner, who quit Green River back in 1985 when he felt the band was becoming too hard rock even then. Arm and Turner decided to reunite and started their own band, Mudhoney, that offered a garagey counterpoint to Lords of the Wasteland. "Well, one of the [goals] was to intentionally simplify things," says Arm, "and I guess go back to our punk rock roots—not just punk rock, but stuff that kind of came before punk rock."

Mudhoney combined prepunk '60s garage rock with the Stooges, as well as the usual early punk rock suspects. The band also drew from rather obscure influences such as Australian postpunk bands Feedtime and the Scientists, San Francisco's bluesy power trio Blue Cheer, and Portland alternative heroes the Wipers. Arm and Turner took all of that and condensed it into straightforward, fuzz-driven riffs.

The budding band added ex-Melvin Matt Lukin to play bass. Arm and Turner had known Lukin for years, back from when they all used to hang together at the Metropolis during the heyday of the Pioneer Square all-ages scene. Lukin was looking for a band after the Melvins moved to San Francisco. The three-piece began to jam together in late 1987. "We'd ask Matt to be in the band, and he never, ever said that he would be in the band," Arm recalls. "But he just kept showing up at practice." Drummer Dan

Peters, who had time to fill after Feast disbanded, rounded out the rhythm section.

Disdaining arena rock posing and guitar solos, Mudhoney welded Arm's wailing vocals to Turner's fuzzed-out riffs. Mudhoney eschewed complicated arrangements in favor of fewer chords and straightforward progressions. "That was the possibility that I ignored in Green River," says Gossard. "That was an eye-opener for me and [it was] exciting to hear how Mark, Steve, and Danny and Lukin played together and [it was] so much more free and heavy and not as overly complex. They were letting it all hang out. And they were groovier, and funner, and more interesting than Green River in my mind."

Mudhoney, in some ways, represented the conclusion of the *Deep Six* era. They combined the heaviness of that sound with tight song structures and an irreverent attitude. Fortunately for the band, they would catch the eye of a label that would take them way beyond Seattle.

Sub Pop: For Real This Time

In April 1988, Bruce Pavitt and Jon Poneman's Sub Pop Records became a full-time entity, and Mudhoney would become their flagship band. Previously, Arm had played Pavitt a barely audible demo tape hoping Mudhoney could record for Sub Pop. That tape, combined with Pavitt's friendship with Arm, and Mudhoney's impeccable punk rock credentials, brought the band on board.

Sub Pop was not the first independent label in Seattle. It was, however, the first label that had serious aspirations beyond the region. Sub Pop would act as a major label, sans the funding. Unlike previous local and national indie labels, Sub Pop would brand and unabashedly hype itself and its bands. Sub Pop bands would emerge in the Mudhoney mold: Play loud and distorted music. Don't be too sincere. And preferably sport long hair, don shorts, and wear Doc Martens.

In short, Sub Pop was bold. Indie labels traditionally flew under the radar, with a low-key approach to marketing themselves. Hip national indies like SST, Touch and Go, and Homestead had cachet because of their bands. Sub Pop bands would be cool because of their *label*.

The codification of all things Sub Pop began with an advertisement in the *Rocket*. Pavitt used a particular word to describe a Green River record.

GREEN RIVER DRY AS A BONE EP
awesome STOOGES/AEROSMITH grunge
6 BUCKS

—Sub Pop advertisement, The Rocket, April 1988

Pavitt created and hyped the term "grunge" to describe Sub Pop's bands. Since Green River had evaporated, the term would fall squarely on Mudhoney. Pavitt's use of the term perfectly described Mudhoney and Sub Pop's early bands. Within a few months, "grunge"—initially used in a joking manner—would take on a life of its own.

As Sub Pop became Seattle's preeminent label, others around town began to take notice. Conrad Uno's Popllama Products could have competed with Sub Pop. Instead, Uno, who got to know Poneman from working the door at the Rainbow, viewed the label's ascent with bemusement. "The whole reason you're doing this stuff," says Uno, "is to have people agree with you that you're cool. And so, they were getting way more people to agree with them that they were cool[er] than everybody else. So, it was kind of like, 'Well, wait a second. We're cool, too!'"

The label defined itself both sonically and visually. In the studio, Sub Pop took note of Jack Endino's production talents. His philosophy fit with what they were going for. "I was a grunge producer really if you think about it," says Endino, "'cause that's almost my definition of grunge—is the bands not concentrating too much on technical perfection, but instead trying to get the emotion and the feeling out."

Sub Pop's visual image began with its logo, which is brilliant in its stark simplicity: the word "SUB" in white with a black background on top of the word "POP" in black with a white background. The logo further distinguishes itself with chevron symbols buttressing the middle letters of each word, reversing on top and bottom. Sub Pop, the logo, came from "Sub Pop," the *Rocket* column, and resulted from the efforts of artist/designers Dale Yarger, Carl Smool, Art Chantry, and others.* Yarger had been putting together the cover for 1986's *Sub Pop 100* LP and couldn't fit "SUBPOP" on the cover where he wanted it. "And [Yarger] said, 'Well, I don't know how to fit this on here,'" says Chantry. "'You got any ideas?' I said, 'Well, stack it.' So I cut it apart and I stacked it, and [put] one [word] on top of the other. Essentially, a cleaned up version of [what] was used on [the *Sub Pop 100*] cover is where the logo came from."

The label presented its bands through the lens of photographer Charles Peterson. Peterson had an uncanny talent for anticipating a moment and capturing it beautifully on film—in stark black-and-white—often while in the midst of a mosh pit. These images ranged from blurry photos of guitar players swinging their long hair to people stage diving. "The way I've always talked about approaching photography is—you have to think fast and slow at the same time," he says. "It's kind of a Zen-like process. . . . It's having that quick reflex . . . and just being able to think quickly on your feet. But at the same time,

---

*The logo evolved over time, but the Yarger/Smool/Chantry version came from the "Sub Pop USA" column design created by Helene Silverman and Wes Anderson.

you have to think slowly too. Because if you don't kind of step back and see the big picture at times, then you're gonna lose out on those moments as well. And sometimes you may lose a moment because you are kind of focusing on the big picture, but the two can play off of each other and it's a matter of trade-offs sometimes. What I mean by that is, let's say, for example, just taking part of the show and focusing on the audience. Well, a performer may do something totally crazy on stage that you missed. But at the same moment you're gonna get the audience reaction, or potentially the band member may jump into the audience or something."

Peterson often accomplished all this while in the midst of slam dancers, with the audience fueled by alcohol and sheer youthful exuberance. He maintained his composure by flowing with the audience and using wide-angle lenses. "The nice thing about wide-angle lenses is: you can just sort of put the camera out there," says Peterson. "A lot of the time, [I'm] not even looking through the camera, per se. At least [I'm] not looking as super-critically as [I] might with a telephoto lens, where you need to tightly compose something."

TAD

Now packaged with a distinctive logo, sound, and photos, Sub Pop needed bands beyond Mudhoney. One of those bands would revolve around Bruce Pavitt's friend Tad Doyle.

By 1988 Doyle's band H-Hour had run its course, and he had already pretty much abandoned playing drums for guitar during recording sessions he had done the previous year. Doyle also became a vocalist, despite lacking what one would call a traditional voice. "I had people tell me like, 'You can't sing dude. Don't even try,'" Doyle recalls. "That was their opinion at the time, and I probably was sounding pretty horrible at first, you know? I'm not one of these natural, perfect, on-pitch type of people. I think that I have something to offer in the quality of the tone of my voice and what I could do with it that sets it apart and makes it unique in its own way. And I definitely wanted to [use] vocals as an instrument, rather than [a] pretty melody . . . and make it do things that [it isn't] usually used for. Like, thirty-second guttural screams without stopping and various textures and harmonics that a normal, pretty pop singer wouldn't use. It was all about trying to break through barriers, you know?"

Doyle had a problem: he didn't have a band after H-Hour's demise. He tried to fit in with Kurt Danielson's Bundle of Hiss, but that didn't work out. At the same time, Bundle of Hiss was splintering since lead guitarist/vocalist Jamie Lane was getting married and moving back East to graduate school, and drummer Dan Peters was playing with Mudhoney. So Doyle and Danielson decided to form a new band. They found guitarist Gary Thorstensen from Poneman's Treeclimbers and added drummer Steve Wied. Since the new band would draw from Tad Doyle's inspiration, it would take the name TAD, all in capitals.

TAD fit nicely into Sub Pop's brand and inspired Pavitt to create a mythology about the band. While Mudhoney would offer long hair-inspired silliness, TAD would scare people. Doyle's sheer girth, combined with Danielson's menacing sneer, gave Pavitt an idea. TAD would be sold as a group of backwoods miscreants, just waiting to invade your homes and murder your children. These misanthropes could not be reasoned with, for they had not evolved much beyond Cro-Magnon man.

The sell would work beautifully during TAD's early years with Sub Pop. Funny thing, though, how perception and reality diverge. In actuality, Doyle is a gifted musician and a soft-spoken, huge-hearted man. He created serious art in his music and envisioned his new band as allowing the musicians to create that art without boundaries. In some ways, TAD melded two completely opposite stylistic approaches: complete freedom and

Throw Ups–like sloppiness, and precise, rhythm-driven songs along the lines of what Vexed had been doing. "It wasn't all about melody," says Doyle. "It was about the essence of just root and rhythm. . . . It was more about hints of melody accentuating the rhythm section and the root, rather than the other way around. . . . [Root is] the basic structure of a song. A lot of songs are written—the chords, the background music is written to support the melody. We wanted to have hints of melody support the background and the backbone of the music."

Danielson didn't fit the pre–*Homo sapiens* mold, either. He had studied English with a creative writing concentration at U-Dub and had a gift for writing as well as an extensive vocabulary. Danielson loved to play up to the joke, however, as exemplified by the following exchange with Dawn Anderson in *Backlash*.

> "We're obviously all healthy young men; we never have any trouble finding something to eat," Danielson told Anderson, "and it's not because we earn enough money to buy food, we just happen to be skillful hunters. We heat our homes with wood. I live in a log cabin myself."
>
> "Uh huh. Where?" Anderson asked.
>
> "The U-District," responded Danielson.

Melvins Roadies

A third band would soon round out Sub Pop's top tier. In January 1988, an unknown guitarist living in Olympia named Kurt called up Endino at Reciprocal. He said he was a friend of the Melvins and wanted to come up and record some songs. Endino said OK. So the guitarist came up, along with a bassist named Chris. They were joined by Melvins drummer Dale Crover. The trio recorded ten songs in five hours. Endino was so impressed that he quickly forwarded the demo tape to Poneman. "We recorded [the songs] . . . before Nirvana even had a name,"

Endino remembers. "They came and did literally their very first demo with me. And that was the tape I gave to Sub Pop."

Nirvana was not an immediate hit with the label. Poneman loved the demo, but Pavitt felt the band sounded too close to heavy metal. Live audiences also had mixed responses to early Nirvana when they began playing Seattle in the spring. Initially, they were viewed as a sort of poor man's Melvins. "I'd seen Nirvana [in 1988], like about two or three times," says the 64 Spiders' James Burdyshaw, "and I didn't really like 'em that much, 'cause I thought they were just like a more dysfunctional version of the Melvins."

Guitarist Kurt Cobain and bassist Chris [later Krist] Novoselic, originally from Aberdeen—a logging town about two hours southwest of Seattle—had spent so much time hanging out with the Melvins, who hailed from nearby Montesano, that their sound approximated that band. "And then this band from Aberdeen would come through every now and then—and they were Melvins' roadies," recalls Doyle. "That's all everybody knew 'em as."

"The first time I saw [Nirvana], they were a little fuzzed out," adds the Fastbacks' Kurt Bloch. "I just didn't quite understand what was all going on."

Producer Steve Fisk, who later engineered Nirvana's *Blew* EP, had been living and working in Eastern Washington. He wasn't initially impressed, either. "When Nirvana played Ellensburg [Washington], I walked out on them," recalls Fisk. "I thought they sucked. . . . Different people would walk away from the same show going, 'I thought they were great. They destroyed everything!' [or] 'Yeah, it really sucked. They destroyed everything!'"

Despite the band's detractors, Nirvana was welcomed by Seattle's musicians and their fans. By the time they arrived in town, Nirvana had added Chad Channing as their full-time drummer. "One of the first [Seattle] shows we ever played—I've heard it's the Central or the Vogue. I'm not really personally myself sure," says Channing, "but there weren't a whole lot of people there. I mean, there was like maybe twelve people, you know, in the whole club. But the people that came to the shows and stuff, they really embraced what we were doing—big time. And, like, it seemed very short lived—the days of the dead shows, so to speak."

Nirvana quickly attracted a following as they hung out after shows and mixed with the local scenesters. "Like, for example, we played some show in the University District," says Channing, "and I'd stay the night in Seattle. The next morning, I went out to get some coffee. So I went into this place—Starbucks or whatever—and I was about to pay for my coffee, and this guy said, 'Hey man, no charge. That was a great show last night.'"

Mudhoney, TAD, Nirvana. In that order, Sub Pop would begin to boost its hipness quotient. Mudhoney would be loud, irreverent, and silly. TAD would frighten the masses. And Nirvana would eventually provide a melodic, pop element, due in no small part to Cobain's association with K Records' Beat Happening.

Screaming Trees

In the spring, as Sub Pop got going with its chosen bands, another group would arrive from Ellensburg playing in a similar vein: Screaming Trees. Unlike the Sub Pop bands, however, the Trees added more melodic structures and psychedelia to their sound. Further, the Trees developed their following and recorded output virtually independent of the Seattle scene. By the time they arrived in Seattle in 1988, the Trees had already recorded with Los Angeles's SST Records, and thus had no need of further street cachet from Sub Pop.

Ellensburg sits in a valley about an hour east of Seattle, on the opposite side of the Cascade Mountains. Despite its close proximity, however, it is a world away from bustling Seattle. Unlike the lush, damp forests and hills of the Seattle region, Ellensburg is basically flat and features an almost desertlike landscape. The mountain road crossing the Cascades can be difficult to navigate during the winter months, further isolating the town.

Ellensburg is home to Central Washington University, which contributes to the town's unusual mixture of students, farmers, and cowboys. Screaming Trees emerged from that environment. Unfortunately for Ellensburg's young rock music fans, country music dominated local radio. Trees' drummer Mark Pickerel lived on the same road as the country-oriented KXLE. "And I literally picked up that country station," Pickerel remembers, "almost from one end of the radio dial to the [other]. It was so bad that country music literally came out of the telephone. . . . And a lot of it was canned. Oftentimes it was the same play lists every day. So it was really just this reoccurring country nightmare."

The Trees' first incarnation—including Pickerel as well as brothers Gary Lee and Van Conner on guitar and bass, respectively—began in 1983, its members barely in high school. The Conners' father, an elementary school principal, set up the band's first gig at a third-grade assembly. "We were literally playing [the Sex Pistols'] 'God Save the Queen' in front of the third graders," Pickerel recalls.

Within a year, Van Conner befriended Mark Lanegan, who tried to replace Pickerel on drums. That didn't last once Lanegan stepped in front of a microphone. As he began to sing, Pickerel and the Conner brothers stared at each other as he effortlessly broadcasted a velvety-smooth baritone reminiscent of the Doors' Jim Morrison. "And a star was born," says Pickerel. "He was great. We immediately knew that he was our singer."

Early Trees sounded like mod-era Who. Soon afterward, the band crossed paths with producer Steve Fisk, who at the time was living in Ellensburg and was working at a new studio in town called Velvetone. In 1985 the band recorded its first EP:

Other Worlds. Fisk was immediately impressed. "They really rocked," Fisk recalls. "It was [a] very wonderful record to record. They set up in a line, like they were on stage, and recorded. . . . And [they] smiled at each other. It was like a performance. I'd never done anything like that in a recording studio. It was very exciting, and very, very different."

Gary Lee became the band's key songwriter, drawing influences from obscure '60s garage and psychedelic rock. The band's sound began to become more raucous, fueled in part by Gary Lee's use of ear-piercing feedback. "The version of Screaming Trees that I helped record was a lot of feedback," says Fisk, "and a lot of shit flying around on stage. And big men jumping up and down and kicking things. And three or four guitar tracks all feeding back at the end of each song."

In 1986 the Trees recorded their first full-length LP: *Clairvoyance*. Shortly thereafter, the band inked a deal with SST. Pickerel had introduced the Trees to SST's Greg Ginn when he gave him a demo tape at a Black Flag concert. That meeting, along with Fisk's connections to SST, got the band a deal with arguably the country's most respected independent label. SST's roster then included Sonic Youth, the Meat Puppets, Hüsker Dü, and Dinosaur Jr.

By 1988, the Trees had already recorded three LPs for SST (who had also re-released *Other Worlds*). The band's prolific recording, combined with its SST panache, gave it instant street cred in Seattle. "In Seattle, Screaming Trees are generally respected," Anderson wrote in the June–July 1988 issue of *Backlash*. "The entire music scene tries to cram itself into the Central Tavern each time they play there."

Coffin Break and the Spirit of '88

Despite the preeminence of the grunge scene, some artists began to move beyond it. One such band was Coffin Break.

Formed in the spring of 1987, Coffin Break could arguably be called the first post-grunge band in that it openly rebelled against slow and heavy. Featuring two songwriters, Coffin Break's guitarist Pete Litwin drew from Black Sabbath and speed metal, while bassist Rob Skinner provided a playful pop/punk approach. They became a three-piece when David Brooks took over on drums. In 1988 the band gigged in Seattle, but soon tired of the still-small club scene and wanted to tour nationally, just as the U-Men, Green River, and the Young Fresh Fellows had done. There was one small impediment, however: Coffin Break had no label, no record, no money, and few contacts.

In the spirit of the times, however, the band welcomed the challenge, and Skinner began booking gigs around the country by cold-calling promoters. He chose locations based on word of mouth and scene reports from the indie punk zine *Maximumrocknroll*. "Three dollars per day—that was our per diem," Skinner recalls. "We got five bucks a day when we were in New York—for three days. That was our big expenditure. We went out with three people and a roadie named Kyle in a '68 Dodge Sportsman. And, [we] just *did* it."

Despite the tour's issues—including van problems, personality conflicts, bad routing, and the like—the band accomplished what it set out to do: get publicity and possibly sell some demo tapes. "And more importantly," Skinner adds, "avoid day jobs."

The Posies and Capping Day

Other bands came from a completely different direction than the Mudhoneys of the world. The Posies' music drew from well-crafted pop song structures that had nothing to do with grunge. Further, the band made no bones about desiring music as a career. In contrast, Mudhoney and their brethren adhered to the (often problematic) punk rock ethos: make music as an end in itself.

Founded by guitarists Jon Auer and Ken Stringfellow, the Posies began life in a similar manner as the Green Pajamas had in 1984. Just as the Pajamas' Jeff Kelly and Joe Ross recorded their first offering, *Summer of Lust*, in Kelly's bedroom and self-released it on consignment at record stores, so went the Posies.

Unlike the Pajamas, however, who were immediately welcomed within the Seattle music community, the Posies were viewed as outsiders. Auer and Stringfellow hailed from Bellingham, a small town about an hour and a half north of Seattle, close to the Canadian border. Despite its small size, Bellingham did not conform to the usual small-town stereotype. Home of Western Washington University, Bellingham became a refuge for ex-hippies escaping the heroin-induced downers of post-'60s California. Auer and Stringfellow, both coming of age during the late '70s and early '80s, grew up in that environ.

The pair became close friends as they began playing and writing songs together during high school. Over the years they developed a distinctive acoustic-based, harmonic vocal style, drawing from such varied influences as the Smiths, the Beatles, and R.E.M. In late 1987 Auer and Stringfellow recorded some songs in Auer's father's home studio. The studio contained vintage '60s gear, and the price of free was cheap enough. The pair played all the instruments. Auer engineered and mixed the songs, having learned his craft by trial and error. The Posies named their debut *Failure*. "The Posies' *Failure* is perhaps the ultimate testament to DIY," says Auer. "I mean, it's not even mixed to a proper mix-down machine. It's mixed to a cassette deck, 'cause that's all I had."

Auer and Stringfellow dubbed copies of their cassette and brought it down to Seattle in 1988, offering it either on consignment at record stores on the Ave or selling tapes out of Auer's backpack. Their efforts soon paid off, as the cassettes began to sell at least modestly. "This little recording," says

Stringfellow, "was meant to be demo'd to get gigs—mainly to try and find some musicians to make a real band with."

The next step was to find a label interested in releasing *Failure*. At the time, Sub Pop's focus didn't match the Posies acoustic ballad style, although according to Auer, Poneman later counted himself as a fan. While Auer and Stringfellow tried to figure things out, the pair caught a Young Fresh Fellows show up in Bellingham. "It was like an off-the-hook crazy rock-and-roll show," Auer recalls, "and this was kind of like, I think, the prime of the Young Fresh Fellows too. . . . In their heyday, I would defy anybody to try to follow the Young Fresh Fellows."

The pair not only loved the Fellows live, they also dug their early Popllama recordings. Both Auer and Stringfellow admired Scott McCaughey's Beatlesque songwriting style. They also knew McCaughey wrote a monthly column in the *Rocket* called "Searchin' USA." Since McCaughey worked at the Cellophane Square record shop on the Ave, Stringfellow handed him a copy of *Failure* in the hopes that he might review it in his column. Falling in love with the tape, McCaughey wrote a glowing review of *Failure* and events began to speed up. He gave the demo to Popllama's Conrad Uno, who was then on tour with the Fellows. "So we were going on a road trip," Uno recalls, "and we put the tape in somewhere out there on the road and freaked out. It was pretty cool . . . hearing that. So of course we had to put it out."

Rereleased as an LP on Popllama, *Failure* sharply contrasted with the burgeoning Sub Pop sound. The record got some play on KCMU, but the acoustic guitars and sweet harmonies fit better on KJET, a commercial station, which began to play the record in regular rotation. Very quickly a local buzz began to surround the Posies, who weren't yet an actual band. About two weeks before a Seattle gig that McCaughey helped schedule, Auer and Stringfellow met bassist Rick Roberts and drummer Mike Musburger and became the Posies, the band.

Gigs began to open up, Posies songs aired regularly on commercial radio, and within a few months the band went from two kids with a homemade demo to a band with serious aspirations. "[We went] from two clueless dorks to two clueless dorks with a song being played on the radio every hour and lots of opportunities," says Stringfellow.

The Seattle music community initially showed the Posies somewhat of a cold shoulder, however. On the surface, the band appeared to run contrary to the punk rock credo: kids from the suburbs playing crafted pop songs with hooks. Some of this resentment drew from the band's early commercial success, as well as the average age of its members being two to three years younger than the typical 1988 Seattle band. Add in the band's desire to make music its livelihood, and the Posies became the anti-Mudhoney. "The idea of playing music as a career and as a living was kind of looked down upon," Musburger recalls, "and we were definitely seen as a careerist kind of band."

In particular, the *Backlash* clique didn't get the Posies, given the fanzine's focus on punk, metal, and the punk/metal grunge hybrid.

The Partridge Family live in Seattle and are now called the Posies. Can someone please exorcise the soul of David Cassidy from their bodies?

—Veronika Kalmar, review of *Failure*, *Backlash*, December 1988

Backlash's scathing review highlighted the Posies' outsider status. "We weren't part of the *scene*," says Auer. "You know, the thing that I really dislike about the whole scene thing is [it] become[s] a little bit like the whole high school vibe. . . . And it's always these people that were nonconformists talking about how they're so about nonconformity and then here comes the scene. And if you don't conform to the scene, you're excluded from it, and it's just like high school all over again."

Despite *Backlash*'s drubbing, players within the music community came to respect the Posies. The scenesters rather quickly began to accept the band within its confines, not only realizing the true DIY nature of *Failure* but understanding the Posies were being true to what they were.

Capping Day in some ways represented a sister band to the Posies, favoring harmonic ballads over loud, crushing rock. Initially an acoustic guitar duo consisting of Laura Weller and Bonnie Hammond, Capping Day displayed dissonant harmonies later popularized by the Indigo Girls. Weller had been DJ'ing at KCMU, hosting *Audioasis*, a show once fronted by Sub Pop's Poneman. KCMU connected her to the scene's up-and-comers. She then met Hammond at U-Dub and began performing at open mike nights.

Before long, bassist Joe Ross from the Green Pajamas and drummer Scott McCullum of Skin Yard approached the pair about forming a real band. So, as with the Posies, Capping Day morphed from an acoustic duo into a full band. McCullum's connection to Jack Endino led the band to Reciprocal, where it recorded "Mona Lisa," a beautiful harmonic, acoustic ballad. KCMU immediately picked up the song and placed it in heavy rotation. Shortly thereafter, the station entered the song in a national college radio contest with EMI records, and the shocked band found out it had won. The winner was supposed to get a record deal with EMI. Not knowing what to do next, the band enlisted the services of Terry Morgan, the one-time Showbox promoter and current Posies manager, to help them with the contract. "[It] was a screwball deal," Morgan recalls. "We ended up renegotiating it, getting them money, and putting out the record independently."

Tom Dyer's Green Monkey Records released "Mona Lisa" as a single the next year. Capping Day would remain viable despite the disappointment. The Posies' Jon Auer had begun recording music and soon steered the band toward Conrad Uno's Egg Studios, where it would begin to flower. Capping Day, like the Posies, would provide a counterpoint to the growing grunge scene.

Experimental Music

The audacious spirit of 1988 not only moved bands into genres other than grunge, it also encouraged experimental music from artists like Couch of Sound, Crypt Kicker 5, and Jack Endino.

Couch of Sound ventured into avant-garde territory, showcasing the talents of multi-instrumentalist Amy Denio, along with guitarist Chip Doring and Soundgarden drummer Matt Cameron. Denio symbolized the sheer openness of the scene at that point. She created music without boundaries, much of it not fitting within the rock idiom. "If I collaborate with all these different musicians," says Denio, "then I'm sure to learn more—to enrich my own understanding of music. So, that's a lot why I like to play with these different people like Matt Cameron or whoever."

"I'm not strictly a rock drummer," Cameron told Anderson in *Backlash*. "So basically this band allows me to do a lot more than just two or four time."

Denio and Cameron's desire to make music together symbolizes the collective communal desire to create music as creative expression. By this time, Cameron's Soundgarden already had their pick of major labels, and thus the drummer didn't need this side project to pad his resume. He just relished the challenge of working with talented musicians, like Denio and Doring, who moved their music into experimental territory.

Doring added his surf-rock influence to Couch of Sound. His main band was another one off the beaten path: Crypt Kicker 5.

By 1988 CK5 was also a three-piece, featuring Jamie Caffery on bass and vocals, and Skin Yard's Endino on drums. "It was surf-rockish. It was surfy," says Endino. "If you can imagine 'prog-surf'—because it was surfy but it was very quirky and weird. So I think the best phrase we had for it was 'Mediterranean Techno-Surf,' which doesn't really do it justice."

In addition to playing guitar in Skin Yard, drums in CK5, and producing Sub Pop bands, Endino also found time to provide a solo offering. *Angle of Attack* came out on cassette in April, with Endino producing and playing most of the instruments. Many of the tracks are instrumentals. Endino instrumentals also periodically popped up in Skin Yard recordings. "Sometimes I have a really hard time writing lyrics," says Endino. "And a lot of stuff I come up with, it just doesn't lend itself to singing. . . . And some [songs], I'd come up with lyrics, and I'd come up with a melody, and it just sounded stupid. And I realized, 'Ah, if I just do a little more work, it'll sound great as an instrumental.' So, yeah, I've always done that."

Angle of Attack's standout track is arguably "Sideways Savannah," an instrumental that features Asian-influenced percussion overlaid with guitar and bass. The percussion sounds came from scrap two-by-fours laid out in a xylophone-like pattern in Endino's basement. Endino and drummer Greg Gilmore (10 Minute Warning) then started playing the blocks of wood at either end simultaneously. "[Gilmore] would come over to my basement, and we would just fiddle around with percussion sometimes," recalls Endino. "We would just hit stuff and make strange percussion tracks using just incidental things—you know: heat vents, chunks of wood, pieces of metal, whatever was laying around in the basement."

The sounds were captured via stereo microphones. Afterward, the pair improvised bass and drum parts together and laid them on top of the initial percussion track. The result is an amazing piece of music that escapes rock's boundaries. "Greg was looking for something that wasn't rock," says Endino, "and [we] just threw the rules out the window."

Major-Label Interest

Seattle's arrival as an independent rock hotbed drew major label interest. Soundgarden became the first most obvious beneficiary. Soundgarden had built up a considerable cachet in Seattle by 1988. That, combined with the majors' intense interest, allowed them to play it coy. The band realized that picking the wrong label could result in giving up creative control or perhaps becoming stylistically pigeonholed. So Soundgarden bided their time and made the majors come to them. "There was a bidding war for Soundgarden," says Beezer. "And I don't think anybody saw that coming. Everybody knew we had some great bands and that [Seattle was] starting to make it and things were happening, but to have [multiple] labels upping the ante on Soundgarden was astonishing."

Soundgarden's transformation from underground punk/metal band to mainstream metal babies was executed in a subtle manner. "Soundgarden made a very conscious and deliberate decision to sell themselves," says Dan Trager, later in A&R with Sub Pop, "and be more commercial to the heavy metal aspect of the industry. And you could literally watch that.... I remember they used to be way more ad hoc and let their experimental and gothic leanings show a lot more. And then gradually it became a lot more about guitars, and vocals, and long hair, and shirtlessness. For a while there, they were big Bauhaus fans. And they'd play Bauhaus covers. And then gradually, the whole Led Zeppelin influence started taking over more and more."

Despite Soundgarden's calculated effort to become more commercial, the band's loyalty to Sub Pop and apparent defiance of major labels earned it respect throughout the Seattle music community. "It's like we're putting off this other aspect of the music business," Chris Cornell told Jeff Gilbert in the *Rocket*. "We can achieve success with our own means and ways, and if that means eventually winding up on a major label, that's fine. Ultimately, we have a better chance for success because we didn't jump right into a major deal."

The band tipped its cap to Sub Pop, even though it had clearly outgrown it, by recording a second record for the label. *Fopp*, a three-song EP highlighted by a cover of Green River's "Swallow My Pride," would hit the stores in July. The record featured the producing talents of Steve Fisk.

Around the same time, the band recorded its first full-length LP with SST. *Ultramega OK* came out in October. Perhaps the record's most powerful track is its opener. "Flower" begins with a dark, paisleyesque psychedelic intro, then heads into a metallic riff reminiscent of *Physical Graffiti*-era Led Zeppelin. The record also contains a reissue of "Incessant Mace," originally released on a 1986 comp called *Pyrrhic Victory*. "Mace" again draws from Zeppelin, this time from the discordant scales of "Dazed and Confused." The album also showcases a cover of Howlin' Wolf's "Smokestack Lighnin'," unfortunately correcting the spelling to "Smokestack Lightning."

Having paid their dues with Sub Pop and SST, and having slowly crossed their sound over to a mainstream metal audience, Soundgarden would soon sign with a major: A&M Records. The band played it brilliantly. Its members could become certified rock stars while, for the most part, retaining the respect and street credibility afforded their peers.

Mother Love Bone's path to major label success contrasted sharply with Soundgarden's. First, the band ditched its original Lords of the Wasteland moniker at singer Andrew Wood's urging. Second, to make themselves more major label–worthy, Mother Love Bone felt an upgrade at drummer was in order.

One day, guitarist Stone Gossard spotted Greg Gilmore walking with a friend on Capitol Hill. Gilmore—a virtuoso drummer formerly with 10 Minute Warning—had just returned from a trip to Asia. Gossard invited him to jam with his new band. Gilmore obliged. There was one issue, however. No one had told original drummer Regan Hagar he was out. Both percussionists found out during a practice session. "We [were] rehearsing in a very dingy basement down near Pioneer Square, and doin' our thing," says Gilmore. "And Regan and somebody came down there—and suddenly—everybody stopped playing and [had] gotten real quiet, and they're putting their guitars away. And I had no idea. They had been playing with Regan. And that's how he found out [he had been replaced]."

The music industry was looking for the next Guns N' Roses, and MLB seemed to fit the bill. The band sent demo tapes to label reps, which led to Geffen Records advancing $5,000 for a demo. Geffen, having pursued and lost out on signing Soundgarden, heavily courted MLB. The band flew to Los Angeles in July to meet with Geffen reps and immediately began contacting agents, publicists, and music attorneys. MLB played Geffen against other labels, eventually signing a deal with Polygram in November. The signing reportedly involved an advance of more than a quarter of a million dollars. Its overt embrace of the business side of rock stardom drew ire from its Seattle peers. Like the earlier Wasted Landlords project, an anti–Mother Love Bone group soon arose—Daddy Hate Box (which included Coffin Break's Pete Litwin on vocals and TAD's Steve Wied on drums).

Punk rock has always had an uncomfortable relationship with commercial success. Yet much of the anti–rock star posing is just that—posing. Even the Ramones, the iconic, original punk rock band, desired stardom. They wanted to sell out. It's just that no one was buying at the time. In the case of Mother Love Bone, the band's "selling out" was a bit too obvious for those within the Seattle music community: you weren't supposed to really *want* to become a rock star.

While Soundgarden and Mother Love Bone pursued major labels in their own ways, Sub Pop began to up the ante. In August the label released a Mudhoney single that in retrospect represents all that was grunge: "Touch Me I'm Sick." This song's magic derives from its simplicity. It displays a blinding, fuzzed-out riff that unequivocally defines Mudhoney. In some ways, grunge begins and ends with "Touch Me I'm Sick." Recorded by Jack Endino at Reciprocal, the record opens with the foreboding buzz of an amplifier. It then lurches into guitarist Steve Turner's fuzzy jumble of chords, accompanied by vocalist Mark Arm's distinctive wail. It is a classic lo-fi recording and garnered attention as far away as England. The single would position Mudhoney as the preeminent underground Seattle band. "That song," says Arm, "is basically the riff from 'Happenings Ten Years Time Ago' by the Yardbirds—which is also the fast part [from] 'I'm Sick of You' by the Stooges. You know, I mean it gets recycled. It's a great riff."

Grunge: The Commodity

The term "grunge," tossed about earlier in the year by Bruce Pavitt, would become ubiquitous by the fall of 1988.

Swallow churn out corroded metal and grungy garage rock at a decibel level that will really stick to your ribs.

—Unknown, *The Rocket*, June 1988

Most of this grunge stuff—for which Seattle has been notorious since the Sonics—is, for me, an object of alien curiosity in the same way rappers Public Enemy and Ice-T fascinate.

—Grant Alden, *The Rocket*, October 1988

MUDHONEY: No Nonsense Seattle Supergrunge

—Headline, *Backlash*, December 1988

This new raging primal grunge band, sure to delight or offend just about everyone, is called Mudhoney.

—Patty Stirling, *Puncture* (San Francisco), Fall 1988

*A nice change of pace from the recent barrage of grunge in this area.**

—Anonymous KCMU DJ review of the Posies' *Failure*

Grunge—the jokey term Pavitt had played around with when describing Green River—had become a bona fide "style"

---

*Used with permission from KEXP, formerly known as KCMU.

of music. Neither he nor anyone else had any idea what the mainstream media would do with the term in the '90s, however (see Chapter 8).

Following Mudhoney, Sub Pop released Nirvana's first single in November. A cover of Shocking Blue's "Love Buzz," the record would become the initial offering of the Sub Pop Singles Club, where subscribers paid a monthly fee to obtain limited-edition vinyl. Sub Pop purposely restricted the number of copies to create an instant collector's item.

The two most striking aspects of "Love Buzz" are its bass line and the melodic, distorted guitar figures. Nirvana disposed of Shocking Blue's sitar to make it more garage-y, yet maintained a melodic hook—a sign of things to come. Surprisingly, Kurt Cobain's vocals are the weakest part of the record.

Sub Pop's Jon Poneman loved the band and the record. Partner Bruce Pavitt remained unconvinced for the time being. "Poneman went along with it," Endino recalls. "He said, 'Well, at least let's let 'em do a single.' I remember, Pavitt just never really liked them that much at the time. It took him a while to come around."

Regardless, "Love Buzz" was an immediate hit within the scene. "And it [blew me away]—I just listened to that single a zillion times," recalls the Fastbacks' Kurt Bloch. "I just wore it out. It was so great. And of course I had the Shocking Blue album too. And I really like that song. Anyways, I [couldn't] believe that somebody [covered] this song. It's so cool."

Bloch got the single from Poneman after seeing Nirvana at the Vogue. "I remember one night seeing [Nirvana] at the [Vogue], and Jonathan is like, 'Hey, I don't have *any* money. If you buy me a cup of coffee, I'll give you this [Nirvana] single next time you're down at Sub Pop that'll just blow your mind.' I was like, 'Sure, I'll buy you a cup of coffee.' [Laughs.]"

Nirvana coalesced as Kurt Cobain moved the band past the wannabe Melvins stage. He was finding his voice. James

Burdyshaw, who after seeing Nirvana in the summer felt they were an inferior version of the Melvins, saw a different band emerging. "I remember standing there with Rob Roth [later with Truly]," says Burdyshaw. "And we were watching [Nirvana] together, and I looked at him and he looked at me. And I said, 'Fuck! I can't *believe* how good these guys sound!' All the sudden, every song was tight. There were these melodies and hooks. I was like, 'What happened?' And this was a change in like a three-month span—where like Cobain all the sudden found himself."

As Sub Pop's flagship bands increased in prominence, the label would release a comp demonstrating to all why Seattle had become an independent rock hotbed. In December the label released *Sub Pop 200*, which unlike *Sub Pop 100*, stuck to regional talent. Issued as three limited-edition EPs, *200* showcased the incredible variety of Seattle music.

BRUCE: Supervisory Chairman of Executive Management
JON: Executive Chairman of Supervisory Management

—from *Sub Pop 200* insert

The record does provide the expected offerings from Sub Pop's top bands Mudhoney, TAD, and Nirvana. TAD's "Sex God Missy" is arguably the standout of the three, featuring pummeling drums and Tad Doyle's wonderfully rough vocals. *Sub Pop 200* also contains helpings from Soundgarden ("Sub Pop Rock City"), the defunct Green River ("Hangin' Tree"), and newer grungy acts like Blood Circus and the Fluid.

The compilation became more eclectic with such offerings as a poetry reading by neo-beat Steven J. Bernstein, a surf rockish effort from Olympia's Beat Happening ("Pajama Party in a Haunted Hive"), an American/Celtic folk rock piece from the Walkabouts ("Got No Chains"), a cover of Green River's "Swallow My Pride" by the legendary Fastbacks, a scary electronic-oriented piece by Steve Fisk ("Untitled"), and a sentimental acoustic rocker from Terry Lee Hale ("Dead is Dead"). The record also features newer Seattle bands such as Cat Butt, Swallow, and Chemistry Set.

While 1986's *Deep Six* documented the beginnings of a sound, *Sub Pop 200* symbolized Seattle's attaining significant music scene status—a scene that, along with Sub Pop, was now nationally and internationally recognized. Sub Pop's definitive document brought considerable attention to Seattle. The city had arrived. "Here we were a bunch of musicians up in the Northwest that weren't good enough to be on records," says Pure Joy's Rusty Willoughby, "[evolving to] to 'Oh my gosh! Half of my favorite bands are my friends' bands!'"

Sub Pop's ascent aligned with Seattle's. Flush with newfound power, Sub Pop found it could—with few exceptions—determine the fate of local bands. If a band fit within Sub Pop's genre, opportunities and attention abounded. The label also helped out friends and their bands, even if they weren't on Sub Pop. If you were not a friend of Poneman or Pavitt, however, doors closed.

Sub Pop's Growing Power

Skin Yard, despite including Sub Pop's producer du jour Jack Endino, landed in the "shunned" column. By 1987 the band had replaced original drummer Matt Cameron with the 64 Spiders' Scott McCullum. McCullum's less precise, hard-hitting punk rock style drove the band away from its prog-rock/postpunk roots and into the garage. In the fall of 1988, Tucson's Toxic Shock label released Skin Yard's second record: *Hallowed Ground*. In contrast to the band's eponymous debut, *Hallowed*

Ground is a noisy, lo-fi, dissonant, and powerful record laced with psychedelia. "And the drummer we got in the band for [*Hallowed Ground*] was actually sort of an ex–punk rock kid [McCullum], who . . . really just like lit a fire under us," says Endino, "and just raised the energy level tremendously, [by not] concentrating so much on careful playing. So we became much thrashier and noisier. . . . [*Hallowed Ground* is] Skin Yard at our most original."

The record's bludgeoning opening track, "Stranger"—also released as a single—reinforces Endino's statement about the album's originality. The title track, however, is probably the album's standout offering. "Hallowed Ground" has the requisite distortion, but it wraps around itself by venturing into dissonant progressions before returning to more traditional rock chords. In some ways, it is every bit of a grunge masterpiece as "Touch Me I'm Sick."

Despite all that, Sub Pop had little interest in Skin Yard. "To those guys, we were a little too much like Black Sabbath or something—not alternative enough," says Endino. "We were a little too close to heavy metal, I think, from the standpoint of the Sub Pop guys."

Skin Yard's vocalist Ben McMillan also didn't fit within the Sub Pop universe. Animosity had existed between him and the label ever since Pavitt had criticized McMillan's vocals on the band's first record. "They basically didn't like our singer," says Endino, "to make a long story short."

The label also didn't get along with Chris Hanzsek, producer and owner of Reciprocal Recording. Hanzsek demanded Sub Pop pay his studio fees, refusing to offer extended credit other vendors provided. As a result of that and Sub Pop's preference for Endino's recording style, Endino, not Hanzsek, got to record Sub Pop bands. "Jack Endino early on," says Hanzsek, "fell in their favor [as a producer] and he benefited greatly. Myself, on the other hand, for some reason—I'd be [recording] a band and the next thing I know they were signed to Sub Pop. And then the band would come to me and go, 'Well, we just got signed to Sub Pop, and they told us that we can't work with you. We have to work with Endino.'

"Once they got as powerful as they got," Hanzsek continues, "then they also proceeded to just exert as much control over the situation as they could. They liked to pull the strings on which bands would make it and which bands wouldn't. And they played favorites. They really ticked some people off and they really kissed other people's butts. And no one could completely understand why they fell exactly on one side or the other."

As Sub Pop's presence increased, the label would not only decide which bands would "make it," but it would also reframe Seattle's musical history. The 1996 film *hype!* illustrates this point. The documentary showcases either Sub Pop's bands or other artists that Pavitt or Poneman favored. Bands (Skin Yard) or people (Hanzsek) they didn't like were simply omitted.

Hanzsek gets no mention in the film. When *hype!* discusses Green River as the prototypical grunge band, it neglects to mention Hanzsek as the person who discovered them and recorded their first demo and album. Further, when the film talks about the *Deep Six* comp, it again omits Hanzsek's name despite the fact that he put it together, produced it, and put it out on his label. Instead, the film shows Daniel House, who ran C/Z after Hanzsek, introducing the record as a "fluke of providence."

Finally, *hype!* displays a photograph of Jack Endino standing in front of Hanzsek's Reciprocal Recording studio, implying that it was his facility. "Who's up there under Reciprocal Recording? Not Chris. Jack Endino," says Tina Casale, who financed *Deep Six*. "Reciprocal [was] Chris. Jack Endino worked at Reciprocal. And I was just, 'Why do they have Jack Endino there?'"

As 1988 began to fade into 1989, the once laughable "rock star" persona became a possibility for some. Bands that enjoyed most favored status with Sub Pop would become internationally known the next year. Others, like Mother Love Bone and Soundgarden, signed huge deals with major labels. A number of bands got neither, but petty jealousies and infighting had—for the most part—not occurred yet. Some people were making fun of Mother Love Bone for selling out, but generally the local music community celebrated those who were now harvesting what they had sown during the lean years. In 1989, when Europe discovered grunge and the money began to roll in for select bands, so did the typical trappings of rock and roll: harder drugs, egos, competition, and the like. 1988 was a special moment and the last in which Seattle had some semblance of innocence. And most people within the music scene got that.

CHAPTER 7

England Is Sending an Emissary!

If you went to the American equivalent of Melody Maker—*which would have been* Rolling Stone *or* Spin—*you wouldn't have been able to find a music critic to treat Sub Pop and all of that kind of hyperbole the same way, because they would've tried to find the truth. And they would've killed it stone dead. And to find the truth would've been missing the most important element of that story—which was the excitement.*

—Everett True, *Melody Maker* music critic who publicized Sub Pop in the UK

Nirvana at Motorsports Garage, 1990. (Photo by Charles Peterson)

The year 1989 was kind of strange. As it turns out, it became a preamble for the coming storm. The scene's continued growth would lead to the inevitable conflict between art and commerce. Sub Pop led the charge toward commercial notoriety, focusing heavily on Europe. Non–Sub Pop bands like Soundgarden—who had by then moved on to a major label—and Mother Love Bone began to see some serious money. Despite these gravitations toward the music business, however, the scene still remained quite healthy, creative, and eclectic. In fact, grunge began to show signs of dissipating in 1989, as bands began to tire of the slow/heavy/sexy sound.

Regardless, Sub Pop's flirtations with Europe—and the UK in particular—amplified the grunge aspect of the scene, although not nearly as much as three years later when Nirvana's *Nevermind* hit number one on the Billboard chart.

London Flirts with Seattle

London had long been a tastemaker, pushing popular culture west to New York, where it then spread through the American heartland, leaving Seattle long behind the cultural curve. The UK's domination of rock and roll, beginning with the '60s classic rock era through '80s postpunk, reinforced the notion of British superiority.

By the mid-'80s, however, that domination began to wane. England had become weary of postpunk's rejection of the guitar and began to look for bands and scenes that actually played rock and roll. By that time, America was bursting with such bands and scenes in cities like Chicago, Los Angeles, Boston, New York, Athens (Georgia), Minneapolis, Austin (Texas), Portland (Oregon), Olympia, and Seattle. The British music press eagerly gobbled up the American underground, writing features on everyone from the Butthole Surfers to Sonic Youth.

Of course Britain's fascination with America is nothing new. England often sneers at a perceived American inferiority, but loves the United States nonetheless. Brits typically idealize America or at least the notion of the sort of wayward individualist, unfettered by a sense of class. It is within these parameters that England took notice of Seattle and Sub Pop.

It began with venerated London DJ John Peel falling in love with *Sub Pop 200* and went from there. The British music media began to take notice that something was happening in Seattle. Sub Pop publicist Anton Brookes accordingly had a suggestion for the label to obtain some UK exposure. He knew of a *Melody Maker* music critic named Everett True, who might be a good person to help create a buzz in Britain. Sub Pop decided to fly True to Seattle in early 1989.

For Sub Pop, the move made total sense. In 1989 the market for American alternative rock remained soft in the United States, but Europe was ready for it.

True turned out to be a strong fit for Sub Pop's aims. A frustrated musician who released a single under his alter ego "The Legend," True had cut his critical teeth working for the *New Musical Express*. In 1988 he left *NME* to work for rival *Melody Maker*. True had never really been a serious rock fan, but began his affection for Sub Pop bands when the label sent him Green River and Soundgarden EPs, as well as *Sub Pop 200*. The grittiness and honesty of the recordings immediately appealed to him.

True arrived in Seattle and received deluxe accommodations on Bruce Pavitt's floor. "My photographer was actually freaked out when he got there," True recalls, "and found out he was expected to share a mattress with me. He checked into a hotel the next day. Never saw him again."

Pavitt and Poneman introduced True to their bands, while filling him with exaggerated tales about TAD and Mudhoney's "backwoods America" background. True understood that reality had little to do with Sub Pop, but was immediately taken with the phony backstory as part of the Seattle put-on sense of humor. "The humor was massively important," says True. "It was part of the music. The funniest stand-up comedian I have ever seen in my life is Mark Arm."

For Seattle, True's arrival meant its little scene had attained international respect, given the high regard musicians held for the British music press. "The whole story about Everett True coming out was kind of like vindication," says Leighton Beezer. "[We thought], 'The taste center in London has sent out an emissary to find out what the fuck it is we're doing out here.'"

After spending about six weeks in town and becoming friends with Sub Pop and their bands, True returned to England. As expected, he wrote all about Mudhoney, TAD, Nirvana, and the other Sub Pop bands in *Melody Maker*.

A mountain of sound. The heaviest man in all creation. The rockiest gnarliest dude you'd ever want to wake up next to. Totally crushing. An enormous talent. From the backwoods of Idaho and trained as a butcher.

—Everett True describing TAD's Tad Doyle, *Melody Maker*,
March 18, 1989

"I picked up a bug on the plane," True recalls. "And I was throwing up the entire way—I was actually throwing up while

I was writing that story. As I think Leighton Beezer—Leighton pointed out, 'That's the real grunge.'"

True willingly led his readers down the primrose path, helping to amplify Sub Pop's mythology of Doyle as the savant logger. "I knew that [Doyle] wasn't really a backwoodsman," says True, "but I didn't give a shit. . . . It was funnier. I've never seen my primary role as a critic—again, this is probably why I was in retrospect perfect to be the person who kind of exposed Sub Pop and Seattle music to the rest of the world—I've never seen my role as a critic to tell the truth. I don't think the truth's got much to do with it. I've always seen my primary role [is] to entertain."

True's efforts to popularize Seattle and Sub Pop's definition of grunge greatly benefited some of Seattle's bands. The first, most obvious beneficiary was Mudhoney, who would lead the Sub Pop charge in the UK. Easier said than done, however; the UK was traditionally a tough market for an underground American band to crack. Fortunately, Sonic Youth, who had already built an audience in Britain, invited Mudhoney to open for them on their 1989 UK tour. (Mark Arm and Steve Turner had befriended Sonic Youth back in their Green River days when they opened for them at venues like the Gorilla Gardens.) "[Sonic Youth] were definitely considered tastemakers [in the UK], for a while there for sure," says Arm. "Also, John Peel was playing our single on his radio show. We never felt like we were beating our heads against the wall."

The position Mudhoney had attained by 1989 cannot be overstated. Nobody was talking about Nirvana—yet. Mudhoney achieved a prominence that no other Seattle independent band had. The band released a split single with Sonic Youth and appeared to reach a level commensurate with that band and others of its ilk, like Big Black and the Butthole Surfers.

Furthermore, Mudhoney symbolized how far Seattle had come in just a few years. Back in 1984, the U-Men were all the rage locally, but there was nowhere for them to go beyond the Northwest. Other than KCMU and the *Rocket*, a support structure didn't really exist. By 1989, however, Mudhoney had become the primary beneficiary of the ambitious Sub Pop label and its connection to the British music press.

Al Bloch, who played in a late-'70s Seattle punk band called the Cheaters with his brother Kurt (the Fastbacks), moved to Los Angeles in 1985. Bloch periodically visited Seattle after that, providing him with a sort of time-lapse view of the city during the latter half of the '80s. He vividly remembers coming up in 1989 and catching a Mudhoney/Nirvana show. "And it was like, 'Whoa!' I mean, people were coming out," Bloch remembers. "The places were packed, and people were excited. And the bands were exciting. It was so different from 1984 and '85."

"And it was all about Mudhoney at that time," says Beezer.

In the UK, Mudhoney immediately connected to British fans who were tired of melancholy postpunk and longing for rowdy punk rock. The band's live set continued in the tradition of other '80s underground acts in that anything was possible on stage. "Mudhoney had a certain intelligent, yet fuck-all sense of humor," adds Dan Trager, who later worked in A&R at Sub Pop. "And they could be accessible and underground at the same time."

Mudhoney blazed the trail, despite modest British sales of "Touch Me I'm Sick" and the corresponding *Superfuzz Bigmuff* EP. Their version of high-energy punk rock immediately warmed British audiences to Sub Pop's version of the Seattle sound, so much so that some have called 1989 the first grunge explosion. Yet Seattle's UK notoriety was rather subdued and paled in comparison to the Nirvana-initiated grungemania of 1991 and '92.

TAD's Balls

It was also a big year for Mudhoney's brethren TAD and Nirvana. Both bands released their debut records, both engineered at Reciprocal by Jack Endino. Endino's raw production techniques fit TAD perfectly, though no one was sure of what to call the final product.

Around the same time, guitarist Tad Doyle and bassist Kurt Danielson attended a bachelor party for friend and former Bundle of Hiss–mate Jamie Lane. The party featured, among other things, a screening of low-rent porno. One movie—called *God's Balls*—caught on with the crowd. A "highlight" featured a priest receiving a blow job. "From a nun," Doyle adds.

"And whenever he was getting a blow job in the film," says Danielson, "he was always screaming out, 'God's balls! God's *ballllsss*!!! God's balls, that feels good!' in a really cheesy deliberate and awkward way—horrible acting. He himself was no stud. And even the chicks were raunchy in this one. But it was pure poetry to my ears."

At the recording sessions, Danielson, with Endino's encouragement, suggested TAD title their first album after the movie.

The record contains elemental TAD, with songs like "Helot" and "Sex God Missy" (previously released on *Sub Pop 200*) showcasing crushing riffs, and a signature effort called "Behemoth." "Behemoth" was based on a violent incident that had occurred the previous summer involving members of TAD and Mudhoney, an African American street gang, and a juniper bush.

Doyle, Danielson, Mudhoney drummer Dan Peters, and a couple of other friends were hanging out at a U-District bar and decided to drop some acid. Danielson was wearing a shirt he designed himself. The front and back displayed raunchy sayings he had written in large block letters in black felt pen. After midnight, the group decided to go outside. "Actually, no,"

Danielson recalls, "we didn't decide, they kicked us out. That's right. [Laughs.]"

The streets were deserted except for an occasional carload of drunken frat boys. The U-District—as it is now—is not the greatest of neighborhoods. The streets were patrolled by an African American gang on the prowl for U-Dub frat boys to harass. The gang members wore weightlifting belts and would terrorize their targets by removing their belts, twirling them over their heads in a frenzy, and then smacking their victims to the ground.

It was under these conditions that Danielson and his acid-riddled friends decided to venture back to his apartment, about four blocks from the bar. As they stumbled along, they noticed a group of large black men coming toward them. They quietly crossed the street to avoid a potential confrontation and continued on their way. As the group neared Danielson's apartment, they discovered one of their friends had lagged back and was now talking to the gang.

Peters immediately ran over to retrieve his friend, who had apparently been soliciting crack. Turns out the gang members were anti-crack warriors. Oops. Before they could realize what was happening, Danielson and his friends were surrounded by men swinging weightlifting belts over their heads like lassos. "So these guys are running right at us," Danielson remembers. "It just freezes the blood in our veins. Remember, we're on acid. It totally is blowing our minds. 'Is this real? Is this really happening?'"

It was all too real. After one friend was knocked unconscious, Danielson hid behind the imposing Doyle. Doyle attempted to placate the attackers, but found himself smacked to the ground and knocked out. "Tad goes *down*," says Danielson, "and the juniper bush that he landed on—died that instant. [It's] dead to this day. I've been by there recently, well, [a] couple years ago. It was still dead. [Laughs.]"

Danielson, now completely exposed, also attempted to negotiate with the gang. Like Doyle, he found himself slapped to the ground and unconscious. "It's like, suddenly this white light and you're out, and you wake up and you're on the ground," says Danielson. "I look, and what's happening, but Dan has made it to the door [of Danielson's apartment]—Dan Peters—and they're all on top of him, 'cause he's fighting back. The rest of us had just crumpled, but Dan was kicking them and hitting them."

Peters' valiant defiance was for naught, however, as the gang members jumped on him and stomped him. Then they picked him up and tossed him through the leaded glass entrance to Danielson's apartment. Peters dislocated his shoulder and required hospitalization. He feared he might not be able to play with Mudhoney on their upcoming UK tour. Fortunately, however, the dislocation was not serious, and Peters was able to go to Europe. "This [experience] became the basis for . . . 'Behemoth,' which I wrote about that night," says Danielson.

Overall, *God's Balls* sounded heavy and brutal with Doyle's grumbly vocals. The band possessed an ingredient the other Sub Pop acts lacked, however. Both Doyle and Danielson held a strong affinity for postpunk bands like Gang of Four and Joy Division. TAD sounded nothing like those bands, but the postpunk connection differentiated their sound from their Sub Pop contemporaries. TAD worked from the rhythm section out, highlighting Danielson's bass lines. Doyle's training as a drummer played into the band's sound as well, even though he was now a guitar player and singer. "What I thought is that they reminded me of Skin Yard," says Endino, "because we had the same sort of postpunk element coming from our bass player Daniel [House]. . . . And they would probably be the only band who were on Sub Pop that had any sort of a postpunk influence at all on what they were doing."

Nirvana's Bleach

Nirvana's first effort, *Bleach*, looms larger in retrospect. At the time, the record was a low-rent effort from a sort of outsider band that was still finding its songwriting voice.

As Nirvana were unable to afford the recording costs, second guitarist Jason Everman lent them $600 to lay down tracks at Reciprocal. Everman, who never quite fit in with the band and was jettisoned in 1989, never played on *Bleach* but got credited anyway.

The standard take on *Bleach* is that it's a bunch of angular grungey songs with one exception: the Beatlesque "About a Girl." Unfortunately, that analysis oversimplifies what is in retrospect a surprisingly strong debut. Standouts include "School," which features two sets of lyrics: "Won't you believe it, it's just my luck" for the verse and "No recess" for the chorus. The bridge, if you can call it that, perhaps showcases Kurt Cobain's faux fondness for adolescence: "You're in high school again!"

Despite "School's" heavy riffs, the song reveals a pop sensibility—one that would come to fruition two years later on *Nevermind*. In addition to "School" and "About a Girl," Cobain's flirtations with pop appear on the Shocking Blue cover "Love Buzz," issued the previous year as a single. "It was entirely the vocals that made them stand out. Nothing else," says Endino. "I mean, it was basically '70s riff rock. It was not punk rock. . . . What [Nirvana] had that set [them] apart from the other bands, notably Mudhoney and TAD, you know—everyone else—was they had a very good, melodic, lead singer, who was not afraid to sing melodies in his gruff voice. . . . Mark Arm's melodies tended to always follow the guitar riff. Nirvana's melodies didn't follow the guitar riff for the most part. They were always a little more sort of developed.

"Compare 'Negative Creep' [from *Bleach*] with [Led Zeppelin's] 'Communication Breakdown,' for instance," Endino adds. "You know, how can you tell me 'Negative Creep' is a punk rock song?"

"Most of the grunge bands back then—they didn't have songs," adds the Posies' Mike Musburger. "They just had riffs. And sometimes the riffs were strung together in very odd ways, I thought. And [Nirvana] was something that was more cohesive."

Packaging *Bleach* became kind of a rush job. Graphic designer Lisa Orth had a band photo she was not terribly impressed with for the cover. So she altered it to a negative image under the "when it doubt, reverse it out" philosophy of the time. Running out of time and money, Orth took the cover design to *Rocket* editor Grant Alden for printing. "She came in one day [to the *Rocket*]," Alden recalls. "She had the type for *Bleach*. . . . And she walks in and says, 'Bruce and Jon [from Sub Pop] want this done today. And I hate this freakin' band. What typeface do you have on the machine? Just set it and whatever you've got— I'll do it.'"

At the time, Alden was doing headlines and had a typeface called Onyx. After the cover came out of the typesetter, the *R* and *V* in Nirvana did not line up properly; the process to fix this is called kerning. Alden offered to kern the letters so they would line up properly. Unfortunately, the procedure required the type to dry before a proper kerning could be effected. Orth refused, citing time and expense considerations. So, *Bleach* went out as is, with an abnormally large space between the R and V. Ironically, the Onyx typeface and off-spacing became the band's signature look. "For 16 dollars and 23 cents," says Alden, "I typed up the Nirvana logo."

The back cover misspelled Kurt Cobain's name as "Kurdt Kobain." The error is yet another example of Seattle humor. Around the same time as *Bleach*'s release, Daniel House's C/Z Records was putting together a compilation called *Teriyaki Asthma*, which featured a Nirvana song called "Mexican Seafood." Unfortunately, as the graphic artists were putting that cover together, they realized they did not know how Cobain spelled his first name.

House attempted to reach the guitarist, to no avail. Graphic designer Art Chantry thought Cobain's first name might be spelled "Kurdt," as he knew of a Kurdt Vanderhoof who, like Cobain, was from Aberdeen. House was not so sure "Kurdt" was correct, but he was running close to press time, so the spelling stuck. Cobain's last name was also spelled with a K, just for fun, and "Kurdt Kobain" showed up on *Teriyaki Asthma*'s (and *Bleach*'s) credits. "And so Kurt thought it was a pretty funny way to misspell it," says Chantry. "So from that point on,* he went way out of his way to misspell his name."

The Post-Grunge Generation

In 1989 a new generation of Seattle bands began to explore other musical avenues besides grunge. Gas Huffer did so with aplomb and accordingly earned respect from their peers. It didn't hurt that the band had guitarist Tom Price, formerly of the U-Men, at its heart. Gas Huffer began life when Price joined forces with drummer Joe Newton, singer Matt Wright, and bassist Don Blackstone. For Price, the U-Men's "beginning with a riff and building from there" songwriting approach had become stale. He had been listening to a lot of soul and R&B, and wanted to present songs to his band that would come out more or less as

---

*At least until *Nevermind*, released in September 1991, when he changed to the real spelling.

he had written them. He knew he had no chance of that happening in the U-Men. Price had also grown tired of grunge. "At the time I started Gas Huffer," says Price, "everything was slow, heavy, and sexy—except for [Tacoma's] Girl Trouble. . . . And I just thought, 'Wouldn't it be kinda neat if there was a band that played really fast, maybe more country-inspired music?' And so that's what we did."

Price's aversion to grunge became evident in Gas Huffer. Abandoning the U-Men's avant-garde jazz leanings, Gas Huffer sped things up and grabbed whatever they could from old-time rock and roll and country, added some garage, and then fused it all together. For one, Gas Huffer could really play. Unlike the grunge aesthetic that championed the notion of passion over technical competence, Gas Huffer clearly had the chops.

Early songs like "Night Train to Spokane" exemplified what Gas Huffer was about. Price begins with a bluesy guitar imitation of a train whistle. Then Newton starts up with a rolling, shuffling beat. The band then speeds up as Wright enters with a punk rock drawl. So within about fifteen seconds, Gas Huffer touches on blues, country, and punk rock.

Similarly, songs like "Robert"* showcased the band's varied approach. The song again sounds punk rock with Wright's vocal style, but its use of varied textures, including acoustic guitar, meant it could easily fit within the Neil Young canon. Then again, it could be the Stooges. Who knows? Gas Huffer defies such categorization.

Girl Trouble's music drew from a similar spring as Gas Huffer, but for many in the Northwest, that band perhaps more closely carried out the Sonics' garage tradition. The term "garage" connotes several terms: loud, raucous, unstructured, genuine. Perhaps the

---

*Both "Night Train to Spokane" and "Robert" show up on *Janitors of Tomorrow*, released on eMpTy Records in 1992.

best word to describe what a garage band is going for is "purity." Never lose that feeling and naïveté when you're young and playing in a tight rehearsal space. Never lose that soul even in the face of increased competence, larger audiences, and the interference of the music business. Girl Trouble were all about that, but possessed the talent to explore beyond most garage bands.

Girl Trouble came into being when Tacoma residents K. P. Kendall (vocals/sax), Dale Phillips (bass), Kahuna (guitar), and Bon Von Wheelie (drums) joined forces in 1983. Situated about forty minutes south of Seattle, Tacoma has two military bases and possesses a much tougher working-class culture than does its larger neighbor to the north. As difficult a going as Seattle punks had in their early days, their Tacoma brethren faced even greater resistance from the police and general community. "We always used to say that a night out in Seattle is a concert, a night out in Tacoma is wrestling," Von Wheelie states via e-mail.

The band quickly became connected to the early Olympia scene and played at the Tropicana alongside such local notables as the Young Pioneers and Beat Happening. During that time, Girl Trouble would venture to Seattle as music fans, catching shows at the Showbox, then still hosting international punk and postpunk acts. The band began making its Seattle presence known in 1985, playing gigs at the Gorilla Gardens with Portland's legendary Wipers. By the time 1989 rolled around, Girl Trouble had become regulars at Pioneer Square's Central Tavern, Belltown's Vogue, and Capitol Hill's Squid Row.

That same year, the band recorded its first LP, venturing to Ellensburg to record at Velvetone Studios (where Screaming Trees made their early records) with producer Steve Fisk. The result was *Hit It or Quit It*, released on Sub Pop. The band attempted to capture not only its live sound, but also that intangible purity of the Sonics. "Musically, we were hoping for the raw sounds we heard in those old Northwest records," Von Wheelie mentions in an e-mail.

Girl Trouble—along with Gas Huffer, Portland's Dead Moon, and Bellingham's Mono Men—represented what might have been a changing of the guard around 1989 and '90, had Nirvana not happened. Those bands represented the harbingers of a new wave of Northwest garage rock—successors to the Sonics. At the very least, Girl Trouble and their brethren demonstrated that the slow/heavy aesthetic had begun to dissipate in Seattle.

Coffin Break was another band that consciously rejected the grunge rules. Formed two years earlier, by 1989 the band had already toured the country and was ready to record their first EP, *Psychosis*, on C/Z Records. The band's offerings, like Gas Huffer's, completely rejected the Sub Pop rules. Instead of slow and sexy, Coffin Break played at varied speeds. Instead of the tongue-in-cheek insincerity of Mudhoney's "Touch Me I'm Sick," Coffin Break wrote songs like "Kill the President,"* tackling politics.

Combining guitarist Pete Litwin's metal leanings with bassist Rob Skinner's pop-punk background, "President" is quintessential Coffin Break. The song begins with a menacing Slayeresque speed metal riff (written by Litwin) that sounds downright scary. Suddenly it stops, and happy major chords (written by Skinner) appear as Skinner sarcastically intones, "I'm so happy, it's sunny outside." The song goes on to not so subtly criticize President George H. W. Bush: "I'm so happy we elected Bush today," Skinner continues. "I'm so happy another criminal. I'm so happy we elected a crook again. I'm so happy . . . wanna kill the president!" Skinner inserted lyrics written by Litwin since they ironically fit with his pop melody. "I was

---

*"Kill the President" appears on Coffin Break's first LP, *Rupture*, released in 1990.

fuckin' pissed—honestly—that Bush got elected," says Litwin. "I could not believe it. Like I thought that with Iran-Contra, there was no fucking way that he could get elected. That he was completely implicated in that,* and there's no way that people would elect him. And I was just shocked, as I was once again in 2000 when his stupid son got in."

Coffin Break drew some ire for their political leanings, and the band responded in kind by making fun of the "cool" people. Litwin and Skinner began composing riffs that sounded similar to other local acts. Examples include "Noise Patch" (a parody of Soundgarden), "Flesh Field" (Skin Yard), and "Pop Fanatic" (Sub Pop).**

Coffin Break displayed their Seattle brand of humor on their DIY tours. For example, the band repeatedly endured calls for the ubiquitous "Free Bird." "It doesn't matter where you play," says Skinner. "You can play Madison Square Garden, you can play Joe's Bar & Grill in front of two people—some idiot's gonna yell, 'Play "Free Bird"!'"

Coffin Break being Coffin Break, they decided to have some fun with it. When a fan would scream out a request for the Skynyrd classic, the band would stop and play it, but in its own

---

*Author's note: the Reagan administration's Iran-Contra scandal, whose crimes included selling arms to Iran and misappropriating profits resulting from those sales, involved high-ups including then Vice-President Bush. By 1988, however, Congress had buried the scandal, and most Americans paid little attention during the presidential election. In 1992, Independent Counsel Lawrence Walsh subpoenaed cabinet meeting notes taken by Reagan's Secretary of Defense Caspar Weinberger-notes which could implicate Bush and Reagan in the scandal. The investigation came to a crashing halt, however, in December of 1992 when Bush pardoned Weinberger and former National Security Adviser John Poindexter.

**"Noise Patch" and "Flesh Field" appear on *Psychosis*, with "Pop Fanatic" on *Rupture*.

irreverent way. Skinner would begin the song by running a beer bottle over the neck of his bass. The band would progress toward the three-chord finale, but Coffin Break would take that and speed it up to the point where it became an unrecognizable blur. "But that was the whole thing," says Skinner. "[We thought] 'OK, fuck you, dude. Here you go. Here's your "Free Bird"!'"

Like Coffin Break, the Walkabouts tackled relevant issues. Instead of coming from a punk rock angle, however, the band approached things from a folk perspective heightened by a punk attitude. Although the Walkabouts were not part of the new generation of bands—they had been playing since 1984—they symbolized the shift Seattle's music was undergoing. By 1989 the band had defined its personality apart from the grunge sound while still actively playing among grunge musicians.

The Walkabouts were certainly different from pretty much everyone else in Seattle. The band employed acoustic guitars, for instance, and other than the Posies, Terry Lee Hale, and the Young Fresh Fellows, not a lot of people were doing that. The band began with a partnership between Chris Eckman and Carla Torgerson: both sang and played a multitude of instruments, but that was where the similarities ended. Eckman, coming from a punk background, showed Torgerson how to play the Buzzcocks and the Jam. Torgerson, coming from a folk background, offered up Bob Dylan and Leonard Cohen. Punk and folk? It's not exactly like mixing chocolate and peanut butter, but the pair decided they could make it work.

Soon they added a rhythm section consisting of Eckman's brother Grant on drums and Michael Wells on bass. After self-releasing an EP called *22 Disasters* in 1985, the Walkabouts recorded their first full-length record, *See Beautiful Rattlesnake Gardens*, for Popllama two years later, and it sounded more folk than rock. Like Coffin Break, the Walkabouts were not afraid to delve into the political realm, with *Gardens* showcasing an odd voiceover called "Robert McFarlane Blues," which again related to the Iran-Contra scandal.

Gardens was intended to be the band's final record, as the group felt burned out after four years of writing and recording. Instead, it represented just a blip in a quarter-century-plus career. Viewed another way, the record became a touchstone for the band, since it had not quite found its voice yet. The eclectic mix that Chris Eckman and Torgerson brought together still sounded like just that: an eclectic mix. "When we started, I think we were really envious of these bands that could only play one way," says Eckman. "Because in a way, it was cool, because they had a sound. They went on stage. They played thirty minutes, and you were enthralled. You were like, 'Wow! That really sounded like something.' We'd play thirty minutes, and it would be like a sampler record."

All of that began to change with the band's next LP, *Cataract*, released on Sub Pop in 1989. Drummer Grant Eckman's friendship with Sub Pop's Bruce Pavitt, combined with Pavitt's appreciation of the band's originality, led to the partnership despite Sub Pop's ties to grunge.

Cataract combined the Walkabouts' diverse backgrounds into one coherent whole, which is quite an accomplishment given the varied instrumentation. In addition to the usual guitar, bass, and drums, you'll find harmonica, keyboards, violin, cello, trombone, and mountain dulcimer. Mountain dulcimer? Yeah, that comes from Appalachia. It's a four-stringed instrument played while sitting down. Nope, this ain't grunge.

The record features guest musicians Terry Lee Hale, Jonathan Segel of Camper Van Beethoven, and Carl Miller of local band Prudence Dredge, as well as Joey Kline and Craig Ferguson of the Squirrels. *Cataract* remains true to Torgerson's folk roots with selections like the wistful "Whereabouts Unknown" and Eckman's rock stylings with "Hell's Soup Kitchen." The record also has a wonderful major/minor chord interplay (later championed by Alice in Chains) in "Whiskey Xxx."

Despite the vast difference between the Walkabouts and bands like Mudhoney, the scene still embraced diversity among its musicians. "At the very least, there were even some—let's say—crossover influences," says Eckman. "You know, Mudhoney listened to Neil Young. We listened to Neil Young. I remember Mark Arm coming to shows that we played. And when we'd do like, Neil Young['s] 'Cortez the Killer' or 'Like a Hurricane,' he would always come up front."

Ron Rudzitis, by then calling himself Ron Nine, remained determined to continue the psychedelic direction of Room Nine. In 1989 the band had run its course, having experienced a not-atypical frustration associated with poorly financed independent labels. So Nine teamed up with drummer Jason Finn (Skin Yard), as well as guitarist Kevin Whitworth and bassist Tommy Bonehead. Taking the name of a Buzzcocks song, the new band would call itself Love Battery.

The interplay between Nine and Whitworth made the band sound quite different from Room Nine. Both talented guitar players, the pair wouldn't designate a lead and rhythm and thus avoided some of the typical rock band ego clashes. Nine had been experimenting with guitar effects. That and the lack of a keyboard made Love Battery sound somewhat akin to the grunge bands, but much more melodic, while maintaining Room Nine's psychedelic aesthetic. Its sound was well represented on the band's first single, "Between the Eyes," released on Sub Pop in 1989.

Finally, a band from Boise brought yet another style into the mix. Descending from the hardcore band State of Confusion, the Treepeople added melodic song structures to create something rather different. Singer/guitarist Doug Martsch's songwriting ability made that band accessible enough that it could have been another Nirvana, if not for internal band issues that led to its demise. "Here was this band that completely appealed to the hardcore underground scene," says Dan Trager, who would later manage the Treepeople's tours, "but really oddball-sort-of-sore-thumb stuck out. Like, the singer was up there—he was kinda balding already, even in his teens—this is Doug Martsch. He was playing an acoustic guitar, yet people were digging it."

While the Treepeople's impact would not extend much beyond the Northwest, its collapse allowed Martsch's songwriting to blossom with his next band, Built to Spill. "And particularly what goes on with Doug," says Trager, "is he's a great arranger—in terms of arranging his songs."

Breakout Shows

In 1989 the audience for all the underground bands began to expand exponentially. Despite much of the scene veering out of grunge territory, however, Sub Pop's preeminence kept the attention squarely on its bands, as evidenced by several pivotal shows occurring that year.

The first of these occurred on June 9 at the Moore Theater. Sub Pop promoted the event as "Lame Fest" and showcased its flagship bands: Mudhoney headlined, with Nirvana and TAD in support. The significance? People filled up the 1,500-capacity facility to see local acts. That was astounding.

The next benchmark slipped beneath the radar, and in retrospect, it mattered only because Nirvana released *Nevermind* in the fall of 1991. Nonetheless, the show represents a key moment in Seattle rock history. Sub Pop held the event at CoCA (Center on Contemporary Art), a downtown venue then located on 1st Avenue and University, about three blocks south of the Showbox. Again, the label showcased Mudhoney and Nirvana. The importance of this performance? Nirvana headlined—not

198 THE STRANGEST TRIBE

Mudhoney. Remember, Mudhoney was the biggest band in Seattle in 1989, other than Soundgarden, who had already moved on to a major label.

At the time, 1st Avenue remained rather sleazy, with CoCA residing next to an exotic dance club called The Lusty Lady. Its warehouse-like structure consisted of two rooms displaying art where bands could perform. The larger room's square footage approximated that of Pioneer Square's Central Tavern without the bar area, so it could hold several hundred patrons.

The Mudhoney/Nirvana show took place on Saturday, August 26 and was actually the second night of festivities. TAD had found themselves sandwiched between the gross-out Dwarves and the alien rock GWAR the previous evening.

Anticipation reached a peak the night of the second show. The Sub Pop lineup, in addition to Mudhoney and Nirvana, consisted of the Black Supersuckers (later Supersuckers) and Cat Butt. The Black Supersuckers opened in the small room, with Cat Butt following in the larger space.

Music fans and members of other bands packed the unair-conditioned venue that night, fueling an almost unbearable heat eclipsing 100 degrees. Space was so limited that the audience could do little more than bounce up and down—moshing was out of the question. Despite the crowd and sweltering heat, the mood remained on the congenial side of rowdy, as most attendees knew each other. CoCA was an all-ages venue, but those in the know could locate a large tub filled with ice and beer behind the stage.

Mudhoney went on after Cat Butt to an adoring crowd. Mark Arm and Co. were on that night and for their finale opened up a box of confectioners' sugar, placed it in front of a fan, and blew it out into the crowd.* The sweaty bodies instantly became sticky

---

*Cat Butt's James Burdyshaw disputes this. He recalls a CoCA organizer heaving the contents at the crowd from the stage, without Mudhoney's participation.

messes. The fans loved it, further adding to Mudhoney's phenomenal live repertoire. Nirvana had to follow that.

Kurt Cobain ventured backstage. There he came across
Cat Butt's James Burdyshaw sitting next to the beer trough,
its ice by then nearly melted. Burdyshaw—drunk and admittedly obnoxious—greeted backstage guests by flicking water in
their faces. While his actions annoyed Mudhoney's Matt Lukin,
Cobain found them amusing. "And then Cobain comes in right
after [Lukin]," Burdyshaw recalls, "and Kurt's like, 'I'd like it
if you'd dunk my whole head in there.' And I was like, 'OK!'
And so, I took his head and I dunked it into this tub of ice water.
And I was gonna pull it back up, but he wouldn't bring it up.
He must have held his head down there for a minute. And then
he brings it up. And he's like, 'Ahhhh . . . ' and he's just like
pourin' with ice water down his face and everything. And he
smiled, and he's like, 'Thank you!' And that's basically how he
got ready for the show."

Meanwhile, bass player Chris Novoselic began to set up his
equipment and noticed the venue had nearly emptied out. Fans
had temporarily exited to escape the heat, but the Nirvana bassist thought he had lost his audience. "I remember," recalls Pure
Joy's Rusty Willoughby, one of the few fans who decided to
remain, "like, seeing Chris Novoselic kinda just like imploring
people like, 'Hey, stick around. We're called Nirvana.'"

Novoselic had no conception of what was going on. Although
Mudhoney had achieved preeminence in underground Seattle,
Nirvana's melding of grunge and melody, combined with
Cobain's impassioned vocals, gave the band an indefinable charisma. Nirvana had been playing in Seattle for just over a year,
but it had already become apparent that this band possessed an
excitement that was about to eclipse Mudhoney's. "I'm watching [Novoselic]," says Willougby. "I can sort of see what's happening and I'm just like, 'He has no fuckin' idea.' And sure

enough, like half [an] hour later they're playing their set and the place is just like—people are like literally hanging from the rafters 'cause that's the only place they can see the band, 'cause the floor is completely packed. There were people sitting on the PA. There were girls on the side of the stage—not like trying to get close to the band—but it was literally the only place they could sit.

"It was like, 'This is a fucking local club show?'" Willoughby continues. "It was the most exciting show I'd ever seen to that point."

Soundgarden and Mother Love Bone's Major Label Debuts

On the major-label front, Soundgarden and Mother Love Bone offered up their debuts in 1989. Released in September, Soundgarden's *Louder Than Love* abandoned any pretense toward punk rock, as they had hired producer Terry Date to provide a big metal sound. Standouts like "Hands All Over" combine elements of Led Zeppelin and Black Sabbath with an added murkiness, while completely ditching the psychedelic elements of the band's earlier work. Despite all the apparent commercial modifications, cries of "sellout" were muted at best. In effect, Soundgarden had put in their time before streamlining their sound for major-label consumption.

Mother Love Bone took a different business approach than Soundgarden. The band had signed with Polygram in 1988 and released its major-label debut EP *Shine* in the spring of 1989. Unlike Soundgarden, Mother Love Bone came into being specifically for major-label success. The fact that its members traced their roots to underground Seattle in bands like Green River and Malfunkshun did little to placate anti–Mother Love Bone sentiment arising within the local community. Further, *Shine* has nothing to do with punk rock, or even metal for that matter. The record sounds closer to Aerosmith than anything and could have fit nicely on regular AOR radio rotation in the '70s. "It had all this sort of '70s nostalgia in it," says Stone Gossard, "and it had all this reverence for sort of completely irreverent rock stars. . . . like Freddie Mercury and T. Rex."

Despite its detractors, *Shine* is a good hard-rock record, highlighted by the epic two-part ballad "Chloe Dancer/Crown of Thorns" showcasing singer Andrew Wood's powerfully sincere delivery. Unfortunately, the backlash against Mother Love Bone would outlast the band and follow its successor, Pearl Jam, when that band exploded in 1991 and '92.

Although Seattle's underground had achieved some level of prominence, the musicians and city often remained at odds, just as they had in the scene's earliest days when the police routinely shut down all-ages clubs. Bands still basically only had three places to play regular gigs: the Central in Pioneer Square, the tiny Squid Row on Capitol Hill, and Belltown's Vogue.

Touring Europe

For some, the best gigs remained on the road. Mudhoney had blazed a trail in Europe, a path soon followed by TAD and Nirvana. In October the two bands set off on their first European tour. British audiences—still enamored with Mudhoney—immediately warmed to their brethren. The musicians spent most of the seven-week tour crammed into a tiny van as it sped its way across the UK and continental Europe. The bands treated each other as equals. At the time, few had any inkling that Nirvana would become a musical fulcrum in two years. "[I] remember sitting around in a van in Europe," Doyle recalls, "when nobody knew who the hell they were, and nobody knew who the hell we were. And we were just having fun just being in Europe together. And I remember sitting down with those guys—we'd jokingly say to each other, 'Hey, man, when you guys make it, don't forget the little guys. Don't forget your brothers.' And, holy crap, it happened to 'em. And they didn't—they didn't forget us."

TAD and Nirvana concluded the trip with a December appearance at Sub Pop's Lame Festival in London, with Mudhoney headlining. The show took place at the iconic Astoria and became a Sub Pop showcase for the British press. TAD and Nirvana were exhausted after driving all night from Belgium and showed up less than half an hour before curtain call. They flipped a coin to see who would go on first. Nirvana won the toss and took the opening slot to get it over with.

For fans in attendance, Nirvana's performance had a dramatic impact. Everett True was one of them. He had seen Nirvana in Seattle earlier in the year and hadn't been especially impressed. "They got on stage. They were absolutely frazzled from driving overnight, really not into playing particularly," True recalls. "So, they just absolutely trashed the stage—just cleared it completely . . . no amps, nothing anywhere. From my perspective, it was just like . . . 'This band absolutely understands rock and roll. They totally get it. They totally understand about spontaneity and electricity and excitement and entertainment. Who gives a fuck what the songs are like?'"

Just before the tour, TAD recorded another EP, this time in Chicago with legendary eccentric independent producer and ex-Big Black front man Steve Albini. Locals had come to know him after Big Black closed out their career in August 1987 at Seattle's Georgetown Steam Plant. After the band's demise, Albini's stature as a producer grew immeasurably when he recorded the Pixies' influential *Surfer Rosa* the following year.

TAD's new EP, *Salt Lick*, had Albini's distinctively raw production stamp. Standouts include "Wood Goblins" (which later became a controversial video, featuring a wild-eyed,

chainsaw-rearing Doyle,* that MTV wouldn't touch) and
"Loser." Sub Pop used the latter song to brand its bands (and
to some extent an entire generation) with a T-shirt that featured the word "Loser" on the front and the Sub Pop logo on
the back. In 1990 Danielson coined the phrase "the loser is the
existential hero of the '90s."

"What could be more ironic than having a loser be a hero? I
mean, it's the ultimate antihero," says Danielson, reflecting on
that comment nearly two decades later. "I said it glibly, and I
meant it and I didn't. And I was fully conscious that it would
sound good. But, in fact I do actually believe [it] in a sense, in so
far as I believe in existentialism—which I don't. [Laughs.]"

TAD's choice of producers had an indelible impact on Nirvana.
For the band's third record (1991's *8-Way Santa*), TAD would
record with Butch Vig at his Wisconsin Smart Studios. Thus
it is no coincidence that the producers of the first three TAD
records—Endino, Vig, and Albini—also happened to engineer
the three Nirvana albums (1989's *Bleach*, 1991's *Nevermind*, and
1993's *In Utero*). "Kurt [Cobain] was always saying, 'Did you
like Albini? Was he good for it?'" Doyle recalls. "You know [we
said], 'Yeah.' So they went and did [*In Utero*] with Albini. And . . .
the same thing with Butch Vig. . . . So we were kinda like testing
the water for those guys in a lot of ways."

Records like the TAD and Nirvana albums made 1989 just
feel different than three years earlier, when the idea of two local
bands debuting with "serious" records was out of the question.
Back then, bands were making records more or less to mark
time. By 1989, however, musical output not only had some distinctive artistic vision, but also some commercial potential as

---

*According to Charles Peterson in the TAD documentary *Busted Circuits and
Ringing Ears*, he had to show Doyle how to operate the saw. The video, however,
played nicely into Sub Pop's fictional backstory of TAD as misanthropic savants.

well. In just three short years, Seattle's underground world had changed irrevocably.

The Beginning of the End

As 1989 faded into 1990, a rather unusual multifaceted dynamic began to envelop Seattle. On the one hand, bands like Mother Love Bone, Soundgarden, Screaming Trees, and the Posies began to get major-label attention. On the other, the Sub Pop bands enjoyed success in Europe and would soon have major labels sniffing them out. Within all that, organically created Seattle music began to turn away from grunge and more toward the garage sounds of bands like Gas Huffer, Tacoma's Girl Trouble, and Bellingham's Mono Men.

Furthermore, the city experienced a veritable explosion of independent labels to support the increasing variety of music. Stalwarts Sub Pop, Popllama, K (Olympia), and C/Z remained in the mix with other labels emerging, such as Green Monkey, eMpTy, Estrus (Bellingham), Nastymix (featuring local rapper Sir Mix-A-Lot), Black Label, and about ten others. Of all the local labels, Sub Pop remained the flagship for grunge, while the others showcased straight-up punk rock, garage, rap, and pop. While the variety of labels exemplified Seattle's musical vitality, an inevitable consequence occurs when the underground becomes financially viable: more expensive drugs.

In March 1990, Mother Love Bone lead singer Andrew Wood died of a heroin overdose. Wood's death, occurring shortly before the planned release of the band's first LP, *Apple*, left the surviving members under a mountain of studio debt with no lead singer to tour with.

In a larger sense, Wood's passing symbolized Seattle's changing drug culture—an inevitable result of commercial success. Sadly, the city has long been saddled with the heroin label. As with most stereotypes, some truth exists in that association.

However, that simplistic cultural view broad-brushes a city in a way that is not only inaccurate, but also taken out of context.

Heroin had long been present in Seattle, but for the most part remained the province of the few within the music community. Certain bands, notably the hardcore Refuzors and the grunge-like Crisis Party, had been tagged as junkie bands. For most people, however, the drugs of choice were beer and pot.

By the late '80s/early '90s, however, heroin had made significant inroads from places like Tacoma, Olympia, and Portland. Unlike beer and pot—or even acid—which often bring people together, heroin typically has the opposite effect. "I never got into the scag," says Scott Vanderpool (Room Nine, Chemistry Set). "[But] a lot of my friends did. It'd get to the point where I'd show up on a Friday night with a half case of beer, and people would be drifting off. Pretty soon I'd be sitting in the living room all by myself, wondering where the hell everybody went. They'd be upstairs nodding off. 'How come you guys are all so sleepy?'"

Heroin had a similar impact upon Seattle as it had upon a number of other music scenes in the US and UK. Dealers came into town after the money hit and proceeded to get their cut while demolishing the music community. Seattle, unfortunately, did not escape this pattern.

In 1990, the city found itself at a crossroads: commercial interest in some of its bands coincided with a shift out of grunge toward garage and other styles. But that year became a crossroads for another reason: Nirvana. While the grunge wave had ebbed locally, Nirvana was about to capture that essence and package it for the masses. Kurt Cobain had no intention of doing so, but he accomplished that end nonetheless.

Nirvana Detonates

In 1990 the band jettisoned drummer Chad Channing, looking for a more precise percussionist who could fit Cobain's evolving songwriting. Robert Roth, a guitar player who saw his band Storybook Krooks crumble the previous year, found himself sharing a cigarette with Cobain. At the time, Roth was a second-guitar candidate for Nirvana, to replace Jason Everman.* "Without saying it, it was sorta obvious to both of us that a new drummer was gonna be necessary," Roth recalls. "I didn't come out and say, 'Chad's not right,' and he didn't come out and say it either, but we both just started talking about what the ideal drummer would be. It's funny, 'cause for Kurt it was [Led Zeppelin's] John Bonham. And he ended up with—eventually—Dave Grohl, which kind of makes perfect sense in a way." Grohl, although lacking some of Bonham's finesse, possesses a similar power and precision.

Cobain had not yet met Grohl, so Mudhoney's Dan Peters turned out to be a temporary solution. Peters recorded a song called "Sliver" with Nirvana that Sub Pop released as a single in early September. Perhaps more than any other cut, "Sliver" encapsulated not only Nirvana's direction, but also where things were going to head within a year. Written in a matter of minutes and recorded in a similar rush job at Reciprocal, the single showcased Cobain's merging of pop sensibilities and childhood angst. His refrain of "Grandma take me home," building to an increasingly anguished crescendo, captured not only the essence of where Seattle grunge had been, but added a melodic structure that would soon be served to the masses.

Nirvana's pop direction was the inevitable result of Cobain's contemporary listening tastes, heavily influenced by Calvin Johnson's K Records and his band, Beat Happening. The Olympia "simple is better" aesthetic, coupled with a pop sensibility, appealed to his songwriting sense. Furthermore, Cobain had

---

Nirvana ended up staying a three-piece for their upcoming tour and major label debut.

the rare ability to take simple chords and weave them together to create something timeless. "We're writing a lot more pop songs like 'About a Girl.' ... some people might think of that as 'changing' into something," Cobain told the *Rocket*'s Nils Bernstein in the December 1989 issue, "but it's something we've always been aware of and are just now starting to express. The stuff we're listening to now are I guess what are called 'cutie bands' in England—Beat Happening, Pixies, Shonen Knife, Young Marble Giants—right now my favorite band is the Vaselines."

The release of "Sliver" whetted fans' appetite for the band's upcoming LP on a label yet to be determined. The local buzz surrounding Nirvana would continue to escalate exponentially following the August 1989 CoCA show. In fact, Nirvana's ascendance would unintentionally pollute Seattle's cultural waters. If they had not happened, Seattle would have inevitably moved beyond grunge by 1990, and likely garage would have predominated. But Nirvana did happen.

On Saturday, September 22, 1990, Nirvana headlined at the 1,500-capacity Motorsports International Garage. Literally a covered parking facility located at the foot of Capitol Hill, the venue occasionally hosted punk rock shows during this period. Nirvana were supported by the Melvins (who had been in San Francisco for three years), the Derelicts, and the Dwarves.

This event became another significant signpost in Seattle's musical progression, in essence receiving the torch from the Moore Theater and CoCA shows. Motorsports Garage was a moment, and most everyone got it at the time: something big, exciting, and scary was about to envelop Seattle. It was almost as if Nirvana threw a party to celebrate (or perhaps mourn) the passing of Seattle's music scene into a new stratosphere.

Anticipation grew as the venue quickly filled beyond capacity. Inside, the Garage turned especially raucous when Nirvana took the stage, ready to show off their new pop direction with songs like "In Bloom" and "Breed," both of which would show up on *Nevermind* the next year. The band, featuring Dan Peters on drums, had no initial lack of self-confidence that night—unlike the CoCA show.

The atmosphere that night was beyond electric. Fans near the band slammed into each other, while others took turns diving into the crowd. The Posies' Mike Musburger and Ken Stringfellow stood near the edge of the pit, close enough to the band to see what was going on, but not too close so as to get sucked into the mayhem. The amused pair watched as diver after diver launched themselves into the crowd's waiting arms. One especially manic fan got on stage fairly close to Cobain and decided to take a running start before heaving himself into the crowd, effectively morphing into a projectile. As he cleared a wave of fans, Musburger and Stringfellow looked up and spotted the human missile heading right toward them. "And the crowd parted," Musburger recalls. "And he landed—literally—face-first on the pavement, and slid to a stop right at our feet. And blood splattered on our shoes."

Posies manager Terry Morgan was also there that night. Nirvana at Motorsports Garage harkened Morgan back to the Showbox nearly a decade earlier, when frenzied PiL front man John Lydon had pushed the crowd to the edge of insanity all the while maintaining his finger on the control button. "[Nirvana] just played and played and played," says Morgan. "Kurt smashed everything. Total chaos. But—again—[he was] totally in control. It was one of those shows where you went home and [said], 'Wow. [I] survived that!'"

Motorsports Garage symbolized the demise of Seattle's music scene as an organic entity and the beginning of its commercialization. In essence, the show was like wishing the Beatles off at their final Cavern gig. Whatever might have naturally happened to Seattle music would soon become overwhelmed by the

Nirvana phenomenon. Almost a year to the date after the show, Nirvana released *Nevermind*. That record would signal to the nation that Seattle had this thing called grunge, a nation that was still listening to Fine Young Cannibals, Michael Jackson, and Poison. In an ironic twist worthy of Seattle, most music fans discovered grunge two to three years after the locals had already moved on.

Addendum: The Legendary Fastbacks

Twenty-three years. That's how long Seattle's Fastbacks remained a going concern—remarkable for a band of any ilk, but especially so for an underground punk act. From 1979 through 2002, the Fastbacks created amazing art. The band made music that lacked pretension, writing songs that became classics. In short, the Fastbacks were Seattle's Ramones.

In fact, the Fastbacks were more punk than even the Ramones. Purists award the Ramones iconic status, even though the world's original punk band made no bones about attaining riches. The Fastbacks, on the other hand, had no plan for commercial success.

The Fastbacks were not technicians. They weren't tight. Their singers weren't always on key. Despite all that, the band captured the basic ingredients of great punk rock: energy, passion, and most of all, fun.

Like the Seattle music scene itself, however, the Fastbacks were more than meets the eye. The band did have serious musicianship, especially at its center: guitarist, producer, and songwriter Kurt Bloch. The songs weren't so simple, either. Just ask the multitude of talented drummers who attempted to master them.

Instead of focusing on monetary gain, the Fastbacks simply wrote songs, performed them, and toured. Beyond that was anyone's guess. During their existence, they released eleven albums, including three live recordings.

The band's life stretched over several Seattle eras, beginning during the Showbox's heyday, when they contributed a track to the first *Seattle Syndrome* compilation; putting out records on Popllama and Sub Pop during the grunge era; and opening for Pearl Jam in 1995 and 1996. During all that time, the Fastbacks remained highly respected within Seattle's confines, but never latched on to any particular musical clique. Nonetheless, they were friends with everyone.

Bloch started the band back in 1979. Before then, he played with his brother Al in an early punk band called the Cheaters. The Cheaters had run its course, and Bloch found himself playing drums in his parents' basement without a band. He asked two friends, Kim Warnick and Lulu Gargiulo, to form a band with him. The trio had all graduated from Nathan Hale High School, located about five miles north of Roosevelt High. Warnick played bass in a band called the Radios and would stick with that instrument in the new band. Gargiulo, who had never been in a band, was still learning how to play guitar. Bloch would play percussion. The singer was Lulu's cousin Shannon Wood. The four-piece would call themselves the Fastbacks upon noticing a Ford Mustang with a fastback nearby.

As the chief songwriter, Bloch would lead the band's direction, which was deeply rooted in early punk rock. Bloch's taste ran from AM radio pop to prog to early-'70s hard rock fare. He found himself somewhat dissatisfied, however, constantly looking for the heaviest, hardest, most obnoxious record he could lay his hands on. "We were always looking for the hardest-rocking music," says Bloch. "Whatever record that came out that we could hear that was like more over the top and just harder, more screaming, and more guitar solos, more distortion, and more of everything."

Bloch's quest led him to bands like Judas Priest, Deep Purple, Sweet, and Montrose. As much as he liked that music, however, something was missing. Then he heard some of the early British punk rock, including the Sex Pistols, the Damned, and the Clash. "And I remember listening to the Sex Pistols," Bloch recalls, "just like thinking, 'Wow, this is the . . . hardest, [most] annoying, blasting, loud music I have ever heard! That's just unbelievable!'"

Warnick and Gargiulo shared Bloch's passions, and soon they were grabbing every import punk rock single they could find. The new band had found its muse. "The hard-rocking '70s British rock bands and stuff still sounded great," says Bloch, "but these [British punk] bands, it's like, 'Wow, this is just people yelling at you, pounding on the drums, and just screaming, and just blasting rhythm guitar. This is what we've been looking for all along!'"

Initially a cover band, the Fastbacks attempted to play Blue Oyster Cult songs, ultimately realizing their then limited ability steered them toward simpler covers: mostly the Ramones, the Damned, and even the Beatles. After rehearsing for a few months in Bloch's parents' basement, the band landed its first gig in early 1980. At the last minute, Wood got cold feet and quit. Without a singer, Gargiulo stepped up and inherited the job. Eventually, Warnick took over the majority of the vocal duties. The playing was quite primitive. "It was terrible. It was just terrible," Warnick recalls.

Shortly thereafter, Bloch moved out of his parents' house, and the three Fastbacks began hanging out in the U-District, then the center of Seattle's punk rock scene. They soon ran into a young Duff McKagan, who had played in a band called the Vains. McKagan liked the Fastbacks and suggested Bloch—a natural guitar player—move to guitar while he took over the drummer's role. Bloch agreed, and the band's sound instantly improved. McKagan thus became the Fastbacks' first real drummer, lasting all of a few months.

The Fastbacks would run through perhaps ten drummers over the next twenty-two years, including Pure Joy's Rusty Willoughby, 10 Minute Warning's Greg Gilmore, Flop's Nate

Johnson, and the Posies' Mike Musburger. The band went through so many percussionists that the "next Fastbacks drummer" became a running gag.

The Fastbacks are still looking for a drummer, and reportedly have set January 1, 1989 as their deadline.

　　　　　　　—Johnny Renton, *The Rocket*, February 1983

The band soon began to incorporate more originals within their sets. Unlike the harshness of some of their British punk influences, however, the Fastbacks displayed a poppier undercurrent. Today, critics would probably call them pop-punk. The band's pop songwriting drew from the eclectic musical environment that was the '70s. "The Jackson Five and Foghat were not that different to me," says Warnick. "It was always just a huge love of all different kinds of music. And all of us can say that. . . . As a kid, I didn't really understand the difference between the Archies and the Rolling Stones. I didn't care. They both had great songs."

The Fastbacks began to gig regularly in 1980, playing the few clubs that existed in Seattle. Unfortunately, the band's raw sound excluded it from premier gigs that groups like the Heats were getting. Even the underground community—where the Fastbacks counted many friends—had not warmed up to the band's music at that point. In the pre-U-Men early '80s, if you wanted a punk following in Seattle, your band had to either play the artsy rock that groups like Student Nurse or the Blackouts were doing, or hardcore like the Fartz or the Refuzors. "We [the Fastbacks] totally didn't fit in," Bloch recalls. "We didn't fit in with the hardcore bands of the day. . . . We weren't slick enough to play in the slick rock clubs. [We played a] hard, loud, overly loud, overly fast, distorted pop music [that] hadn't found its scene at that time, I guess."

Venturing up to Vancouver, the Fastbacks soon found a home away from home, playing alongside bands like D.O.A. Early-'80s Vancouver seemed to pigeonhole its bands less than Seattle did. Shortly thereafter, the Fastbacks found a similarly welcoming audience in San Francisco.

Around the same time, the band began to record some songs. Neil Hubbard, who was putting together *Seattle Syndrome, Vol. 1* in 1981, took notice of the Fastbacks' talents and invited the band to record for the comp. With McKagan playing drums, the Fastbacks contributed the peppy "Someone Else's Room."

Over the next few years, the Fastbacks' output continued to come from home recordings. During this period of time, the band recorded one of its standout tracks. "3 Boxes," unlike much of the other early recordings, was done on twenty-four-track and sounded fairly polished for an independent band. The song begins as a sentimental ballad and slowly builds toward a crescendo as the once sweet guitar begins to acquire an edge of nastiness. Before the listener realizes, the Fastbacks are in full-on punk rock mode with loud, disjointed chord progressions, punctuated by rolling drum fills. The craziness soon passes, and the song ends wistfully.

In 1986 when bands like Soundgarden and Green River began to rear their heads, the Fastbacks connected with Conrad Uno, who wanted to release their first full-length offering, *. . . and His Orchestra*, on his Popllama label. At the time, Popllama was best known for the Young Fresh Fellows and the Squirrels. "He's just such a great guy," says Warnick. "Then of course we knew the Young Fresh Fellows. Again, it was just all the same scene. So it made total sense."

. . . and His Orchestra, recorded at Egg Studios and two other locations on four-track and eight-track, featured some early

Fastbacks classics, notably the wonderful pop ditty "K Street." The CD reissue also offered—at least to the unsuspecting—a sort of odd cover: the Grass Roots "Midnight Confessions." The Grass Roots—a '60s pop band—seems like an unusual choice for a punk rock band to cover, but, with the Fastbacks' affinity for pop music, "Midnight Confessions" made perfect sense. Bloch and Co. recorded a stripped-down version of the Grass Roots classic.

As the Sub Pop scene heated up in the late '80s, the band found itself on temporary hiatus due to internal drug problems. During this time, Bloch joined the Young Fresh Fellows, while Popllama released another Fastbacks LP, *Very Very Powerful Motor*. The band began to reconvene just as Nirvana and grungemania broke in Seattle in 1991 and '92.

During that time, Warnick was answering phones for Sub Pop, then viewed by America as the hip grunge label. One day, she was playing a cassette of Fastbacks songs when Sub Pop co-owner Jon Poneman walked by. Upon hearing the tape, Poneman turned to her and asked what she was playing. She said it was her own band. "Who's putting it out?" Warnick recalls him asking. "[I responded], 'I don't know. Nobody puts our stuff out.'"

So Sub Pop did. The compilation, entitled *The Question Is No*, included Fastbacks songs recorded from 1980 through 1992. Notables included the aforementioned "Someone Else's Room" and "3 Boxes."

For outsiders, Sub Pop and the Fastbacks did not belong in the same sentence. Why would a grunge label show interest in a poppy punk band? The answer is simple. They were all friends. Poneman liked what he heard and wanted to support local music.

During the height of 1990s grungemania and the associated popularity of Nirvana, Pearl Jam, Soundgarden, and Alice in Chains, hordes of young kids descended on Seattle. They donned long hair and flannel shirts, determined to "make it" by becoming the next popular grunge band. The Fastbacks did not fit the mold, but there must have been a temptation to become a grunge band, right? "There's no way we could've changed anything about us," says Warnick. "We were stubborn kids that couldn't sound any other way. It would have been physically impossible."

So the Fastbacks, unlike some of their friends' bands at the time, were ignored by the major labels. Why? They weren't grunge, and the band members were already in their thirties, and thus too old to fit the corporate definition of hip. The Fastbacks realized their plight and dealt with it, except for one minor gripe. "It is very strange," says Bloch, "we never got taken out to dinner . . . by any record label except Sub Pop."

In the '90s, the band finally settled on a sort of full-time drummer. Mike Musburger split time between the Posies and Fastbacks during the first half of the decade, then dedicated most of his time to the Fastbacks in the second half. For drummers, playing Fastbacks songs live represented a serious challenge. Unlike many rock bands that play at a moderate pace showcasing midtempo songs with breaks in between, the Fastbacks provided a full-on frontal assault. There is—in the words of one drummer in a private remark—no "space." Space within a song allows a drummer to create his own fills, as well as providing a physical break from an already taxing job.

For Musburger, the transition from the Posies' tight song structures and pop hooks to the Fastbacks' style of in-your-face punk rock became the ultimate test of endurance. "It was a physical, demanding workout," says Musburger. "It really changed my technique drastically. . . . everything—how high I sit, my posture, my hands—everything is totally different. It was having to learn how to play that intensely, and that fast, for that amount of time without falling over. 'Cause I have carpel tunnel and my hands would go numb from overuse. And I had to figure out ways around that."

"I used to get cramped—my right arm that used to play a high hat—I would frequently cramp up," Nate Johnson adds, "because it was such a manic pace and I was holding the sticks so tightly. And every once in a while, I would feel my arm start to swell up—about the third song—and somehow I'd still manage to get through the whole concert. It was a real physical workout."

After *The Question Is No*, the band began regularly recording in studios and put out three records on Sub Pop: *Zucker* (1993), *Answer the Phone Dummy* (1994), and *New Mansions in Sound* (1996). In 1995 Pearl Jam—at the height of their popularity—invited the Fastbacks to open for them on a West Coast tour. The following year, the Fastbacks opened for Pearl Jam again on a twenty-seven-city tour that took them across the United States and over to Europe, including Turkey. "We've known those guys forever," says Warnick. "Eddie [Vedder] really liked us. I just couldn't believe that they took us as the sole support. . . . It was magical. Every night was magical."

The Pearl Jam tour did not translate into record sales or major popularity for the Fastbacks, however. Nonetheless, the stadium tour represented a highlight of the Fastbacks experience. "I spent most of the time just looking around at those giant stadiums," Warnick recalls, "and just remembering as a kid going to see Elton John when I was like thirteen. Now I know what he saw. . . . To be actually up there, and have the lights be dimmed, and hear that *wooshhhh* sound of the crowd be excited for the show to start. And to be led up on stage by a flashlight in the dark. It's like, 'I'm now living the dream.' . . . A lot of people [say], 'I just like playing the small, intimate places.' I don't. I hate that. I want to play the giantest place every night."

For the most part, the Fastbacks' version of high-energy punk rock—replete with Kurt Bloch manically jumping around on stage—was received rather well by Pearl Jam's audience. "For a band like the Fastbacks," says Musburger, "that's like a dream come true. You get to play stadiums, and gigantic basketball arenas every night to a whole lot of people. Granted, you're in front of like people's favorite band *ever*."

The band only experienced serious resistance in London and Rome. In Rome, the audience reacted by tossing unusual objects on stage. "They threw things like glasses and clothes," Musburger recalls. "I think a sandwich dinged off my head. But I think Kim actually ended up walking off stage with a really nice jacket. She's like, 'This is great. People can throw stuff at us anytime they want.' I think Lulu even like picked up a pair of prescription glasses and really liked the frames. . . . It's like stage shopping."

The Fastbacks continued to record and tour, releasing a live album in 1996 and a recording, *The Day That Didn't Exist*, in 1999. In 2002 Warnick left the band rather abruptly. She had reached her own end point. Warnick's sudden departure was like being out to dinner with friends; after dinner, dessert, and coffee, she became the first one to wipe her mouth with her napkin, ask for the check, and get up. "You know, it's kind of funny," says Warnick. "That Pearl Jam tour, in a way was almost my undoing because I didn't want to come back from that world. I just didn't want to play clubs anymore."

Two years later, Warnick quit music altogether and hung up her bass. Bloch released the band's final, posthumous musical statement that year: *Truth, Corrosion and Sour Biscuits*. Following that, he ventured onward, forming Thee Sergeant Major III with Musburger and the Young Fresh Fellows' Jim Sangster. Bloch's new band plays the occasional Fastbacks song, with Warnick sometimes popping up in the audience.

The Fastbacks legacy reaches beyond cultlike status. The band's impact can be felt by anyone who has ever wanted to start

a band, make records, and tour. The Fastbacks proved that talent, passion, and sheer will can overcome adversity to make your
own imprint on the world. They never became famous, and perhaps that's better. Fame would have resulted in the inevitable
escalating ego clashes. In fact, fame would have clearly brought
down a band that outlasted its peers. "There [were] no expectations on us," says Warnick. "We weren't being told to go back
and write the single. We weren't on the treadmill of like, 'Go on
tour and starve.' You know, 'Play at fucking shitty sports bars
all across the country and then come home and make the next
record so we can tell you again: write the next single.' We didn't
have to do that. We all saw friends of ours become disillusioned
in that whole world. . . . Both Lulu and I loved Kurt's songs so
much. It was always so much fun to learn a new song. [We were
all] friends from a long time ago."

CHAPTER 8

After the Gold Rush

*It turned from being a music scene into a cluster fuck if
you ask me.*

—Blake Wright, owner, eMpTy Records

*Green River reunion, 2008. From left: Jeff Ament (Pearl Jam);
Mark Arm (Mudhoney); Alex Shumway; Stone Gossard (PJ);
Steve Turner (Mudhoney). Not shown: Bruce Fairweather
(Love Battery).* (Photo by Stephen Tow)

Nirvana did not come out of nowhere. Similar to the way Sub Pop capitalized on the mythology surrounding TAD, the national media latched on to the notion of Kurt Cobain and his bandmates as backwoods savants from Aberdeen, Washington. Cobain himself played up the idea of Nirvana as "the chosen rejects." The facts reveal quite a different story, however.

By the dawn of 1991, the band had generated enough of a buzz to have its pick of major labels. Eventually, Nirvana chose DGC Records, a Geffen subsidiary, mostly because it had Sonic Youth.

Following the Motorsports Garage gig, the band found its final drummer, Dave Grohl of the DC hardcore band Scream. Scream imploded in Hollywood, and Grohl got in touch with Nirvana through their old friend Buzz Osborne of the Melvins. Cobain had seen Scream before that in San Francisco, and Grohl's power and precision had immediately impressed him. "I'm standing with Kurt [at the San Francisco show]," recalled the late Ben McMillan, of Skin Yard and Gruntruck. "And I'm standing there with fuckin' Buzz, right? And here comes on fuckin' Scream. . . . And Kurt is like, 'Fuckin' get him!'"

On September 24, almost one year to the date after the Motorsports Garage show, Nirvana released their major-label debut, *Nevermind*. DGC initially pressed fifty thousand copies, which would have been a strong number for any obscure band's debut. No one was prepared—not the record company, not the band, not the band's management, or anyone else—for *Nevermind* to sell twenty times that figure in the United States alone. Cobain's negative reaction to the record's mammoth sales not only reflected an artist's uncomfortable relationship with commercial success, but also Seattle's misgivings about it. As the band toured Europe that fall, it got the unexpected news that, with the release of the anthemic "Smells Like Teen Spirit," *Nevermind* was climbing the charts at an increasingly rapid pace. "When we were in Amsterdam [in November]," said McMillan, whose band Skin Yard opened for Nirvana, "and [*Nevermind*] hit five hundred thousand, right? I said, 'Kurt, your fuckin' album's doing great. You know, you're gonna make money.' He's like, 'I don't wanna fuckin' talk about it.'"

Back in Seattle, *Rocket* staffers got advance copies of the record, and it literally blew their minds. "After a while, we just listened to *Nevermind* over and over," recalls Art Chantry. "We went, 'Damn! That's a good record. Who's that again? Little Kurt's band?'"

By January 1992, *Nevermind* had reached number one on the Billboard album chart, toppling Michael Jackson's *Dangerous* from the top spot. The album, with its now ubiquitous cover of a naked baby pursuing a dollar underwater, had its songs constantly playing on commercial radio and its videos in regular MTV rotation. Nirvana's unexpected ascent literally turned the page on rock history overnight. In an instant, Jackson and hair metal were out, and all things loud, angry, and flannel were in. Nirvana had changed the world, with all kinds of expected and unexpected consequences.

---

*4 months in rotation? This little brat probably has armpit hair by now!**

—Anonymous KCMU comment about *Nevermind* and its cover

---

*Used with permission from KEXP, formerly known as KCMU.

Nationally, Nirvana appealed to a disaffected Generation X who found modern music out of touch with their everyday angst. Furthermore, Nirvanamania created a river that caught Seattle in its all-powerful current. Pearl Jam, whose first record, *Ten*, had preceded the release of *Nevermind*, caught fire in Nirvana's wake. The national media co-opted grunge and applied it to both bands, as well as compatriots Soundgarden and Alice in Chains. Nirvanamania had morphed into grungemania and Seattlemania. For young people caught up in it, grunge meant flannel and long hair accompanied by loud, distorted guitars. The national media effectively altered the definition of grunge.

In reality, grunge was more an approach to playing than an actual style of music. Distorted guitars certainly were a prerequisite, but the grunge aesthetic meant passion and fire more than it did hard rock and long hair. Mudhoney's "Touch Me I'm Sick" equated to the real grunge. Sub Pop successfully marketed Mudhoney to Europe and the American underground, but they would never become a made-for-the-masses kind of band. Their music had few catchy hooks, lead singer Mark Arm wasn't melodic enough, and, quite frankly, he wasn't cute enough. All of the big-four Seattle bands presented themselves nicely because they all possessed, in varying degrees, songs with melodic hooks. Furthermore, all of the singers—Nirvana's Cobain, Pearl Jam's Eddie Vedder, Soundgarden's Chris Cornell, and Alice in Chains' Layne Staley—were good-looking dudes. Hooks and looks. An easy sell to the masses.

Of the four, Nirvana allied most closely to the grunge aesthetic. Even though *Nevermind* presented a cleaned-up and accessible version of the genre, Nirvana still tapped into the spirit of grunge. By the time Soundgarden went major label in 1989, it had evolved into a mainstream metal band. Its third LP, *Badmotorfinger*, released contemporaneously with *Nevermind*, showcased a more sophisticated Soundgarden as the band's rhythmic dynamics, propelled by drummer Matt Cameron, veered toward prog-metal territory.

Alice in Chains had little to do with underground Seattle. The Eastside band first played in town as "Alice 'N' Chains" back in 1987. At the time they presented themselves as a glam-metal act. Following Nirvana's success, however, Alice in Chains made a conscious decision to move from hair metal toward a darker arena. This transformation becomes evident upon comparing their 1990 major-label debut *Facelift* with 1992's *Dirt*. Any resemblance to hair metal fades by the 1992 effort, and the band fits neatly into the accepted Seattle canon. In reality, as good as AIC was, they had little connection to the punk community that generated what became known as grunge. They were, quite simply, a suburban metal band made to sound more grungelike. "This label rep is bringing in their new signee—Alice in Chains—and these dudes are all looking exactly like Soundgarden," says longtime scenester Scott Vanderpool, then a DJ with Walla Walla's KXRX, "with the combat boots and the little cutoff pants. I was kind of like, 'What the fuck is this all about?'"

Nirvana enjoyed the scene's wholehearted support, since they were lauded as a local band who made good. Cobain's lack of pretense and abhorrence of major rock stardom endeared him to the locals despite his band's enormous success. Soundgarden's "selling out" had been quite subtle, and the band had generated so much hype just being themselves, that they could afford to take their time before jumping to a major. In addition, Soundgarden's climb to the top came in stages. *Badmotorfinger*, although a terrific record, was quickly overshadowed by *Nevermind*. The band didn't actually achieve rock star popularity until 1994's *Superunknown*. Therefore, Soundgarden, for the most part, were also given a free pass by the locals. Alice in Chains were never part of the scene to begin with, so few cared how popular they became.

And then there was Pearl Jam. For most folks outside Seattle, grunge conjures simultaneous images of Nirvana and Pearl Jam, neither having more or less legitimacy than the other. Not so within Seattle. Pearl Jam quickly became the band to hate, and that distaste became palpable.

Local animosity toward Pearl Jam harkened back to Green River's 1987 split and the band's successors, Mudhoney and Mother Love Bone. Mudhoney made a deliberate effort not to become rock stars. The band didn't play hooks, the singer (Arm) screamed and wailed as he saw fit, and the guitar player (Steve Turner) subscribed to the punk rock ethic of eschewing solos. Even after Seattle exploded, Mudhoney refused to change their sound to appeal to the growing market. On the other hand, Mother Love Bone became in a sense an all-star Seattle band bent on commercial success. It folded after singer Andrew Wood's March 1990 death, leaving the band with an enormous debt for studio time.

In November and December 1990, members of MLB and Soundgarden recorded a tribute record to Wood called *Temple of the Dog*. The players came in contact with a Californian named Eddie Vedder, who guest-sang on "Hunger Strike," and Pearl Jam was born. Vedder became the front man, hooking up with ex-MLB/Green River guitarist and bassist Stone Gossard and Jeff Ament, respectively. The three-piece added lead guitarist Mike McCready, who hailed from the Eastside metal band Shadow, and drummer Dave Krusen. The new band had a much harder edge than MLB, drawing from McCready's metal background as well as matching Gossard and Ament's tastes. In short, Pearl Jam was an arena-ready hard rock band. "Even just the band names and all that: Mother Love Bone, *Temple of the Dog*, Pearl Jam," comments photographer Charles Peterson, "versus like Mudhoney.... It was more like, 'Oh, they wanna be a serious rock band.'"

Pearl Jam's massive success, not to mention *Ten*'s accumulation of classic '70s-style rock riffs and solos, put the band within the crosshairs. "The backlash was just a lot of people being upset that a band would so explicitly go for a stadium rock model," says Jack Endino. "Because frankly, the first—I personally really don't like the first Pearl Jam record. I still don't like it. I never liked it. And a lot of people didn't like it, even though millions of people bought it. It really sounds like a Bad Company album, in a lot of ways. And partly that, I'm afraid, is due to the production. It's a strange record. It's got too much reverb, and just as a producer I'm offended by it. I think the second and third Pearl Jam records are infinitely better records production-wise and I actually like them. But the first record really—it just sounds like a massively overproduced, really ponderous, bloated arena rock album. That was how it sounded to us in 1992 or 1991. It certainly didn't sound like it had anything to do with anything coming from Seattle."

Yet the Seattle folks didn't get something.

In 1992 most American music fans had little awareness of the underground. This generation had been raised on MTV, Michael Jackson, and Madonna. By the early '90s, however, the glittery videos of the previous decade seemed out of place. The aftermath of the Gulf War had left a group of kids—many of whom were the products of divorce—bored and disillusioned. Thus the angst-fueled passion generated by Pearl Jam's music didn't seem all that different from Nirvana to them. For most outsiders, Pearl Jam sounded refreshing. They had little inclination to delineate real alternative rock from the mainstream; the record just sounded good.

At the time, though, Cobain shouted vitriol at Pearl Jam, accusing them of selling out. The media, of course, played that up into a rivalry. "Like the whole thing between Nirvana and them—that was a strange misunderstanding," says Endino. "I wish they had had a chance to work it out. 'Cause Eddie [Vedder] really is a nice guy, you know? I mean, they're all nice guys. . . . They're just lovely people, the Pearl Jam guys."

Seattle's anti–Pearl Jam stance didn't last. After the band's initial success, it explored many avenues musically. Furthermore, the members' commitment to charitable work, combined with their lack of airs, eventually endeared them to their Seattle brethren.

Back in 1998, longtime punk rocker and ex–Thrown Ups bassist Leighton Beezer planned a trip to Hawaii. After he heard Mudhoney would be opening for Pearl Jam during his stay, he called up his friend Mark Arm and asked if he could hang out. Arm said yes, and Beezer ended up partying with both bands the day before the show. "The next night," says Beezer, "we went to the show. And Neil Young was backstage, and a bunch of other celebrities. And I got to sit backstage and look at the audience from Pearl Jam's perspective. I have never seen more beautiful twenty-year-old cheerleaders pulling their shirts off in my life. And the guys in Pearl Jam, who[m] I had ridiculed for taking the path they chose ten years before that, could not have been more gracious. They welcomed me. They introduced me to people. Made sure I was having a good time. Suddenly, the lightbulb went off. And it's like, if I could go back, I would just go right ahead and sell out my principles. Because, you know, they were right. You know that's a hard thing to say."

Selling out your principles is a rather nebulous concept and reveals itself on different levels. The minute a band charges admission to a show or desires money for a record, the selling-out process has begun. Yet if your music becomes popular, is that so distasteful? Clearly, the guys in Pearl Jam wanted to make the music they were playing. They also desired popularity, but they didn't change their MO to achieve that popularity. Pearl Jam did play the business game, hiring agents, attorneys, managers, etc. But so did Nirvana and Soundgarden. Those bands were just more subtle about it. "I mean, that's a common arrow to sling, that someone [sold] out," says Mother Love Bone drummer Greg Gilmore. "But what the hell does that mean? In its most negative connotation, sell-out means you're prostituting yourself—what?—for money? Is that it? You'll do anything for money. Well, I wouldn't say those guys have done that. I mean . . . they've done what they wanted to do, which was make a certain kind of band and make it popular. And it's a certain kind of band that they are into. . . . I think a lot of us find a lot in that to envy. I certainly have a lot of respect for 'em over it."

Pearl Jam has thoroughly endeared themselves to the community, inviting their friends Mudhoney and the Fastbacks to tour with them and playing regular gigs with less famous locals they have known for years. In 2008 Gossard and Ament joined members of Mudhoney and Mother Love Bone to reunite as Green River, coinciding with Sub Pop's twentieth anniversary celebration. And Ament has re-formed Deranged Diction, his pre–Green River hardcore band. "[The] connection to the past is something that I'm interested in exploring—I know Jeff is," says Gossard. "And revisiting old relationships and looking at your artistic choices at one period of time, and then being able to go back and sort of revisit those, and reassess sort of how you were thinking. And it's really a cool experience. So, it's [an] honor to be able to play music with them. For the band that was so influential [Green River], and you look at Mudhoney and where they went, and Jeff and I where we went with Mother Love Bone and with Pearl Jam. And it just shows you how wide of a variety musical experience can be, even [among] people that start out in a band together. All of us have so much potential to do different sorts of collaborations."

Further, Pearl Jam has made it a regular effort not only to do charity work, but to focus on giving back to the local community. "All those guys are just the best," says the Fastbacks' Kim

Warnick. "And they're kinda like the best ambassadors this city's had for a rock band. Just the things they do for this city. . . . It's pretty phenomenal. . . . They turned out to be the most punk rock band ever."

The Unmaking of Alternative Rock

Two rather unfortunate consequences resulted when the national media combined Pearl Jam, Nirvana, Soundgarden, and Alice in Chains into one grunge lump. First, the definition of grunge became forever changed. Grunge became equated with anything heavy coming from Seattle, as opposed to the actual organic version created in the '80s. Second, and perhaps even more regrettable, the very definition of alternative rock irrevocably changed. Prior to Seattle's explosion, alternative rock meant simply that: rock bands whose songs did not receive play on commercial radio and whose videos did not show up on MTV. After Seattle, alternative rock became a commodity. Anyone who sounded like Nirvana became the new alternative rock.

After the early-'90s grunge explosion, the major labels fed us Nirvana clone after Nirvana clone; Nickelback and Puddle of Mudd come to mind. The formula: take an attractive, but sort of rough-looking lead singer—preferably blonde—with a grumbly but melodic voice and have him scream on key. Add ear-piercing, distorted guitars to a tuneful melody, and voilà, you have the next alternative rock band.

Meanwhile, back in Seattle, the grunge explosion was greeted at first with bemusement, and then with disgust. As Nirvana and Pearl Jam's initial success enveloped the city, waves of media—from MTV to the *New York Times, Spin,* and even *People* magazine—came to town, attempting to grab their angle on the Seattle sound. "Just to see that sort of culture explosion happen around you was fascinating," recalls author Gillian Gaar, then with the *Rocket.* "I mean, I used to talk with Art

Chantry a lot about that kind of thing, and other cities' scenes and that sort of thing—and never thinking that it would happen here. So when it did, it was amazing. And it just seemed to go into this other realm. Where people were saying, 'Oh, it was like when Athens [Georgia] got famous or Minneapolis got famous.' But, in those instances, it was pretty much limited to the music. And with Seattle, it was just sort of everything— it was, you know, your whole lifestyle and the flannel shirts, the grungewear. And they had the high-fashion grungewear, which was really funny . . . and embarrassing."

As waves and waves of TV crews, music media, and A&R people infiltrated the town, the locals' bewilderment continued. The media horde would hit any place they could dig up a potential rock star to interview. Typical targets included Sub Pop, C/Z Records, and the *Rocket*. "One day we had—like some Italian fashion magazine," recalls Art Chantry, then the *Rocket*'s art director. "We had some Japanese TV crew come through. We had the *Christian Science Monitor* come through, and the *New York Times* and some other magazine came through. [They] came in with their cameras, barked at the front desk . . . anybody that was wearing flannel and jeans all the sudden got nailed as a rock star. And they wanted to take the pictures and interview them. You know, I got interviewed. It was by somebody who spoke Italian and I didn't speak any Italian. They didn't speak any English. It was ridiculous. We thought it was hilarious. You know, we'd sit there and [say], 'Yeah, yeah, yeah, I'm Nirvana.'"

"Writers would come in from all over the world—all over the world—and wanna do an interview," adds Kim Warnick, then working at Sub Pop. "And like [Jon Poneman would say], 'Well, there's one right there [pointing toward Warnick]. You can talk to her. She's in a band.'"

In 1992 Seattle became a star in *Singles*, a film about young people trying to find love in the '90s. The mostly lighthearted romantic comedy starred Bridget Fonda, Matt Dillon, and Kyra Sedgwick, and showcased performances by Soundgarden and Alice in Chains. In addition, Pearl Jam's Gossard, Ament, and Vedder joined with Dillon in a fictional band called Citizen Dick. The band had a hit song called "Touch Me I'm Dick," a play on the Mudhoney classic "Touch Me I'm Sick."

Singles did create an unfortunate consequence. The film reinforced, or perhaps helped create, the Seattle grunge stereotype. Dillon and his Citizen Dick mates ambled around town with the requisite long locks, scruffy facial hair, and flannel shirts. In effect, *Singles* did more to codify the grunge look than any other event.

Tacoma's Girl Trouble witnessed the phenomenon from the front row—or in this case, the front door. By 1992 the band had been playing regular gigs at the Off Ramp, a club that opened in the summer of 1990 about a block from the Motorsports Garage. Girl Trouble was well entrenched within the Seattle music community and knew almost everyone in it. "One of our friends told us about how this *Singles* movie had come out," GT drummer Bon Von Wheelie states in an e-mail, "and suddenly everybody was wearing the uniform of jeans and flannel shirts. . . . We thought whoever told us this story was crazy. So to prove they were just making it up, we sat at the table by the door [of the Off Ramp] and watched people come in. What a laugh riot! There was this sea of young guys sporting the same grunge uniform. It was unbelievable. And we'd never seen these people before. It wasn't like it was anybody we knew. . . . It was just a long line of flannel. I'll never forget it."

As the hysteria escalated, Seattle's initial bewilderment began to turn to disgust. As word spread that major labels were signing every local band that moved, hordes of young musicians descended on the city, looking to become the next Nirvana or Pearl Jam. The notion of making music for its own sake had evaporated. In its place was a scene entirely based upon fame and riches. "This [was] a scene, all right," comments TAD's Kurt Danielson, "but [it was] a totally artificial one, and synthetic. The real actual scene was more of a state of mind that occurred a few years before. And this was a crystallization of that, but in a crass, commercial, calculated way."

Furthermore, because of the popularity of the major-label version of grunge, local clubs began to focus their lineups on bands that fit the mold. People who had been veering into other musical directions through the normal organic process soon found themselves on the outside of things—in their own town. "If you didn't fit the mold of what was grunge—let's say from the years '90 through about '95 or '96—if you didn't fall in the Seattle sound mold," says producer and studio owner Chris Hanzsek, "you were pissed off, because no one knew what to make of you. They used to put stickers on just about everybody's album that said, 'This is from Seattle.' And distributors would do that, and labels would do that, just so they could attract the buyer to the idea that, you know, 'Hey, here's another one of those Seattle sounds.' And there were bands that didn't fit that at all. And so, they were confused. They felt like they were being pressured to make their guitar all distorted, and get someone to scream a little bit less intelligibly than they were."

As nongrunge bands like the Walkabouts (and again, most of the locals weren't playing grunge after 1990) toured America, they began to notice the expectations of what a Seattle band should sound like. "I remember, like, [a] pretty full club, which was pretty exciting . . . but suddenly you see the guys with the backwards baseball caps," recalls the Walkabouts' Chris Eckman, "and the flannel shirts in the front with their arms crossed. And, you know, we start some song—some traditional folk song or something. And, you know, three or four songs later they're no longer there. And, possibly, there's about thirty other people that have left also."

Even bands that played from a genuine grunge approach found themselves in a weird place—unless, of course, they possessed hooks and looks. TAD became symbolic of not only what happened to Seattle, but what can happen when major labels invade any town looking for the next big thing.

Unlike independent record labels, which typically look to support local art, the majors view their bands entirely as product. And also unlike the indies, the majors are almost always behind the cultural curve. The big labels find out about the next cultural event at around the same time as most of us, and—like the kids coming to Seattle in flannel—they ride into a city hoping to capitalize on what's hot. They send out their A&R reps like armies of ants, hoping to sign up the next big thing. These A&R people typically have little understanding of what actually exists musically within the scene. They want product. They want another Nirvana. They want hooks and looks.

Like some of the other local bands, TAD was approached by a major—in this case, Giant. As is typical of A&R people, the band was promised the moon: a big advance, touring support, etc. In 1993 TAD began concentrating on *Inhaler*, their major-label debut. Controversy began almost immediately, initially over an album poster featuring President Bill Clinton holding a joint with the accompanying caption: "It's heavy shit."

Problems can run deeper, though, with a band like TAD on a major label. While the A&R rep promised the band it could keep its artistic integrity, the label demanded songs with pop structures. TAD didn't deliver that product. "And I remember, our manager at the time had just got off the phone with the A&R person," recalls lead singer/guitarist Tad Doyle. "And he said, 'Well, the label's saying they're not hearing a single.' And we all looked at each other and started bustin' out laughing [and we said], 'Well, that's because there isn't a single. What the fuck do you want? Are you insane? I mean, you got a band on your label [whose] first record is called *God's Balls*. You know? We toned [the title] down with *Inhaler*, but that's about as far as it goes.'"

The label soon dropped TAD while they were on tour in Europe supporting Soundgarden. All their funding instantly evaporated. They had a similar experience with another major. Bands typically don't realize A&R reps, who often bounce around the industry, are their only contact with the label. So when an A&R person quits or gets fired, the band becomes a nonentity. After the second major dropped TAD, their manager attempted to call the record company without success, finding employees there had not even heard of the band. Other Seattle bands had similar experiences with the majors.

In addition, the hard drugs that had arrived in Seattle by the late '80s had escalated. More people began to die, some of them famous. Cobain committed suicide after injecting himself with heroin in 1994. Eight years later, broken junkie Layne Staley of Alice in Chains was found dead in his apartment. "Being that close to the hub of a culture explosion wheel—I've never seen anything like it," says Chantry. "I don't ever want to see it again. It was, at first, exhilarating, hilarious. Then it became frightening, and then it became deadly."

Girl Trouble, then at the forefront of the local garage movement, had a rather close perspective on Seattle's angst. The band remained fiercely independent, refusing to sign to a major even when many of their friends did. "We concentrated on trying to ignore the whole thing and just play shows," Von Wheelie comments in an e-mail. "We felt lucky to play Seattle and then be able to just go home. And actually when grunge imploded, it was fortunate for us to not be around it. Everybody seemed to be either way too drugged up (the heroin thing was really bad), or bickering, or worrying about record contracts, etc., and we just stayed in Tacoma and heard the rumors. It was better to be out of town. I like to say that when the grunge was over, it imploded. It really did seem to fall in on itself. Everybody got too full of themselves, too worried about contracts or dealing with big companies, doing bad drugs and not getting along. It was very depressing there for awhile. It was stressful for bands. We've always said that dealing with what those bands did would have cracked us like an egg. In hindsight, we were lucky to avoid it."

By the late '90s, the smoke began to clear, and Seattle effectively moved beyond the grunge hype and the resultant national backlash against it. Even Sub Pop had long shed its original branding to sign artists (the Shins, Sunny Day Real Estate, No Age, etc.) with little connection musically to the Mudhoneys of the world. Meanwhile, Seattle expanded economically by leaps and bounds, powered by software behemoths Microsoft and Adobe and coffee giant Starbucks. As the twenty-first century dawned, the city had grown up.

Today, Seattle has become a proper big city, with little resemblance to what it had been during the germination and growth of its underground music scene in the '70s and '80s. Downtown is gleaming, upscale, and beautiful. Lake Union is crowded with pricey watercraft. Similarly, Capitol Hill, Belltown, and Ballard have become upscale enclaves with tony boutique restaurants and shops and yuppie-friendly expensive condominiums. In addition, unlike during the music scene's late-'80s heyday—during which bands might get gigs at three or so clubs—Seattle today has many places for bands to play original music.

The Walkabouts' Chris Eckman has seen Seattle emerge, explode, implode, and flourish throughout his career. His band began during the doldrums of 1984, lasted through the grunge era and beyond, and continues to record. He now resides in Slovenia, where he performs, tours, and produces. During his long career, Eckman has seen the world. As he has played his many gigs over the years, he has heard complaints from people about how their town is so boring and has no music scene or cultural community to speak of. "In Athens, Greece, in Barcelona, and in Scotland and Boston . . . I've said it so many times," says Eckman, "'Well, if you think your hometown is bleak, let me tell you a story.'"

LITTLE-KNOWN SEATTLE RECORDS YOU SHOULD LISTEN TO

Individual Artists

1. The Blackouts, *History in Reverse* (K, 2004)

Wonderful retrospective from a truly great Seattle band.

2. The U-Men, *Solid Action* (Chuckie-Boy, 1999)

The entire magic that was the U-Men is difficult to capture on record. That being said, one listen and you'll at least have an inkling about the band's wonderfully managed mayhem. Brace for the opening tracks "Gila" and "Shoot 'em Down," and hear for yourself the unabashed creativity and insanity that was the U-Men.

3. Mr. Epp and the Calculations, *Ridiculing the Apocalypse* (Super Electro Sound Recordings, 1996)

What's better than a Mr. Epp compilation? The record opens with DJ Stephen Rabow's famous "world's worst rock-and-roll band" commentary.

4. The Young Fresh Fellows, *Fabulous Sounds of the Pacific Northwest/Topsy Turvy double-CD set* (Popllama, 1988)

As Conrad Uno commented, "What's not to like?"

5. Jim Basnight, *We Rocked & Rolled: 25 Years of Jim Basnight & The Moberlys* (Disclosed, 2008)

Basnight's catchy, melodic songwriting ability is well captured on this retrospective. Standouts include "Rest Up," "Sexteen," "Live in the Sun," and "Blow Your Life Away."

6. The Fastbacks, *The Question Is No* (Sub Pop, 1992)

It's hard to pick just one Fastbacks record. *The Question Is No* is a wonderful early Fastbacks sampler, spanning recordings from 1981 through 1992.

7. The Walkabouts, *Cataract/Rag & Bone* (Glitterhouse, 1989)

Just a fabulous, well-recorded folk meets punk meets . . . from the Walkabouts.

8. The Squirrels, *Scrapin' for Hits* (Popllama, 1996)

While it's tempting to include *The Not-So-Bright Side of the Moon*, this "greatest hits" sampler provides a nice introduction to this singular band.

9. Green River, *Come on Down* (Homestead, 1985)

This record, issued prior to *Deep Six*, perhaps represents grunge's opening document.

10. The Posies, *Failure* (Popllama, 1989)

Failure, like the Green Pajamas' *Summer of Lust*, represents a wonderful effort that can come only from young musicians unfettered by the vagaries of the world.

11. Screaming Trees, *Anthology: SST Years 1985–1989* (SST, 1991)

The Trees' SST efforts come well represented on this compilation from the band's first EP and the three SST LPs that followed it.

12. Red Dress, *The Collection* (Popllama, 1994)

This is not a rock record in any shape or form, but the two-disk collection contains a studio and live recording of Conrad Uno's favorite band. He describes them as "Captain Beefheart meets James Brown."

13. Upchuck, *Gone But Not Forgiven* (dadastic!, 2009)

A well-recorded collection of Bowie-esque glam rock from a Seattle legend.

14. Skin Yard, *Hallowed Ground* (Toxic Shock, 1988)

Take dissonant chords, distorted hooks, a powerful drummer, and a singer who could sing like Ozzy Osbourne, and you get *Hallowed Ground*.

15. Jack Endino, *Angle of Attack* (Bobok, 1992)

While Endino's 2005 *Permanent Fatal Error* delves into more of a Skin Yard prog-meets-punk aesthetic, *Angle of Attack* is far more experimental and thus more exciting.

16. Coffin Break, *Rupture/Psychosis* (C/Z, 1990)

These two records showcase Coffin Break as their irreverent selves.

17. Gas Huffer, *Janitors of Tomorrow* (eMpTy, 1991)

For those who think Seattle was all about Soundgarden and Alice in Chains, put this record on and prepare for the requisite *huh?*

18. Mudhoney, *Every Good Boy Deserves Fudge* (Sub Pop, 1991)

While *Superfuzz Bigmuff* defines early Mudhoney, *Fudge* is the consistently superior record.

19. Love Battery, *Dayglo* (Sub Pop, 1992)

It's hard to pick just one Love Battery record, since most of them are excellent, but I have a soft spot for this one, recorded at Conrad Uno's Egg Studios.

20. Truly, *Fast Stories . . . from Kid Coma* (Capitol, 1995)

This record came out well after this book's narrative, but I had to include it because it's that good.

Compilations

1. *Seattle Syndrome, Vol. 1* (Engram, 1981)

The first *Seattle Syndrome* provides a nice cross-section of Seattle's variety at the dawn of the '80s.

2. *Lowlife* (Ironwood, 1986)

Lowlife never got the street cachet *Deep Six* received, but overall, it's a much better record.

3. *Secretions* (C/Z, 1988)

Just preceding *Sub Pop 200*, *Secretions* became overshadowed by it, but may be the superior comp, with selections from Skin Yard, Couch of Sound, Capping Day, Vexed, Crypt Kicker 5, Pure Joy, Coffin Break, and H-Hour (with TAD's Tad Doyle on drums).

4. *Sub Pop 200* (Sub Pop, 1988)

In many ways, *Sub Pop 200* is the comp all others are measured by. While the label then narrowly defined itself in terms of the Mudhoney/TAD/Nirvana grunge axis, this record goes beyond all that to provide a valid document of late-'80s Seattle.

5. *Bite Back/Live at the Crocodile Café* (Popllama, 1996)

Even though *Bite Back* documents a 1995 show, it should be in your collection. The record features selections from some of the Northwest's most amazing artists, including Gas Huffer, the Presidents of the United States of America, the Young Fresh Fellows, the Minus 5 (with members of the Young Fresh Fellows and R.E.M.), Love Battery, the Walkabouts, Flop, Girl Trouble, Mudhoney, TAD, the Fastbacks, Mad Season (with members of Pearl Jam, Alice in Chains, and Screaming Trees), and Built to Spill. Get this record if at all possible.

INDEX

About the Author

Stephen Tow is a historian specializing in American history and popular music. He teaches at a college near Philadelphia.